Fraiche AND SIMPLE

EASY PREP AND MAKE-AHEAD
RECIPES FOR REAL LIFE

Fraiche and Simple

Tori Wesszer, RD

PENGUIN
an imprint of Penguin Canada, a division of Penguin Random House Canada Limited

Canada • USA • UK • Ireland • Australia • New Zealand • India • South Africa • China

Penguin, an imprint of Penguin Canada
A division of Penguin Random House Canada
320 Front Street West, Suite 1400
Toronto, Ontario, M5V 3B6, Canada
penguinrandomhouse.ca

The authorized representative in the EU for product safety and compliance is
Penguin Random House Ireland, Morrison Chambers, 32 Nassau Street, Dublin D02 YH68,
Ireland, https://eu-contact.penguin.ie

LIBRARY AND ARCHIVES CANADA CATALOGUING IN PUBLICATION

Title: Fraiche and simple : easy prep and make-ahead recipes for real life / Tori Wesszer.
Names: Wesszer, Tori, author
Description: Includes index.
Identifiers: Canadiana (print) 20250268051 | Canadiana (ebook) 2025026806X |
ISBN 9780735250239 (hardcover) | ISBN 9780735250246 (EPUB)
Subjects: LCSH: Quick and easy cooking. | LCSH: Cooking. | LCGFT: Cookbooks.
Classification: LCC TX833.5 .W47 2026 | DDC 641.5/55—dc23

Book and cover design by Kelly Hill
Typeset by Terra Page
Photography by Rachelle Beatty
Food and prop styling by Tori Wesszer and Team Fraîche
Interior backgrounds: (canvas) © andersphoto, (cross pattern) © Olgastocker,
(floral border; blue stripes) © Limolida Studio, (yellow gingham) © Pacha M Vector,
(green plaid) © theeve, (grey plaid; green checks) © Lara, (green stripes) © katyamaximenko,
(brown stripes) © Hanna, (yellow polka dots) © Hiro, all Adobe Stock

Printed in China

10 9 8 7 6 5 4 3 2 1

Penguin Random House
PENGUIN CANADA

DEDICATION

To my boys, Charlie and Max, who are growing up into such wonderful humans so very fast. May you always remain curious and kind. I hope your childhood memories are filled with the cozy smells of your favourite home-cooked meals that your dad and I have enjoyed preparing for you over the precious years. No matter where life takes you, never forget that food is love.

To the love of my life, Charles. I'm so grateful that the kitchen is our happy place. I hope to be singing Frank Sinatra over wine at the stove together until we are old and grey. We were meant for each other.

ACKNOWLEDGMENTS

My heritage includes a mix of Ukrainian, German, French, and English ancestry; my husband Charles's is a combination of German and Hungarian. Charles and I were both raised on good food made with love and throughout the years have enjoyed cooking meals from a variety of cultures outside of our own, some of which have inspired recipes you will find in this cookbook.

Food is a beautiful, important part of people's identities and should be treated with respect. I hope you love my versions of these recipes, and I encourage you to explore the authentic recipes and beautiful cultures that they were inspired by.

Contents

SHEET-PAN MEALS

SIMPLE SWEETS

STAPLES

INTRODUCTION

I co-wrote my first two cookbooks, *Fraiche Food, Full Hearts* and *Fraiche Food, Fuller Hearts*, with my cousin Jillian Harris. They were beautiful projects to create with someone I love like a sister, and books I'll cherish forever. And now, I can't believe I'm sharing another cookbook with you, one of my very own, to help you simplify mealtimes and bring more joy to your kitchens and homes. It's a dream come true! Thank you from the bottom of my heart for choosing my cookbook to grace the shelves of your kitchen. I hope it earns the honour of splattered, dog-eared pages, the ultimate cookbook compliment, as you cook your way through it.

As I write this cookbook, I see my own life—and the lives of those I love—changing so quickly before me. Perhaps you are feeling the same. It feels like yesterday that I was a new mom, and now my oldest son Charlie is officially taller than I am . . . with a moustache! Time seems more precious than ever, which was my motivation for writing this book. I want to help you reclaim time, and the best way I know how starts in the kitchen.

If you're anything like me, you've had those 5 p.m. moments—standing in front of the fridge, hungry kids circling like sharks, and no clue what's for dinner. And I'm a dietitian! Trust me, I've been there more times than I'd like to admit. Over the years, I discovered that a bit of proper planning goes a long way, and it completely changed how I approach cooking for my family. I only wish I had started earlier.

At the top of the list of daily life stresses? Dinner. Figuring out what to feed your family night after night is no small task. It's easy to get stuck cycling through the same handful of recipes. Not because they are your favourites, but because you're too tired to think up something new. You want to switch things up, but you simply don't have the time to craft a plan each week, so you wing it and hope for the best. By midweek, takeout or cereal for dinner starts sounding pretty good.

And it's not for lack of recipes. We have endless access to recipes, yet we are cooking less than ever. But I don't think it's the cooking that is getting in the way: *it's everything that comes before it*. Deciding what to cook, catering to everyone's needs and preferences, grocery shopping . . . it's a lot! On top of everything else you're juggling, you can easily end up feeling like you're drinking from a fire hose.

But I believe that it goes even deeper. We are hardwired to nourish our loved ones and have been since the beginning of humanity. It is critical to our survival as a species. That's why it hits hard when we miss the mark on mealtimes—and why it feels so incredibly rewarding when we get it right.

I struggled a lot until I created my digital meal planning tool, Fraîche Table. I realized there had to be a better way, a solution to occupy that awkward space between fumbling through a week trying to figure it out on my own and calling for pizza delivery. My way of meal planning became my lifesaver—not just to save time, but to take the stress out of deciding what to eat every day. It's how I went from dreading dinnertime—and the panic that came with it—to looking forward to it. A plan gives you more control over your week and frees up your precious mental space for more important things.

This cookbook, along with my online meal plan FraicheTable.com, was created with that in mind. Picture a world where you walk into each new week with a plan for all your meals, your fridge is stocked with exactly what you need (and nothing more), and the basics are prepped so you can cruise into dinnertime each evening without the regular stress and mental load of what to make for dinner.

This isn't just a cookbook—it's a key to calm in the kitchen. A system to help you plan less and enjoy more. A way to feed yourself and the people around you with more ease and intention. *Fraiche and Simple* is so much more than a collection of recipes; it's everything I've learned about bringing joy and delicious food to the table, even when life feels full.

Inside, you'll find the meals my family loves most—recipes that are simple, flexible, and made to fit real life. But just as important, I've included the tips, strategies, and planning tools that make cooking feel less like a chore and more like something you can actually look forward to.

Whether you're feeding a hungry family, cooking for one, or somewhere in between, this book is designed to help you:

- get organized without feeling overwhelmed
- save time with smart shortcuts and prep-ahead tricks
- stay inspired with fresh, approachable meals
- adapt with ease because life (and dinner) doesn't always go as planned.

My hope is that this book helps you feel like a total rock star in your kitchen, even on the busiest weeknights. Cooking at home isn't about perfection. It's about connection, creativity, and giving yourself grace. Whether you're feeding picky eaters, hosting friends, or simply craving a cozy night in, I hope this book inspires you to cook great food with more confidence—and far less stress—regardless of your kitchen skills.

Here's to more family dinners, fuller hearts, and food that actually fits your life. Let's bring the joy back to your kitchen.

So, let's get cooking.

With love,

tori
xo

MY NUTRITION PHILOSOPHY

Few things can appear more confusing than nutrition. Thank you, internet. The truth? For most of us, eating well is so simple. I believe Michael Pollan, American author, journalist, and professor known for his work on food, nutrition, and the environment, said it best: "Eat food. Not too much. Mostly plants."

I'm the first one to take an extra helping of kale, but there are also times when I want to dig my fork into something like Baked Chicken Parmesan (page 264) or a slice of Orange Creamsicle Cake (page 300). The key to healthy living is moderation and balance, and my splurges aren't from a package with a mile-long ingredient list.

Eating home-cooked food with those you love is one of the simplest joys in life, yet it is often the first thing to go when schedules get busy. I hope the recipes in this cookbook give you the inspiration and tools to create more moments to connect with those you love over good food.

BUILDING NOURISHING MEALS

One of the easiest ways to create a balanced meal is to use your plate as a simple visual tool—no need for special equipment. The "Perfect Plate" concept is a straightforward guide to help you build nourishing meals. Do your best to include variety whenever possible. Different foods provide a unique mix of vitamins, minerals, antioxidants, and other nutrients that work together to support your immune system, energy levels, and overall health.

Veggies and Fruit

Packed with fibre, vitamins, minerals, and antioxidants, fruits and vegetables should take up 50 percent of your plate to help fuel your body with essential nutrients. Your veggie options can range from leafy greens to roasted carrots—whatever you love.

Carbohydrates

Carbs are a key energy source (our brain's preferred fuel source) and contribute essential fibre and nutrients. They should make up about 25 percent of your plate, with a focus on complex carbs such as quinoa, whole-grain pasta, brown rice, or sweet potatoes.

Fats

Healthy fats are crucial for everything from skin health to supporting your nervous and immune systems. The quality of fats is more important than the amount. My preferred sources of fats include extra-virgin olive oil, avocados, and avocado oil (for high-heat cooking), to name a few.

Protein

Protein has a long list of benefits, but is essential for repairing tissues, supporting muscle health, and keeping you feeling full. Fill about 25 percent of your plate with protein-rich options such as lean chicken, fish, or eggs or plant-based choices such as beans, lentils, or tofu.

Not all recipes in this book may pass the "Perfect Plate" test on their own. Here are some ways to add more vegetables to any meal.

1. Add a salad: My Herby Green Salad (page 119) is my go-to, but the Simple Salads section of this book is filled with nourishing, interesting salads for you to choose from. A salad will always be a welcomed addition to the table; having it prepped ahead is key.

2. Serve a platter of veggies and dip: Pile the platter with your family's favourite fresh-cut veggies (prep them ahead) and a bowl of Herb Ranch Dressing (page 133), with your meal. Bonus: It's a hit with all ages!

3. Serve steamed or sautéed veggies: A quick steam or sauté can bring out the best in your most-loved vegetables (like green beans, carrots, and broccoli) and unlock nutrients.

4. Leverage frozen veggies: Think of frozen veggies as your secret weapon. Keep bags of your favourites in the freezer so you're always ready to add a nutritious boost to any meal in no time. Frozen veggies are nutrient-rich and can be just as—or even more—nutritious than fresh ones.

For example, to balance out a hearty dish like my Jalapeño Popper Chicken Pasta (page 183), I'd add a crisp leafy salad like my Herby Green Salad (page 119) for freshness and nutrients. Or serve Sheet-Pan Breakfast Sandwiches (page 57) or Protein Egg Bites (page 44) with slices of fresh fruit or Fruit Salad with Coconut Lime Yogurt Dressing (page 76). Any comforting casserole pairs perfectly with a simple side of steamed veggies like broccoli or cauliflower.

HOW TO USE THIS BOOK

The first thing you should know is that I don't believe in all-or-nothing thinking, especially when it comes to getting food on the table. There is no pass or fail; you are simply doing your best. Some nights are harder than others, and for those nights, having an SOS-style meal or two in your back pocket will mean the difference between ordering in (between tears of frustration) and getting a home-cooked meal on the table while barely lifting a finger. The goal is to feed your crew with as little stress as possible.

Meal planning isn't about being perfect or having it all together—it's about giving yourself a little more breathing room. It's one of the most powerful, practical tools for creating a sense of order within the chaos of everyday life.

When you have a plan, even a loose one, everything shifts. You save time. You save money. You waste less. You open the fridge and feel in control rather than overwhelmed. You feed yourself and the people you love with more ease, intention, and nourishment. But maybe most importantly, meal planning frees up precious mental space. No more last-minute scrambles or stressful grocery runs at the end of a long day. No more decision fatigue. You can stop asking "What's for dinner?" every single night—because you already know.

This book is here to help you make meal planning feel simple, approachable, and sustainable. The plans are flexible, the prep is manageable, and the recipes are designed to work together to make your week feel lighter—not more complicated. You deserve meals that bring more joy and less stress, and a kitchen that feels like a soft place to land at the end of the day.

I designed this cookbook to work in two ways, whether you're someone who thrives with a structured meal plan or you're a free-spirited cook who loves choosing recipes on the fly. If you love having a plan (or need one!), I've put together eight weeks of meal plans to take the guesswork out of mealtime. Four weeks focus on cozy, comforting meals perfect for fall and winter, while the other four feature lighter warm-weather-friendly dishes that require less oven time—ideal for spring and summer. For solo cooking, you'll find main dishes organized by cooking method—think sheet-pan meals, one-pot wonders, casseroles, and more—along with sections dedicated to breakfasts, soups, salads, sweets, baking, and staple recipes. Flip through the pages or head straight to the contents page to find exactly what you're looking for.

The recipes serve four to six people and are designed to be creative yet as simple as possible, using wholesome ingredients that are easy to find at your local grocery store. I added recipes for homemade versions of popular staples such as quick pickles (pages 327–331), Spicy Mayo (page 332), and SOS Spaghetti Sauce (page 312), but feel free to use store-bought options of these staples.

Think of each section in the book as another tool in your meal planning toolbox—a collection of over 100 recipes designed to help you tackle mealtime challenges with ease. The recipes are organized in the following sections:

BIG-BATCH BREAKFASTS

Let's be real—most mornings don't leave much room for slow, from-scratch breakfasts. That's where big-batch breakfasts save the day. These recipes are designed to make your mornings smoother, with Make Ahead, Freezer-Friendly, and grab-and-go options that are perfect for busy weekdays. Cook once, enjoy all week—and start each day with something nourishing, stress-free, and totally delicious.

EASY BAKING

It wouldn't be a cookbook of mine without a section on baking. From tender Greek Yogurt Biscuits (page 109) to beautifully crispy Focaccia Muffins (page 94) to Milk and Honey Bread (page 89), this section will have your house smelling like a bakery, and leave you feeling like the hero you are when you pull these no-fuss baked goods out of the oven.

SIMPLE SALADS

This might just be my favourite section—and once you dig in, you'll see why. These crunchy, vibrant salads are anything but boring, packed with hearty ingredients that hold up beautifully in the fridge. Paired with flavour-packed dressings (that also double as marinades for chicken or tofu!), they make eating your veggies something to truly look forward to.

MAKE-AHEAD SOUPS

Soup is the ultimate comfort food—warm, wholesome, and endlessly satisfying. These make-ahead soups are as nourishing as they are simple, perfect for stocking your freezer or prepping in advance for a stress-free meal. Most freeze beautifully, so go ahead and make a double batch—your future self will thank you.

NO-FUSS CASSEROLES

The beauty of no-fuss casseroles lies in their ease and simplicity. Many are "dump-and-bake" dishes, making them incredibly convenient. Plus, they freeze well and they're perfect for feeding a crowd.

ONE-PAN AND ONE-POT MEALS

Who actually wants *more* dishes? Certainly not me—and probably not you either. These one-pan and one-pot meals are here to make your life easier, without skimping on flavour or comfort. From my Cheeseburger Chili (page 229) to my Smashed Chicken Caesar Tacos (page 197), these meals are simple to prep, easy to clean up after, and perfect for busy weeknights. These recipes are true kitchen heroes that save the day (and your sanity).

SHEET-PAN MEALS

Crank up the oven and grab that trusty sheet pan—it's time to make dinner the easiest part of your day. These simple, flavour-packed meals, like Crispy Hot Honey Chicken Sliders (page 247), come together on a single pan with barely any cleanup.

SIMPLE SWEETS

This chapter is all about desserts that deliver joy without the fuss. From everyday favourites to special-occasion showstoppers, these easy-to-make treats prove that sweet doesn't have to mean complicated. From my Orange Creamsicle Cake (page 300) to my Old-Fashioned Coconut Oatmeal Cookie Bars (page 287), you'll find something for everyone.

STAPLES

If you run out of a basic ingredient or simply enjoy making your own, this section has you covered. From my Flax Egg (page 317) for vegan substitutes, to Enchilada Sauce (page 316), these simple, better-than-store-bought recipes will save you a trip to the grocery store.

At the top of each recipe, you'll find useful indicators calling out whether the recipe is one or more of the following: Prep Ahead, Make Ahead, Freezer-Friendly, and SOS (for when you're short on time).

Prep Ahead
Can be partially prepped ahead and finished later.

Make Ahead
Can be fully made ahead.

Freezer-Friendly
Can be covered and frozen for up to 1 month or as indicated in the recipe.

SOS
Short on time and need dinner on the table in a pinch? These easy recipes take 30 minutes or less to make.

I know that food is not one size fits all. To help you flex the recipes, wherever possible I include adaptations to make recipes vegan or vegetarian, dairy-free, gluten-free, or nut-free. At the beginning of those recipes, I give one or more of the following dietary indicators, and a dietary adaptation option appears at the bottom of the recipe.

Vegan
The recipe does not contain any animal products such as meat, eggs, fish, dairy, or honey.

Vegetarian
The recipe does not contain any meat, chicken, or fish, but may contain dairy products or eggs.

Dairy-Free
The recipe does not contain dairy products.

Gluten-Free
The recipe does not contain gluten. Be sure to read labels to make sure you are using certified gluten-free ingredients.

Nut-Free
The recipe does not contain any nuts.

You'll find helpful tips throughout the cookbook, plus notes on prepping ahead, making ahead, storing, and freezing for later. The book also includes a feature called

Re-Fraiche

To level up your leftover game, I have added ways to reinvent meals or their components to create something clever and different with extras while reducing food waste and minimizing the need to make new meals from scratch.

KEY INGREDIENTS USED IN THE BOOK

These are some of the key ingredients commonly used throughout the book:

Salt: I use fine sea salt in my recipes. Fleur de sel or flaky sea salt like Maldon is also great to have on hand for finishing dishes.

Flour: Unless otherwise specified, when a recipe calls for all-purpose flour, I used unbleached all-purpose flour.

Oil: Extra-virgin olive oil is my preference, for both taste and nutrition, but compared with other oils it has a distinct flavour and a lower smoking point that makes it unsuitable for some recipes. Avocado oil is a good choice for cooking at high heat and is neutral in taste with a healthy fatty acid profile, but other vegetable oils will work as well. When a recipe calls for coconut oil, I used virgin coconut oil (not neutral-tasting refined coconut oil).

Butter: I used salted butter when developing the recipes in this book.

Milk: I used 2% cow's milk during recipe development, but unsweetened oat milk, soy milk, or almond milk will also work for most recipes.

Cream: Either table (18%) or heavy/whipping (35%) cream will work in most recipes calling for cream. (Depending on the brand, heavy cream can range from 33% to 35% fat. You can use any of these, even though my recipes call for 35%.) Cashew Cream (page 332) can be used as a plant-based substitute in most of the recipes.

Stock: I personally love the Better Than Bouillon brand of stock concentrates for their convenience and flavour. They are high in sodium, though, so be sure to taste a dish before adding any extra salt—it likely will not need it!

Eggs: I used large free-range eggs in the recipes.

Sugar: I used white organic cane sugar when a recipe calls for sugar. You can substitute an equal amount of coconut sugar in most recipes, though the taste will not be identical.

Honey: I used pure liquid honey (not creamed) in my recipes. I suggest buying locally sourced honey if possible. Pure maple syrup can be substituted where indicated.

Greek Yogurt: When called for, I use full-fat Greek yogurt; typically 2% to 5% fat.

MEAL PLANNING FOR SUCCESS

Meal planning can be broken down into three main components:

PLAN: Plan out your meals.
PURCHASE: Make your list and shop for the ingredients (I do a lot of my grocery shopping online to save time).
PREP: Do steps ahead for stress-free cooking.

Getting into the habit of doing these three simple steps each week will put your meal planning on autopilot and help take away the mental load of "what's for dinner" day after day.

Meal planning doesn't have to be complicated. Spending just a half hour on the weekend to map out the plan for the week ahead and complete an online grocery order will save so much time, stress, and money, reducing extra trips to the grocery store and giving precious hours back to your week.

Even if you're not a meal planner (yet!), these simple tips will make your life so much easier.

1. SET YOURSELF UP FOR SUCCESS

Organize Your Kitchen and Pantry: This sets the foundation for cooking healthy meals for your family. Organize your fridge to keep perishable items at eye level and in clear or labelled containers so they don't go unnoticed. Clean out the pantry: Throw out anything expired and wipe down the surfaces. Invest in clear storage containers with labels to keep everything visible.

Stock the Basics: Simply put, cooking goes faster when you have all the ingredients on hand. And since many foods are shelf-stable and can be stocked up (where space allows), a well-stocked pantry takes the heavy lifting out of your weekly meal prep and grocery shopping.

If you've forgotten or don't have time to meal plan (it happens!), try this 2-3-4 method. Purchase the following to stock your kitchen with key basics that can be transformed into a number of simple meals in a pinch:

- *2 quick-cooking proteins* (canned beans or lentils, chicken or rotisserie chicken, tofu, fish, shrimp, or ground meat)
- *3 starches* (quinoa, rice, couscous, pasta, bread, baby potatoes)
- *4 vegetables* (fresh or frozen spinach, carrots, sweet peppers, zucchini, cherry tomatoes, cucumber).

These ingredients will give you the ammunition you need to put together a variety of dishes throughout the week, like stir-fries, soups, pasta dishes, and salads. Frozen vegetables are just as nutritious as fresh and help make healthy eating convenient. I recommend always having them on hand.

Gather Storage Containers: When it comes to meal planning, having the right storage containers on hand is just as important as the recipes themselves. The right containers make prepping, storing, and reheating meals a breeze, while the wrong ones (hello, lidless mismatched chaos) can be a source of stress.

A well-rounded set of storage containers will cover all your bases, from pre-chopped veggies to full meals. Clear containers make it easier to see what is inside, and purchasing containers with uniform lids is helpful. Look for these types:

- *Ovenproof glass containers with lids:* Best for casseroles, leftovers, and fridge-to-oven baking. Choose a mix of small (1 cup/250 mL), medium (2 to 4 cups/500 mL to 1 L), and large (6+ cups/1.5+ L).
- *Mason jars (various sizes):* Best for dressings, smoothies, overnight oats, and pantry storage. Wide-mouth jars are easier to clean and scoop from.
- *Stackable plastic or silicone storage containers:* Best for storing batch cooking, kids' lunches, and snacks. Make sure they are ovenproof and BPA-free.
- *Reusable silicone bags:* Best for marinating, freezing fruit, and storing produce.

2. MAKE A WEEKLY MEAL PLAN

Match Meals to Your Schedule: Adjust your meal plan around *your* schedule and cooking preferences. Choose quick meals for busy days, such as Smashed Chicken Caesar Tacos (page 197) or Pizza Pasta (page 225), and make more involved dishes when you have the extra time. If you're following the meal plans (page 25), review the recipes and make swaps or flex the recipes to fit your family's preferences and tastes. Scale the recipes to fit your needs—for instance, a family with young children will have very different food demands compared with a family with teenagers. Plan and cook accordingly.

Keep a Short "Go-To" Meal List: Have a list of easy family-favourite recipes to rotate through when you're short on time. For instance, if your family loves the Bolognaise Flatbread (page 243), keep the pizza crust, grated cheese, and a batch of the sauce in the freezer. Add fresh veggies, bake, and dinner is served!

Write It Down: Writing out your weekly menu helps keep you organized and prevents last-minute scrambles. Put your meal plan somewhere visible in your kitchen so everyone knows what's for breakfast, lunch, and dinner!

Scan this QR code to download my meal planning template.

3. SHOP SMART

Never shop hungry—it leads to impulse buys. Spread out meal planning tasks: grocery shop one day, prep another. Order groceries online: it saves time and prevents unnecessary purchases. Use the done-for-you grocery lists for the meal-planned weeks (page 25).

Scan this QR code to download the grocery lists for the meal plans.

4. MEAL-PREP EFFICIENTLY

Don't make meal prep something you dread. Here are a couple of ways you can make it fun and efficient.

Don't Tackle It All at Once: I meal-plan and grocery shop one day and prep another day. Dividing up the work this way means I don't feel I'm spending the majority of my weekend thinking about meals for the week.

Create Workstations: When prepping ingredients or recipes, work in stations. For instance, cut and prepare all your vegetables first and finish with your protein, as you will want to sanitize your cutting boards and cooking utensils at that point. Have your storage containers on the counter ready to go, and consider using masking tape and a felt pen to label the containers. Place a discard bowl on the counter to collect compostable scraps.

5. ROTATE MEALS

You don't have to cook something new every night! While you may feel pressure to always cook something new, there is nothing wrong with keeping a solid rotation of the same meals that you know your family loves. To give you inspiration, I include eight sample meal-planned weeks using my recipes on page 25. Half of these meal-planned weeks are designed with warmer months of the year in mind, with lighter flavours and less baking and oven use, and the other half of the weeks are filled with cozier recipes geared towards the cooler months of the year. Many of the meals I include are Freezer-Friendly; consider doubling some of those recipes to pop in the freezer to make mealtimes easier for your future self.

6. BATCH-COOK AND FREEZE MEALS

Investing a few hours into batch cooking Freezer-Friendly meals when you have time is a game-changer. When you're making a batch of Cheeseburger Chili (page 229), Apple Raisin Bran Muffins (page 113), or SOS Spaghetti Sauce (page 312), why not make a double batch and freeze extras for those busy days ahead? Look for the "Freezer-Friendly" label at the top of a recipe, which indicates it can be made ahead and frozen. Cook grains, proteins, and veggies in bulk along with a sauce or dressing, such as Better-for-You Bolognaise (page 315) or Simple Caesar Dressing (page 197), for easy mix-and-match meals throughout the week.

7. LEVERAGE LEFTOVERS

Cook once, eat twice! Make extra for lunches or freeze portions for future meals. Look for the "Freezer-Friendly" label for recipes that freeze well. Getting creative with leftovers is a game-changer in the kitchen. Many leftovers can be reinvented to create a brand-new dish, reducing food waste and saving time. For instance, leftover Pot Roast (page 231) can become Cottage Pie (page 169) or French Dip Sandwiches (page 239). Leftover Greek Yogurt Biscuits (page 109) or Sour Cream and Onion Biscuits (page 106) can be toasted to make a delicious breakfast sandwich the following day or cut up and baked for croutons for topping a hot bowl of soup like Pierogi Soup (page 156). Leftover sauce from the Better-for-You Bolognaise (page 315) can be frozen to make a future Bolognaise Flatbread (page 243) that will leave your family fighting for the last slice. Or why not create a bowl out of leftover sheet-pan meals for a satisfying lunch the following day?

8. SUNDAY PREP DAY (OR YOUR PREFERRED PREP DAY)

If you have time, prep a meal or two for breakfast and lunch for the week that keep well, and freeze any fresh ingredients that won't keep for more than a few days (not all are Freezer-Friendly). Cut up a container of fresh vegetables for veggies and dip, and make a salad with hearty ingredients to last a few days to make healthy eating convenient. Bonus: The dressings can double as marinades for protein!

While any day of the week works, I find that Sundays are a great day to make and enjoy recipes that take a bit more time but can be repurposed throughout the week. For example, Roast Chicken Dinner (page 235) or Pot Roast (page 231) can be used in a variety of ways in other recipes, simply tucked into a sandwich, or tossed into a soup or salad.

9. DIY SALAD BAR

You will usually find a big bowl of salad in our fridge and some cut-up veggies for the family to snack on. I make a big-batch salad almost every week so there's always something healthy on hand. It's a great opportunity to use up smaller amounts of vegetables at the beginning or end of the week. Having nourishing, ready-to-grab options prepped ahead means it's much easier to make smarter food decisions. Salads are also great to serve alongside lunches or dinners.

To create a salad bar, tear up your washed greens in a large bowl (or resealable bag). I tend to use a base of kale because it's sturdy enough to last the week, but you could use green lettuce, spinach, or romaine lettuce; it just might not last as long. Then add hearty ingredients—feta cheese, sweet peppers, celery, beans—anything you like to create your base. Each night, we switch things up with different toppings (see below). Set out a few different options to create your own family salad bar—what a fun way for everyone to enjoy salad! Drizzle on the dressing when ready to eat. See my Simple Salads section (pages 119 to 140) for a feast of delicious salad recipes.

Here is my three-step formula for a DIY Salad Bar or big-batch salad.

Make a Base

Arugula
Cabbage
Canned beans (black beans, chickpeas, kidney beans)
Coleslaw
Cooked pasta
Couscous
Iceberg lettuce
Kale
Quinoa
Romaine lettuce
Shaved brussels sprouts
Shredded beets
Shredded carrots
Spinach

Add Toppings

Apples
Avocado
Cheese (feta, cheddar, or other)
Chopped dates
Chopped walnuts
Corn
Cucumber
Dried cranberries
Fresh herbs (cilantro, parsley, dill)
Grapes or other fruit
Hard-boiled eggs
Hemp hearts
Protein Crunch Salad Topper (page 311)
Pumpkin seeds
Radishes
Red, orange, or yellow sweet peppers
Sliced almonds
Sprouts
Sunflower seeds
Tortilla chips

Drizzle with Dressing

Make a batch or two of your favourite dressing and store in a resealable container in the fridge for up to 5 days. Dressing ideas include:

Creamy Caper Dill Dressing (page 120)
Herb Ranch Dressing (page 133)
Mediterranean Dressing (page 129)
Sesame Peanut Dressing (page 135)
Simple Caesar Dressing (page 197)
Southwest Dressing (page 123)
Strawberry Dressing (page 139)

No-Recipe Salad Combinations

ANTIOXIDANT POWER SALAD

Spinach; blueberries; red, orange, or yellow sweet peppers; almonds; hard-boiled eggs; avocado; sunflower seeds, walnuts, or Protein Crunch Salad Topper (page 311)

SOUTHWEST SALAD

Romaine lettuce; chopped pitted dates; black beans; avocado; corn; tomato; red, orange, or yellow sweet pepper; cilantro; feta; tortilla chips; lime wedges (for squeezing)

CALIFORNIA SALAD

Spring mix greens; strawberries; feta; pecans; cucumber; avocado; red, orange, or yellow sweet pepper

10. BUILD A BOWL

Bowls are a fantastic and versatile way to make the most of leftovers. Plus, they're easy to prepare, making them a convenient option for quick, balanced meals. Repurpose proteins, grains, and vegetables from previous meals to easily create something entirely new and exciting. For instance, effortlessly transform leftover roast chicken, quinoa, and steamed veggies into a hearty grain bowl by adding fresh greens and a drizzle of dressing or a dollop of hummus.

The beauty of a bowl is that there are no rules—just endless possibilities! Mix and match your favourite ingredients to create something delicious every time. Below is my go-to formula for creating the perfect bowl. To further inspire you, on page 22 you'll find a few mix-and-match bowls that repurpose leftovers of recipes in this cookbook.

Choose a Base

Start with a satisfying foundation to build your bowl. Some great options include:

Barley

Brown or white rice

Couscous

Farro

Mixed greens or shredded kale (for a lighter option)

Quinoa

Roasted potatoes or sweet potatoes

Tip

Take your grains up a notch by:

- Cooking them with stock instead of water for extra flavour
- Mixing in a splash of lime or lemon juice for freshness
- Stirring in fresh herbs such as chopped cilantro, parsley, or basil
- Adding a sprinkle of toasted sesame seeds for a savoury boost

Add Protein

A good source of protein makes your bowl filling and balanced. Use leftovers or prepare fresh options such as:

Chickpeas, black beans, or lentils

Grilled or roasted chicken

Hard-boiled eggs

Marinated tofu or tempeh

Salmon, shrimp, or canned tuna

Load Up on Veggies

Veggies bring colour, crunch, and nutrients to your bowl. Try a mix of raw, roasted, or sautéed options such as:

Avocado for creaminess

Roasted broccoli, cauliflower, or brussels sprouts

Shredded carrots or red or green cabbage for crunch

Sweet peppers, cucumbers, or cherry tomatoes for freshness

Add Some Crunch

A little texture takes your bowl to the next level. Try adding:

Crushed tortilla chips

Pita Croutons (page 322)

Protein Crunch Salad Topper (page 311)

Roasted chickpeas

Sliced radishes

Toasted nuts or seeds (almonds, sesame seeds, pumpkin seeds, sunflower seeds)

Drizzle with Dressing

Dressings are one of my favourite ways to bring new flavours to leftovers. They can transform a simple meal into something exciting; add just before enjoying. Dressing ideas include:

Mediterranean Dressing (page 129)

Sesame Peanut Dressing (page 135)

Herb Ranch Dressing (page 133)

Bowl Recipes

SANTORINI BOWLS

Cooked quinoa

Lemon Dill Chicken (page 193), chopped

Quick Pickled Red Onions (page 331)

Big Crunchy Greek Kale Salad (page 140)

Tzatziki

Hummus

Chopped fresh flat-leaf parsley

Mediterranean Dressing (page 129; optional)

FISH TACO BOWLS

Cooked rice (pan-fry to make crispy, if desired)

Crispy Fish Burgers (page 269)

Coleslaw

Pico de gallo

Chopped fresh cilantro

Quick Pickled Cabbage (page 327)

Spicy Mayo (page 332)

SESAME TOFU BUDDHA BOWLS

Cooked quinoa

Sesame Tofu Croutons (page 135)

Sesame Peanut Dressing (page 135)

Diced mango

Diced red pepper

Shredded carrots

Chopped fresh cilantro

Roughly chopped salted peanuts

Lime wedges

MANGO COCONUT SHRIMP BOWLS

Coconut Rice (page 249)

Coconut Shrimp (page 249)

Spicy Mango Sauce (page 249)

Diced English cucumber

Diced fresh mango

Quick Pickled Red Onions (page 331)

Chopped fresh cilantro

CHIPOTLE SHRIMP PINEAPPLE FAJITA BOWLS

Rice or Coconut Rice (page 249)

Lime Crema (page 263)

Chipotle Shrimp and Pineapple (page 263)

Diced avocado

Quick Pickled Red Onions (page 331)

Chopped fresh cilantro

Lime wedges

HOT HONEY CHICKEN BOWLS

Cooked rice

Crispy Chicken (page 247), chopped

Hot Honey Sauce (page 247)

Herb Ranch Dressing (page 133)

Dill Pickle Slaw (page 247)

Diced avocado

Chopped fresh cilantro

CHICKEN PARMESAN BOWLS

Baked Chicken Parmesan (page 264), chopped

Caesar Salad (page 197)

Simple Caesar Dressing (page 197)

Cherry tomatoes, cut in half

Finely chopped fresh basil

SHAWARMA BOWLS

Cooked rice

Chicken from Shawarma Chicken Pita Wraps (page 254), chopped

Diced English cucumber

Diced tomato

Shredded lettuce

Chopped fresh flat-leaf parsley

Garlic Yogurt Sauce (page 254)

LUMPIA RICE BOWLS

Cooked rice

Lumpia Filling (page 195)

Spring Roll Crisps (page 195)

Sweet Chili Sauce (page 195)

Shredded carrots

Finely shredded cabbage

Chopped fresh cilantro

Spicy Mayo (page 332)

THE MEAL PLANS

The meal plans are designed to give you variety and balance with as little work as possible. Each plan is intended to feed four people, with portions designed for family-style cooking and shared meals. Similar ingredients are leveraged throughout the week with suggestions for leftovers and instructions for freezing extras to help reduce waste.

Any recipes that can be prepped ahead are included in Sunday Prep Day. Light prep tasks are spread throughout the week as needed, so you're set up for success every day.

As a five-day meal plan, I recommend following a Monday-through-Friday schedule, but if you end up ordering dinner in on Wednesday that's okay! Just adjust the schedule as needed.

Many foods can be frozen for use at a later date. If you do switch the days of the week in the meal plan, be mindful of how long prepped food remains safe to eat. For example, you might need to freeze your taco filling to be pulled out when you're ready to eat it at a later date.

I intentionally left weekends open to allow for flexibility. Because life happens!

A DIETITIAN'S APPROACH TO MEAL PLANNING

As a dietitian (and a busy mom), creating meal plans isn't just about making dinner easier—it's about bringing balance, variety, and nutrition to your table in a way that *actually* works in real life.

Every meal plan in this book is thoughtfully designed with a few key goals in mind:

- **Balanced Nutrition:** I aim for every meal to include a source of protein, plenty of vegetables or fruit for fibre and micronutrients, healthy fats, and satisfying carbohydrates. This helps support energy, fullness, and overall well-being.
- **Variety Without the Overwhelm:** A good plan keeps things interesting but not chaotic. You'll find a mix of flavours and ingredients from week to week, so meals never feel repetitive, but your fridge and pantry still feel manageable.
- **Protein-Forward Meals:** Including enough protein helps stabilize blood sugar, support metabolism, and keep you feeling fuller longer. You'll see a range of sources of protein throughout these plans, both plant-based and animal-based.
- **Vegetables Made Doable:** I believe in finding simple ways to work more veggies into meals. Whether they're hidden in sauces, blended into soups, or roasted to perfection, vegetables play a starring (and delicious) role in these meals.

Ultimately, this is food you can feel good about—nourishing, balanced, and still full of flavour and joy. Because healthy eating should never feel like a chore.

SPRING AND SUMMER MEAL PLAN

Week 1	BREAKFAST	LUNCH	DINNER
MONDAY	Cheddar Bacon Chive Breakfast Quesadillas (page 51) From Sunday prep	Pierogi Soup (page 156) From Sunday prep	Lumpia Lettuce Wraps (page 195) Double to Re-Fraiche for Tuesday's lunch
TUESDAY	Peach Crumble Breakfast Bars (page 80) From Sunday prep	Lumpia Rice Bowls (see page 22) Re-Fraiche from Monday night	Tuscan Orzo (page 189)
WEDNESDAY	Cheddar Bacon Chive Breakfast Quesadillas (page 51) From Sunday prep	Pierogi Soup (page 156) From Sunday prep	Flank Steak with Feta Salsa (with Grilled Peppers and Onions) (page 181) and Garlic Bread (page 321) Double to Re-Fraiche for Thursday's lunch
THURSDAY	Peach Crumble Breakfast Bars (page 80) From Sunday prep	Flank Steak with Feta Salsa Sandwiches (see page 182) Re-Fraiche from Wednesday's dinner	Smashed Greek Chicken Tacos (page 201)
FRIDAY	Raspberry Lemon Overnight Oats (page 67) From Thursday prep	Big Crunchy Greek Kale Salad (page 140) From Thursday prep	Corn Chowder Seafood Cakes (page 259)

Suggested Dessert
No-Bake Chocolate Cheesecake Jars (page 292)

Optional Batch Cook

Stock the freezer this week by doubling any of the following recipes: Cheddar Bacon Chive Breakfast Quesadillas, Filling for Lumpia Lettuce Wraps, Peach Crumble Breakfast Bars, and/or Corn Chowder Seafood Cakes.

Sunday Prep

Cheddar Bacon Chive Breakfast Quesadillas (page 51)
Peach Crumble Breakfast Bars (page 80)
Pierogi Soup (page 156)

Weekday Prep

Thursday: Raspberry Lemon Overnight Oats (page 67) and Big Crunchy Greek Kale Salad (page 140)

SPRING AND SUMMER MEAL PLAN

Week 2	BREAKFAST	LUNCH	DINNER
MONDAY	Citrus Ricotta Pancakes or Waffles (page 59) From Sunday prep	Santa Fe Pasta Salad (page 123) From Sunday prep	Thai Kale Salad with Sesame Tofu Croutons (page 135) Double the tofu and dressing to Re-Fraiche for Tuesday's lunch
TUESDAY	Pierogi Breakfast Bake (page 43) From Sunday prep	Sesame Tofu Buddha Bowls (see page 22) Re-Fraiche from Monday's dinner	Creamy Dill Salmon and Baby Potatoes (page 213)
WEDNESDAY	Citrus Ricotta Pancakes or Waffles (page 59) From Sunday prep	Santa Fe Pasta Salad (page 123) From Sunday prep	Smashed Chicken Caesar Tacos (page 197) Double for leftovers for Thursday's lunch
THURSDAY	Pierogi Breakfast Bake (page 43) From Sunday prep	Smashed Chicken Caesar Tacos (page 197) Leftover from Wednesday's dinner	Cajun Skillet Shrimp Boil (page 214) Double for leftovers for Friday's lunch
FRIDAY	Smoked Salmon Bagel Sandwiches (page 52)	Cajun Skillet Shrimp Boil (page 214) Leftover from Thursday's dinner	Jalapeño Popper Chicken Pasta (page 183)

Optional Batch Cook

Stock the freezer this week by doubling the Citrus Ricotta Pancakes or Waffles.

Suggested Dessert
Cherry Turnovers (page 305)

Sunday Prep

Citrus Ricotta Pancakes or Waffles (page 59)
Santa Fe Pasta Salad (page 123)
Thai Kale Salad with Sesame Tofu Croutons (page 135)
Pierogi Breakfast Bake (page 43)

SPRING AND SUMMER MEAL PLAN

Week 3	BREAKFAST	LUNCH	DINNER
MONDAY	Mediterranean Protein Egg Bites (page 44) From Sunday prep	Lemon Chicken Orzo Soup (page 146) From Sunday prep	Chicken Ricotta Meatballs (page 209) with Garlic Bread (page 321) Double to Re-Fraiche for Tuesday's lunch
TUESDAY	Almond Baked French Toast (page 64) From Sunday prep	Chicken Ricotta Meatball Subs (see page 209) Re-Fraiche from Monday's dinner	Broccoli and Cheese Orzo (page 190)
WEDNESDAY	Mediterranean Protein Egg Bites (page 44) From Sunday prep	Lemon Chicken Orzo Soup (page 146) From Sunday prep	Mango Coconut Shrimp Tacos (page 249) Double to Re-Fraiche for Thursday's lunch
THURSDAY	Almond Baked French Toast (page 64) From Sunday prep	Mango Coconut Shrimp Lettuce Wraps (see page 249) Re-Fraiche from Wednesday's dinner	Everything Bagel Salmon (page 257) Double the salmon to Re-Fraiche for Friday's lunch
FRIDAY	Strawberry Cheesecake Bagel Sandwiches (page 55)	Everything Bagel Salmon Salad (page 120) Re-Fraiche from Thursday's dinner	Ranch Cobb Salad (page 133)

Optional Batch Cook

Stock the freezer this week by doubling the Lemon Chicken Orzo Soup (cook and freeze orzo separately) and/or Chicken Ricotta Meatballs.

Suggested Dessert
Orange Creamsicle Cake (page 300)

Sunday Prep

Mediterranean Protein Egg Bites (page 44)
Lemon Chicken Orzo Soup (page 146)
Almond Baked French Toast (page 64)

SPRING AND SUMMER MEAL PLAN

Week 4	BREAKFAST	LUNCH	DINNER
MONDAY	Tropical Breakfast Cookies (page 75) and Fruit Salad with Coconut Lime Yogurt Dressing (page 76) From Sunday prep	Dill Pickle Tuna Salad (page 130) From Sunday prep	Crispy Hot Honey Chicken Sliders (page 247) Double to Re-Fraiche for Tuesday's lunch
TUESDAY	Santa Fe Breakfast Quesadillas (page 51) From Sunday prep	Hot Honey Chicken Bowls (see page 22) Re-Fraiche from Monday's dinner	Thai Green Curry Pot (page 222)
WEDNESDAY	Tropical Breakfast Cookies (page 75) and Fruit Salad with Coconut Lime Yogurt Dressing (page 76) From Sunday prep	Dill Pickle Tuna Salad Wraps (page 130)	Smashed Dumpling Tacos (page 203) Double for leftovers for Thursday's lunch
THURSDAY	Santa Fe Breakfast Quesadillas (page 51) From Sunday prep	Smashed Dumpling Tacos (page 203) Leftover from Wednesday's dinner	Lemon Dill Chicken and Potatoes (page 193) Double for leftovers for Friday's lunch
FRIDAY	Strawberry Cheesecake Bagel Sandwiches (page 55)	Lemon Dill Chicken and Potatoes (page 193) Leftover from Thursday's dinner	Cheeseburger Nachos (page 244)

Optional Batch Cook

Stock the freezer this week by doubling any of the following recipes: Tropical Breakfast Cookies, Lemon Dill Chicken (marinate and freeze), and/or Santa Fe Breakfast Quesadillas.

Sunday Prep

Tropical Breakfast Cookies (page 75)
Coconut Lime Yogurt Dressing (page 76)
Dill Pickle Tuna Salad (page 130)
Santa Fe Breakfast Quesadillas (page 51)

Suggested Dessert
Strawberry Yogurt Lemon Loaf (page 277)

FALL AND WINTER MEAL PLAN

Week 1	BREAKFAST	LUNCH	DINNER
MONDAY	Peanut Butter and Jam Breakfast Cookies (page 71) From Sunday prep	Curried Coconut Squash Soup (page 145) From Sunday prep	Buffalo White Chicken Chili (page 221)
TUESDAY	Farmer's Sausage Breakfast Sandwiches (page 57) From Sunday prep	Buffalo White Chicken Chili (page 221) Leftover from Monday's dinner	Bolognaise Flatbread (page 243)
WEDNESDAY	Peanut Butter and Jam Breakfast Cookies (page 71) From Sunday prep	Curried Coconut Squash Soup (page 145) From Sunday prep	Cajun Chicken Sheet-Pan Burgers (page 266) Double the chicken to Re-Fraiche for Thursday's lunch
THURSDAY	Farmer's Sausage Breakfast Sandwiches (page 57) From Sunday prep	Cajun Chicken Lettuce Wraps (page 266) Lettuce wrap Re-Fraiche option from Wednesday's dinner	Pizza Beans (page 226) Double for leftovers for Friday's lunch
FRIDAY	Mocha Overnight Oats (page 68) From Thursday prep	Pizza Beans (page 226) Leftover from Thursday's dinner	Garlic Butter Pork Chops with Creamy Mushroom Sauce (page 217)

Suggested Dessert
Pear Gingerbread Bundt Cake (page 280)

Optional Batch Cook

Stock your freezer this week by doubling any of the following recipes: Peanut Butter and Jam Breakfast Cookies, Sausage Breakfast Sandwiches, Curried Coconut Squash Soup, Buffalo White Chicken Chili, Better-for-You Bolognaise, and/or Pizza Beans.

Sunday Prep

Peanut Butter and Jam Breakfast Cookies (page 71)
Apple Chicken Sausage Patties (page 48)
Sheet-Pan Eggs (page 57)
Sausage Breakfast Sandwiches (page 57)
Curried Coconut Squash Soup (page 145)
Optional: Buffalo White Chicken Chili (page 221)

Weekday Prep

Monday: Better-for-You Bolognaise (page 315)
Thursday: Mocha Overnight Oats (page 68)

FALL AND WINTER MEAL PLAN

Week 2	BREAKFAST	LUNCH	DINNER
MONDAY	Greek Yogurt Pancakes (or waffles; page 63) From Sunday prep	Herby Green Salad (page 119) with Protein Crunch Salad Topper (page 311)	Skillet Enchiladas (page 186) Use leftovers for Tuesday's lunch
TUESDAY	Fiesta Tortilla Breakfast Egg Cups (page 47) From Sunday prep	Skillet Enchiladas (page 186) Leftover from Monday's dinner	Coconut Curry Lentils (page 206) Double to have leftovers for Wednesday's lunch
WEDNESDAY	Greek Yogurt Pancakes (or waffles; page 63) From Sunday prep	Coconut Curry Lentils (page 206) Leftover from Tuesday's dinner	No-Layer Gnocchi Lasagna (page 177)
THURSDAY	Fiesta Tortilla Breakfast Egg Cups (page 47) From Sunday prep	Herby Green Salad (page 119) with Protein Crunch Salad Topper (page 311)	Shawarma Chicken Pita Wraps (page 254) Double to Re-Fraiche for Friday's lunch
FRIDAY	Protein Crunch Salad Topper (page 311) with yogurt and berries	Shawarma Bowls (see page 22) Re-Fraiche from Thursday's dinner	Gyoza Soup (page 159)

Optional Batch Cook

Stock your freezer this week by doubling any of the following recipes: Greek Yogurt Pancakes (or waffles), Fiesta Tortilla Breakfast Egg Cups, Skillet Enchiladas, or Coconut Curry Lentils.

Suggested Dessert
Apple Slab Pie (page 273)

Sunday Prep

Greek Yogurt Pancakes (or waffles; page 63)
Fiesta Tortilla Breakfast Egg Cups (page 47)
Protein Crunch Salad Topper (page 311; omit the cayenne)
Tamari Dressing (page 119)
Marinate and freeze chicken for Shawarma Chicken Pita Wraps (page 254)
Optional: Skillet Enchiladas (page 186)

FALL AND WINTER MEAL PLAN

Week 3	BREAKFAST	LUNCH	DINNER
MONDAY	Farmer's Sausage Protein Egg Bites (page 44) From Sunday prep	Butter Chicken Soup (page 149) From Sunday prep	Mom's Sneaky Meatloaf Muffins (page 174) Use leftovers for Tuesday's lunch
TUESDAY	Triple Berry Coconut Crisp (page 291) with yogurt From Sunday prep	Mom's Sneaky Meatloaf Muffins (page 174) Leftover from Monday's dinner	Everything Bagel Salmon (page 257) Double to Re-Fraiche for Wednesday's lunch
WEDNESDAY	Farmer's Sausage Protein Egg Bites (page 44) From Sunday prep	Everything Bagel Salmon Salad (page 120) Re-Fraiche from Tuesday's dinner	Creamy Pesto Tomato Tortellini (page 205)
THURSDAY	Triple Berry Coconut Crisp (page 291) with yogurt From Sunday prep	Butter Chicken Soup (page 149) From Sunday prep	Chipotle Shrimp Pineapple Fajitas (page 263) Double to Re-Fraiche for Friday's lunch
FRIDAY	Apple Cinnamon Creamy Steel-Cut Oats (page 79)	Chipotle Shrimp Pineapple Fajita Bowls (see page 22) Re-Fraiche from Thursday's dinner	Buffalo White Chicken Chili (page 221)

Suggested Dessert
Pumpkin Cheesecake Bars (page 283)

Optional Batch Cook

Stock your freezer this week by doubling any of the following recipes: Butter Chicken Soup and/or Mom's Sneaky Meatloaf Muffins.

Sunday Prep

Farmer's Sausage Protein Egg Bites (page 44)
Butter Chicken Soup (page 149; freeze half)
Triple Berry Coconut Crisp (page 291)
Optional: Mom's Sneaky Meatloaf Muffins (page 174)

Weekday Prep

Tuesday: Creamy Caper Dill Dressing (page 120)

FALL AND WINTER MEAL PLAN

Week 4	BREAKFAST	LUNCH	DINNER
MONDAY	Chocolate Hazelnut Breakfast Cookies (page 72) From Sunday prep	Curry Chicken Pasta Salad (page 125) From Sunday prep	Baked Chicken Parmesan (page 264) Double to Re-Fraiche for Tuesday's lunch
TUESDAY	Jalapeño Popper Protein Egg Bites (page 44) From Sunday prep	Chicken Parmesan Bowls (see page 22) Re-Fraiche from Monday's dinner	Butternut Squash Ravioli Lasagna (page 167)
WEDNESDAY	Chocolate Hazelnut Breakfast Cookies (page 72) From Sunday prep	Curry Chicken Pasta Salad (page 125) From Sunday prep	Crispy Fish Burgers with Oven Fries (page 269) Double to Re-Fraiche for Thursday's lunch
THURSDAY	Jalapeño Popper Protein Egg Bites (page 44) From Sunday prep	Fish Taco Bowls (see page 22) Re-Fraiche from Wednesday's dinner	Sweet and Sour Chicken Casserole (page 163) Double to Re-Fraiche for Friday's lunch
FRIDAY	Mocha Overnight Oats (page 68) From Thursday prep	Sweet and Sour Chicken Lettuce Wraps (see page 163) Re-Fraiche from Thursday's dinner	Sneaky Sheet-Pan Taquitos (page 253)

Optional Batch Cook

Stock your freezer this week by doubling any of the following recipes: Chocolate Hazelnut Breakfast Cookies, Butternut Squash Ravioli Lasagna, and/or Sneaky Sheet-Pan Taquitos.

Suggested Dessert

Deep-Dish Chocolate Banana Cake (page 284)

Sunday Prep

Chocolate Hazelnut Breakfast Cookies (page 72)
Curry Chicken Pasta Salad (page 125)
Jalapeño Popper Protein Egg Bites (page 44)
Butternut Squash Ravioli Lasagna (page 167)

Weekday Prep

Thursday: Mocha Overnight Oats (page 68)

STORING FOOD PROPERLY

Keeping your ingredients fresh and properly stored helps reduce waste, saves time and money, and makes weeknight cooking feel effortless. Here's how to store common ingredients to extend their life and get the most out of your grocery haul.

Apples and Pears: Store in the fridge, away from leafy greens, as they emit ethylene gas that can cause other produce to spoil faster.

Avocados: Unripe avocados will ripen on the counter. Once ripe, store in the fridge to extend freshness. If you've cut one, brush it with a squeeze of lemon or lime and store it, with or without the pit, in a resealable container in the fridge.

Bananas: Store at room temperature. If you want to slow ripening, wrap the stem in plastic wrap. Overripe bananas? Peel and freeze in a container or bag for smoothies or baking.

Berries: Don't wash until just before eating. Store in a breathable container lined with paper towel and keep them dry to avoid mould. For strawberries, remove any mushy ones right away to prevent them from spoiling the rest.

Carrots, Celery, and Radishes: Prep and store submerged in cold water in a sealed container to maintain crispness. Refresh the water every few days.

Citrus Fruits: Store lemons, limes, and oranges in the fridge—ideally in the crisper drawer, loose or in a breathable produce bag—to help them stay fresh much longer than if left on the counter. You can also freeze extra zest or juice in small portions for easy use later.

Cheese: Wrap blocks of cheese in parchment or wax paper, then place in a resealable bag or container in the fridge. Don't use plastic wrap—it traps moisture and can lead to faster spoilage.

Eggs: Store in their original carton in the coldest part of the fridge (not the door!). This keeps them fresher longer and prevents temperature fluctuations.

Fresh Herbs: Treat tender herbs (such as parsley, cilantro, dill) like flowers: trim the stems, place them in a glass of water, loosely cover with a reusable bag, and store in the fridge. Change the water every couple of days. For hardy herbs (such as rosemary and thyme), wrap them in damp paper towel and store in a resealable bag in the crisper drawer.

Grains: Keep in resealable containers in a cool, dark place. Use clear containers if possible so you can easily see what you have.

Leafy Greens: After washing and drying (a salad spinner works wonders), layer your greens in a container lined with paper towel to absorb moisture. Keep in the fridge and replace the towel every few days.

Nuts and Seeds: Store in the fridge or freezer in resealable containers to prevent oils from turning rancid, especially flaxseeds, walnuts, and pine nuts.

Milk and Plant-Based Milks: Keep in the back of the fridge where it's coldest. Once opened, be sure to seal tightly and use within the recommended time.

Potatoes, Onions, and Garlic: Store in a cool, dark, well-ventilated space. Keep potatoes and onions separate—if stored together, the gases they release cause spoilage faster.

Tomatoes: Keep at room temperature, stem side down, away from sunlight. Refrigeration will dull their flavour and make them mealy.

NOTE: Store leftovers in resealable containers, labelled with the date. Most cooked foods last 3 to 4 days in the fridge. Reheat only the amount you'll eat to avoid repeated cooling and reheating.

CHAMPAGNE

KITCHEN AND PANTRY STAPLES

A well-stocked pantry and kitchen will make a world of difference to your cooking game. Here are some of the pantry staples, kitchen tools, and equipment that I recommend you keep on hand.

FATS

Avocado oil
Butter (salted)
Extra-virgin olive oil
Sesame oil
Vegetable oil or canola oil
Virgin coconut oil

NUTS, SEEDS, AND BUTTERS

Almond butter (smooth natural)
Chia seeds
Ground flaxseed
Hazelnut butter
Hemp seeds
Peanut butter (smooth natural)
Poppy seeds
Pumpkin seeds
Raw almonds, whole and sliced
Raw cashews
Raw pecans
Raw walnuts
Sesame seeds
Sunflower seeds
Tahini

DRIED HERBS AND SPICES

(Purchase spices in small amounts so they'll be as fresh as possible)

Allspice
Black pepper (ground)
Cayenne pepper
Chili powder
Cinnamon (ground)
Cumin (ground)
Garam masala
Garlic powder
Ginger (ground)
Ground turmeric
Nutmeg (ground)
Onion powder
Oregano
Paprika (smoked and sweet)
Red chili flakes
Salt (sea salt, table salt, fleur de sel)

CANNED AND BOTTLED GOODS

Beans (black beans, chickpeas, navy beans)
Chicken, beef, and vegetable stock or bouillon concentrate (I like the brand Better Than Bouillon)
Diced and crushed tomatoes
Full-fat coconut milk and coconut cream
Hot sauce
Marinara sauce
Soy sauce or tamari
Tomato paste
Vinegars (white wine vinegar, red wine vinegar, white vinegar, apple cider vinegar)

FROZEN FOODS

Corn kernels
Mixed berries
Peas
Shrimp
Puff pastry
Vanilla ice cream

REFRIGERATED FOODS

Berries (blueberries, strawberries, raspberries)

Buttermilk

Capers

Cream cheese

Dijon mustard

Dill pickles

Extra-firm tofu

Herbs (basil, cilantro, flat-leaf parsley, rosemary, sage)

Fresh ginger

Lemons and limes

Mayonnaise

Milk (2% cow's milk or unsweetened plant-based alternative)

Mustard (Dijon mustard, yellow mustard)

DRY, CANNED, AND BOTTLED GOODS

Active dry yeast

Baking powder

Baking soda

Coconut (sweetened and unsweetened shredded)

Cornstarch

Dutch-process cocoa powder

Dried cranberries

Flour (unbleached all-purpose flour, whole wheat flour)

1:1 gluten-free flour blend (if needing gluten-free)

Medjool dates

Panko crumbs

Pasta (spaghetti, orzo, bow ties, and any other shape you love)

Pure local liquid honey

Pure maple syrup

Quinoa

Raisins

Rice (jasmine rice, brown rice)

Rolled oats (old-fashioned, quick)

Sugar (brown sugar, white cane sugar)

BAKING TOOLS

18 × 13-inch (45 × 33 cm) large baking sheet (half sheet pan; this is my go-to baking sheet used throughout the book, except where I specify otherwise)

15 × 10-inch (38 × 25 cm) baking sheet (jelly roll pan)

Loaf pans (9 × 5-inch/2 L and 8 × 4-inch/1.5 L)

12-cup muffin tin

Silicone giant muffin tins (for freezing soups, sauces, and such in individual portions)

Bundt pan (10-cup/2.5 L)

13 × 9-inch (3.5 L) ceramic baking dish

13 × 9-inch (3.5 L) metal baking pan

9-inch (23 cm) square ceramic baking dish

9-inch (23 cm) square metal baking pan

Mixing bowls (various sizes)

Hand-held electric mixer or stand mixer

Spring-release cookie scoops (various sizes)

Wire whisk

Rolling pin

Rubber spatulas

Kitchen scale

Parchment paper

Plastic wrap

Aluminum foil

Paper muffin liners

MEAL PLANNING TOOLS

Glass jars (various sizes)

Glass or plastic resealable storage containers (various sizes)

Resealable storage bags

COOKING TOOLS

Chef's knife (the best you can buy; a 6-inch/15 cm) is my preference)

Colander and fine-mesh sieve

Citrus juicer

Electric hand mixer or stand mixer

Food processor

Garlic press

Heavy-bottomed pots with lids

High-speed blender

Immersion blender

Instant-read thermometer

Microplane zester

Nonstick frying pans (small, medium, large)

Ovenproof frying pan (large) with lid

Paring knife

Vegetable peeler

Wooden spoons

Big-Batch BREAKFASTS

MAKE AHEAD | FREEZER-FRIENDLY

PIEROGI BREAKFAST BAKE

Vegetarian Option • Gluten-Free Option • Nut-Free

Serves 6 to 8

TIME	
Prep:	15 MINUTES
Cook:	25 MINUTES
Total:	40 MINUTES

8 frozen hash brown patties

½ pound (225 g) thick-cut bacon, diced

1½ cups (375 mL) finely diced yellow onion

4 cups (1 L) roughly chopped spinach

¼ cup (60 mL) sliced green onions (white and light green parts only), plus more for garnish

¼ cup (60 mL) chopped fresh dill, plus more for garnish

12 eggs

½ cup (125 mL) sour cream, plus more for garnish

½ teaspoon (2 mL) salt

¼ teaspoon (1 mL) pepper

1½ cups (375 mL) grated cheddar cheese

STORAGE

Store the cooled breakfast bake in a resealable container in the fridge for up to 4 days or in the freezer for up to 3 months. If frozen, thaw in the fridge overnight, then reheat in the oven or microwave until warmed through.

I could gladly eat pierogies to start my day, and this breakfast bake lets me do exactly that. All the flavours of pierogies, but in a delicious breakfast casserole. This Ukrainian gal's dreams have truly come true! This dish is great for every day as well as for hosting a hungry crowd. Make it ahead and prepare to *wow* your lucky guests, or slice it up for a grab-and-go breakfast on busy mornings.

1. Preheat the oven to 425°F (220°C) and grease a 13 × 9-inch (3.5 L) baking dish.

2. Line the prepared baking dish with the hash brown patties to cover the bottom, trimming where necessary. Bake until golden brown and crispy, about 25 minutes. Remove from the oven. Reduce the oven temperature to 350°F (180°C).

3. **Meanwhile, make the Filling:** In a medium frying pan over medium heat, cook the bacon until slightly crispy and the fat is mostly rendered, 3 to 5 minutes. Drain off all but about 1 tablespoon (15 mL) of fat from the pan. Return the pan to the heat, add the yellow onion, and cook, stirring frequently, until the onion is soft and translucent, 3 to 4 minutes. Add the spinach, green onions, and dill and cook, stirring, until the spinach is just wilted, about 1 minute. Set aside to cool.

4. In a large bowl, whisk together the eggs, sour cream, salt, and pepper.

5. Sprinkle the cheese over the crispy hash browns, then scatter the bacon mixture on top. Pour the egg mixture evenly over the filling. Bake until the eggs are set and the edges are golden brown and puffed up slightly, about 25 minutes. Garnish with sour cream, dill, and green onions if desired.

Vegetarian: Omit the bacon and fry the onions in 1 tablespoon (15 mL) of avocado oil.

Gluten-Free: Use certified gluten-free bacon. Omit the hash brown patties (and cooking in step 2) and replace with 2 cups (500 mL) diced cooked peeled russet or yellow potatoes.

MAKE AHEAD | FREEZER-FRIENDLY

PROTEIN EGG BITES

Vegetarian Option • *Gluten-Free Option* • *Nut-Free*

Makes 12 egg bites

TIME
Prep: 15 MINUTES
Cook: 20 MINUTES
Total: 35 MINUTES

10 eggs

½ cup (125 mL) 2% cottage cheese

2 tablespoons (30 mL) heavy (35%) cream

¼ teaspoon (1 mL) salt

¼ teaspoon (1 mL) pepper

FILLING ADD-INS **(each makes enough for 1 batch; optional)**

Mediterranean

¾ cup (175 mL) finely chopped spinach

½ cup (125 mL) finely diced sweet pepper (yellow, orange, or red)

¼ cup (60 mL) crumbled feta cheese

Jalapeño Popper

½ cup (125 mL) crumbled cooked bacon

¼ cup (60 mL) finely diced seeded jalapeño pepper

½ cup (125 mL) cream cheese, room temperature

Farmer's Sausage

1 cup (250 mL) diced cooked sausage

½ cup (125 mL) sautéed sliced mushrooms

2 tablespoons (30 mL) sliced green onion (white and light green parts only)

Prepare to have these protein-packed egg bites on repeat. Better than those found at your favourite coffee chain (you know who you are!), these egg bites are cost-effective and a great high-protein option to make ahead of a busy week. I've created three dynamite flavour combinations, but feel free to modify the add-ins as you wish (just use roughly the same volume). Enjoy them on their own as you fly out the door, with toast, wrapped in a tortilla, or with a smoothie.

1. Place a rimmed baking sheet on the middle rack of the oven and fill halfway with hot water. Preheat the oven to 350°F (180°C). Grease a 12-cup muffin tin.

2. In a high-speed blender, combine the eggs, cottage cheese, cream, salt, and pepper. Blend on high speed until smooth, 30 to 60 seconds.

3. Divide the desired add-ins evenly among the muffin cups. Carefully pour the egg mixture evenly over the add-ins.

4. Carefully place the muffin tin on the baking sheet in the oven (it will sit in the water). Bake until the eggs are set, about 20 minutes. Remove the egg bites from the pan and transfer to a rack until ready to serve.

Vegetarian: Omit the meat from the variations.

Gluten-Free: Use gluten-free sausage for the Farmer's Sausage add-ins.

STORAGE
Store cooled egg bites in a resealable container in the fridge for up to 4 days or in the freezer for up to 3 months. If frozen, thaw in the fridge overnight, then reheat in the microwave for 30 to 60 seconds until warmed through.

MAKE AHEAD | FREEZER-FRIENDLY

FIESTA TORTILLA BREAKFAST EGG CUPS

Vegetarian Option • Dairy-Free Option • Gluten-Free Option • Nut-Free

Makes 12 egg cups

TIME	
Prep:	10 MINUTES
Cook:	25 MINUTES
Total:	35 MINUTES

6 medium (7-inch/18 cm) flour tortillas

Avocado oil or vegetable oil, for cooking

2 fresh chorizo sausages (4 ounces/115 g each; not cured or dried), casings removed

½ cup (125 mL) refried beans

½ teaspoon (2 mL) ground cumin

8 eggs

¼ cup (60 mL) salsa

½ teaspoon (2 mL) salt

¼ teaspoon (1 mL) pepper

½ cup (125 mL) grated Monterey Jack or cheddar cheese

For serving

Guacamole

Sour cream

Salsa

Finely chopped fresh cilantro

Finely chopped green onions

STORAGE

Store cooled egg cups in a resealable container in the fridge for up to 4 days or in the freezer for up to 3 months. If frozen, thaw in the fridge overnight, then reheat in the microwave or in an air fryer until warmed through.

These tortilla egg cups bring the fiesta to your breakfast table! Packed with Mexican flavours and protein-rich ingredients like eggs and refried beans, they're the perfect make-ahead solution for hectic mornings. Wholesome, satisfying, and customizable—just add your favourite toppings and enjoy a delicious breakfast on the go or at home.

1. Preheat the oven to 325°F (160°C) and grease a 12-cup muffin tin.

2. Cut the tortillas in half. Gently press a tortilla half into each muffin well, pressing up the sides to create a cup.

3. Heat a drizzle of avocado oil in a small frying pan over medium heat. Add the sausage, breaking the meat into small pieces with a wooden spoon, and cook until browned, about 5 minutes. Remove from the heat and set aside.

4. In a small bowl, stir together the refried beans and cumin.

5. In a medium bowl, whisk together the eggs, salsa, salt, and pepper.

6. Divide the refried beans evenly among the tortilla-lined muffin cups. Scatter the cooked sausage over the refried beans. Pour the egg mixture evenly into the cups. Top with a sprinkle of cheese. Bake until the eggs are set and the edges of the tortillas are golden brown, about 25 minutes.

7. Remove the baked tortilla cups from the tin and transfer to a rack to cool slightly. Serve with guacamole, sour cream, salsa, cilantro, and green onions.

Vegetarian: Omit the chorizo sausage.

Dairy-Free: Omit the chorizo sausage. Use vegan cheese and vegan sour cream.

Gluten-Free: Use gluten-free tortillas.

APPLE CHICKEN SAUSAGE PATTIES

Dairy-Free • Gluten-Free • Nut-Free

Makes 6 patties

TIME	
Prep:	10 MINUTES
Cook:	10 MINUTES
Total:	20 MINUTES

1 pound (450 g) ground chicken
½ cup (125 mL) grated peeled apple
2 tablespoons (30 mL) pure maple syrup
1 teaspoon (5 mL) garlic powder
1 teaspoon (5 mL) onion powder
½ teaspoon (2 mL) dried oregano
½ teaspoon (2 mL) salt
¼ teaspoon (1 mL) pepper
Extra-virgin olive oil, for cooking

STORAGE
Store cooled patties in a resealable container in the fridge for up to 3 days or in the freezer for up to 2 months. If frozen, thaw in the fridge overnight, then reheat in a frying pan on the stovetop or in an air fryer until warmed through.

Once you make your own breakfast sausage patties, it's hard to go back. Especially when you see how simple it really is! My family loves the savouriness and sweetness of these Apple Chicken Sausage Patties. These are great to serve with a traditional breakfast or add to a sandwich like my Sheet-Pan Breakfast Sandwiches (page 57).

1. In a medium bowl, mix together the ground chicken, grated apple, maple syrup, garlic powder, onion powder, oregano, salt, and pepper until well combined.

2. Heat a drizzle of olive oil in a large frying pan over medium heat. Working in batches, scoop about ⅓-cup (75 mL) portions of the mixture into the pan and press down with a spatula to form patties about ½ inch (1 cm) thick. Cook until golden brown and cooked through, about 4 minutes per side. Serve hot.

BREAKFAST QUESADILLAS

Vegetarian Option · *Gluten-Free Option* · *Nut-Free*

Makes 12 quesadillas

TIME
Prep: 10 MINUTES
Cook: 20 MINUTES
Total: 30 MINUTES

12 eggs

½ teaspoon (2 mL) salt

¼ teaspoon (1 mL) pepper

12 medium (7-inch/18 cm) flour tortillas

Extra-virgin olive oil, for cooking

FILLING ADD-INS (each makes enough for 1 batch; optional)

Sausage Feta Spinach

1 cup (250 mL) crumbled cooked Italian sausage or Apple Chicken Sausage Patties (page 48)

1 cup (250 mL) chopped spinach

¾ cup (175 mL) crumbled feta cheese

Cheddar Bacon Chive

1 cup (250 mL) grated cheddar cheese

½ cup (125 mL) crumbled cooked bacon

¼ cup (60 mL) chopped fresh chives

Santa Fe

1 cup (250 mL) grated jalapeño Jack cheese

¾ cup (175 mL) canned black beans, drained, rinsed, and mashed

½ cup (125 mL) finely diced red, yellow, or orange sweet pepper

½ cup (125 mL) chopped fresh cilantro

2 tablespoons (30 mL) diced red onion

For serving

Sour cream

Guacamole

Salsa

Hot sauce

My son Charlie has recently become quite the young chef! His favourite meal to make for himself is breakfast, and these quesadillas are top of his list. It's easy to see why. They are simple to make, easily customizable with fillings you love (or perfect for a "clean out the fridge" moment), and you can even prep a big batch ahead of time—simply reheat them in a frying pan to get them crisp. I like using whole wheat or sprouted grain tortillas—they are a great way to sneak in some extra fibre.

1. Preheat the oven to 200°F (100°C) and set aside a baking dish. In a medium bowl, whisk together the eggs, salt, and pepper.

2. Heat the olive oil in an 8-inch (20 cm) frying pan over medium heat. Add ¼ cup (60 mL) of the whisked eggs to the hot pan, rotating the pan to form about a 7-inch (18 cm) circle, and cook until the egg starts to set, about 30 seconds. Place a tortilla on top of the egg and continue cooking until the egg is set on the bottom, about 20 seconds. Slide a spatula under the egg and quickly flip the tortilla.

3. Evenly spread about ¼ cup (60 mL) of the desired filling over one half of the egg, then fold the empty half of the tortilla over the filling to create a half-moon. Press down on it slightly so the two halves adhere, and continue cooking, flipping halfway through, until the cheese has melted and the tortilla is golden brown on both sides. Transfer the quesadilla to the baking dish, cover with foil, and keep warm in the oven. Repeat with the remaining tortillas and filling.

4. Serve immediately with sour cream, guacamole, salsa, and hot sauce as desired.

Vegetarian: Omit the bacon and sausage or use plant-based alternatives.

Gluten-Free: Use gluten-free tortillas. Use gluten-free bacon and sausage, if using.

STORAGE

Individually wrap cooled quesadillas, without toppings, in plastic wrap, then place in a resealable container and store in the fridge for up to 4 days or in the freezer for up to 2 months. To reheat from frozen, unwrap the quesadillas and microwave until just thawed, about 1 minute. Crisp up the quesadillas in a frying pan over medium heat if desired.

SMOKED SALMON BAGEL SANDWICHES

Gluten-Free Option • *Nut-Free*

Serves 4

TIME | *Prep:* 10 MINUTES

Smoked Salmon Spread

7 ounces (200 g) cold-smoked salmon, chopped

1 package (8 ounces/250 g) cream cheese, room temperature

½ English cucumber, seeded and finely diced

¼ cup (60 mL) finely diced red onion

¼ cup (60 mL) finely diced dill pickles

¼ cup (60 mL) finely chopped fresh dill

1 tablespoon (15 mL) drained capers, chopped

2 teaspoons (10 mL) fresh lemon juice

For assembly

4 bagels

Arugula or baby spinach

PREP AHEAD
The Smoked Salmon Spread can be made up to 4 days ahead and stored in a resealable container in the fridge.

This smoked salmon sandwich spread features all the ingredients of a classic smoked salmon bagel, but chopped up and ready to be spread onto your favourite bagel for an easy breakfast. This chopped version is so easy to prep ahead and has the perfect ratio of each ingredient in every single bite. My preference is to use everything-seasoned bagels, but any savoury bagel flavour will work. If sweet things are more your thing, try my Strawberry Cream Cheese (page 55).

1. **Make the Smoked Salmon Spread:** In a medium bowl, mix together the smoked salmon, cream cheese, cucumber, red onion, dill pickles, dill, capers, and lemon juice until well combined.

2. **Assemble:** Slice the bagels in half horizontally. Toast until lightly browned. Smear the spread on each of the bottom halves of the bagels, then top with some arugula. Close with the bagel tops.

Gluten-Free: Use gluten-free bagels.

STRAWBERRY CHEESECAKE BAGEL SANDWICHES

Vegan Option • Vegetarian • Dairy-Free Option • Gluten-Free Option • Nut-Free

Serves 4

TIME | *Prep:* 10 MINUTES

Strawberry Cream Cheese

1 package (8 ounces/250 g) cream cheese, room temperature

1 cup (250 mL) diced fresh strawberries

2 tablespoons (30 mL) pure liquid honey

1 teaspoon (5 mL) lemon zest

1 tablespoon (15 mL) fresh lemon juice

½ teaspoon (2 mL) pure vanilla extract

For assembly

4 bagels

Fresh mint leaves, for garnish (optional)

PREP AHEAD
The Strawberry Cream Cheese can be made up to 4 days ahead and stored in a resealable container in the fridge.

Don't we all wish we could eat strawberry cheesecake for breakfast? Good news: It takes only 5 minutes to make your very own Strawberry Cream Cheese! Perfect for a thick spread on bagels, but it doubles as dip for fresh fruit: Simply add a spoonful of vanilla Greek yogurt to thin if desired. This spread also tastes divine served on top of Almond Baked French Toast (page 64) or Greek Yogurt Pancakes (see page 63).

1. **Make the Strawberry Cream Cheese:** In a medium bowl, mix together the cream cheese, strawberries, honey, lemon zest, lemon juice, and vanilla until well combined.

2. **Assemble:** Slice the bagels in half horizontally. Toast until lightly browned. Divide the mixture evenly among the toasted bagel halves and spread evenly to cover. Garnish with mint if desired.

Vegan: Use vegan cream cheese. Use sugar instead of honey.

Dairy-Free: Use vegan cream cheese.

Gluten-Free: Use gluten-free bagels.

SHEET-PAN BREAKFAST SANDWICHES

Vegetarian Option · *Gluten-Free Option* · *Nut-Free*

Serves 8

TIME
Prep: 10 MINUTES
Cook: 20 MINUTES
Total: 30 MINUTES

Sheet-Pan Eggs

12 eggs

½ cup (125 mL) 2% cottage cheese

2 tablespoons (30 mL) table (18%) cream or heavy (35%) cream

½ teaspoon (2 mL) salt

¼ teaspoon (1 mL) pepper

TOPPING ADD-INS **(each makes enough for 1 batch; optional)**

Mediterranean

1 cup (250 mL) halved cherry tomatoes

½ cup (125 mL) crumbled feta cheese

¼ cup (60 mL) finely chopped fresh basil

Jalapeño Popper

1 jalapeño pepper, seeded and finely diced

½ cup (125 mL) cream cheese, room temperature

½ cup (125 mL) crumbled cooked bacon

Farmer's Sausage

1 cup (250 mL) crumbled cooked breakfast sausage or Apple Chicken Sausage Patties (page 48)

1 cup (250 mL) grated cheese (cheddar, Havarti, or similar)

1 cup (250 mL) chopped spinach

This breakfast sandwich is a morning game-changer! I love how you can mix and match the toppings in the same pan to make everyone happy (a tall order some days). Take *just* 10 minutes on the weekend to meal-prep these hearty, protein-packed breakfast sandwiches on a sheet pan, then simply nestle slices of the eggs into English muffins, buns (great with the Focaccia Cheese Buns, page 101), biscuits (try the Sour Cream and Onion Biscuits, page 106), or wraps, and store them in the fridge or freezer for the week (or month) ahead. Your future self will thank you. For added nutrition, layer on extra veggies before cooking the sheet-pan eggs. This is also a great dish for using up small amounts of veggies you have in your fridge such as sweet bell pepper, zucchini, or fresh herbs.

1. Position the racks in the upper and lower thirds of the oven. Half fill a small ovenproof dish with hot water and place on the lower rack. Preheat the oven to 350°F (180°C).

2. Spray a 15 × 10-inch (38 × 25 cm) baking sheet with cooking spray, then line with parchment paper. Set aside.

3. **Make the Sheet-Pan Eggs:** In a high-speed blender, combine the eggs, cottage cheese, cream, salt, and pepper. Blend on medium-high speed until smooth, 30 to 60 seconds.

4. Pour the egg mixture into the prepared baking sheet. Sprinkle the desired toppings, if using, evenly over the top. Bake on the upper rack until the eggs are set, 15 to 20 minutes.

Recipe and ingredients continue . . .

Garlic Aioli (optional)

½ cup (125 mL) mayonnaise

1 clove garlic, minced

1 teaspoon (5 mL) fresh lemon juice

¼ teaspoon (1 mL) salt

For assembly (optional)

Bagels

Greek Yogurt Biscuits (page 109)

Sour Cream and Onion Biscuits (page 106)

English muffins

Flour tortillas

STORAGE

Individually wrap cooled sandwiches in parchment paper or foil, then place them in a resealable bag and store in the fridge for up to 4 days or in the freezer for up to 2 months. If frozen, thaw in the fridge overnight, then reheat in the oven or an air fryer until warmed through.

5. **Meanwhile, make the Garlic Aioli, if using:** In a small bowl, whisk together the mayonnaise, garlic, lemon juice, and salt. Refrigerate until ready to use.

6. Cool the eggs slightly before cutting into 8 equal pieces. Serve as is or assemble into breakfast sandwiches with a spread of the Garlic Aioli (if using) on a split bagel, Greek Yogurt Biscuit, Sour Cream and Onion Biscuit, or English muffin, or wrap in a flour tortilla.

Vegetarian: Omit the sausage and bacon.

Gluten-Free: Use gluten-free bread, bacon, and sausage, if using.

MAKE AHEAD | FREEZER-FRIENDLY

CITRUS RICOTTA PANCAKES OR WAFFLES

Vegan Option • Vegetarian • Dairy-Free Option • Gluten-Free Option • Nut-Free

Makes about 12 pancakes or 8 waffles

TIME
Prep: 15 MINUTES
Cook: 20 MINUTES
Total: 35 MINUTES

2 eggs
2 cups (500 mL) buttermilk
½ cup (125 mL) ricotta cheese
¼ cup (60 mL) butter, melted
1 teaspoon (5 mL) lemon zest
1 teaspoon (5 mL) orange zest
2 tablespoons (30 mL) fresh lemon juice
2 tablespoons (30 mL) fresh orange juice
1 teaspoon (5 mL) pure vanilla extract
2½ cups (675 mL) all-purpose flour
½ cup (125 mL) sugar
1 tablespoon (15 mL) baking powder
½ teaspoon (2 mL) baking soda
¼ teaspoon (1 mL) salt
Vegetable oil, for cooking

These irresistibly light, fluffy, and tender pancakes are bursting with fresh citrus flavour. Ricotta cheese is creamy and delicious, and it packs a punch with protein and calcium—making these pancakes a filling and satisfying breakfast that will keep you fuelled all morning. This elevated take on a pancake or waffle is perfect for a cozy weekend brunch or a special morning treat topped with a drizzle of maple syrup, a dollop of yogurt, or a dusting of powdered sugar. Serve them with fresh berries for a vibrant, flavourful start to your day! Both the pancakes and waffles freeze beautifully. If you don't have buttermilk, make your own (see page 317).

1. Preheat the oven to 200°F (100°C) and line a baking sheet with parchment paper. If making waffles, heat a waffle iron according to the manufacturer's directions.

2. In a large bowl, whisk the eggs. Add the buttermilk, ricotta, melted butter, lemon zest, orange zest, lemon juice, orange juice, and vanilla. Whisk to combine.

3. In a medium bowl, stir together the flour, sugar, baking powder, baking soda, and salt.

4. Add the dry ingredients to the wet ingredients and fold to combine. Do not overmix. The batter will look slightly lumpy.

5. **To Make Pancakes:** Heat a small amount of vegetable oil on a griddle or in a large frying pan over medium heat. Using a ladle or measuring cup, for each pancake scoop about ⅓ cup (75 mL) of batter into the pan. Cook until bubbles appear on the surface of the pancakes, 3 to 4 minutes; peek at the underside to make sure it is nicely browned before flipping. Flip and continue to cook until golden brown on the bottom, another 3 to 4 minutes. Transfer the pancakes to the baking sheet and keep warm in the oven while you cook the remaining pancakes.

Recipe and ingredients continue . . .

For serving

Butter

Icing sugar or pure maple syrup

Fresh berries

STORAGE

Store cooled pancakes or waffles in a resealable container in the fridge for up to 5 days or in the freezer for up to 2 months. If frozen, thaw at room temperature. To reheat, arrange the pancakes or waffles in a single layer on a baking sheet lined with parchment paper, cover loosely with foil, then heat in a 350°F (180°C) oven until warmed through, 5 to 7 minutes. Alternatively, heat in a toaster, or microwave in 20-second intervals, until warmed through.

6. **To Make Waffles:** Coat a waffle iron generously with cooking spray. Using a ladle or measuring cup, scoop about ½ cup (125 mL) of batter into the waffle iron, spreading it to cover the entire surface. Close the iron and cook until the waffle is light golden brown, about 3 minutes. Transfer the waffle to the baking sheet and keep warm in the oven while you cook the remaining waffles.

7. Serve the pancakes or waffles with butter, a sprinkle of icing sugar or a drizzle of maple syrup, and fresh berries.

Vegan: Use a store-bought egg replacer or Flax Eggs (page 317) instead of eggs. Make the vegan option of the Buttermilk (page 317). Use non-dairy yogurt instead of ricotta. Use vegan butter.

Dairy-Free: Make the vegan option of the Buttermilk (page 317). Use non-dairy yogurt instead of ricotta. Use vegan butter.

Gluten-Free: Use a 1:1 gluten-free flour blend.

Tip

To make sheet-pan pancakes, grease a 15 × 10-inch (38 × 25 cm) baking sheet, then line with parchment paper. Pour the batter into the pan and spread evenly. Bake in a 350°F (180°C) oven until light golden brown around the edges and a wooden skewer inserted into the centre comes out clean, about 30 minutes.

Tip

To make Greek yogurt waffles, in step 1 heat a waffle iron according to the manufacturer's directions. In step 5, coat the hot waffle iron generously with cooking spray. Using a ladle or measuring cup, scoop about ½ cup (125 mL) of batter into the waffle iron, spreading it to cover the entire surface. Close the iron and cook until the waffle is light golden brown, about 3 minutes. Transfer the waffle to the baking sheet and keep warm in the oven while you cook the remaining waffles. (Makes about 8 waffles.) For a fun way to eat them, cut the waffles into sticks and dip them into maple syrup and vanilla yogurt—a winner with kids!

MAKE AHEAD | FREEZER-FRIENDLY | SOS

GREEK YOGURT PANCAKES

Vegan Option • Vegetarian • Dairy-Free Option • Gluten-Free Option • Nut-Free

Makes about 12 pancakes

TIME
Prep: 10 MINUTES
Cook: 15 MINUTES
Total: 25 MINUTES

2 cups (500 mL) all-purpose flour

1½ cups (375 mL) oat flour or whole wheat flour

¼ cup (60 mL) sugar

4 teaspoons (20 mL) baking powder

2 teaspoons (10 mL) cinnamon (optional)

1 teaspoon (5 mL) baking soda

½ teaspoon (2 mL) salt

2 eggs

2 cups (500 mL) plain full-fat Greek yogurt

2 cups (500 mL) buttermilk

¼ cup (60 mL) butter, melted

1 tablespoon (15 mL) pure vanilla extract

For serving

Whipped cream or Chantilly Cream (page 333)

Pure maple syrup

Fresh berries

STORAGE

Store cooled pancakes, without toppings, in a resealable container or plastic bag in the fridge for up to 5 days or in the freezer for up to 3 months. To heat from frozen, microwave on high until just thawed, about 30 seconds, then toast in the toaster until crisp.

School day mornings are no joke in our house, and these pancakes can turn around the wildest of mornings. I keep a stash in my freezer and love that the kids can pop them in the toaster themselves. Everyone is a fan of these pancakes, and I especially like that they have an extra boost of protein from the Greek yogurt that will keep your busy crew fuelled for the day. If you don't have buttermilk, make your own (see page 317).

1. Preheat the oven to 200°F (100°C) and line a baking sheet with parchment paper.

2. In a large bowl, whisk together the all-purpose flour, oat flour, sugar, baking powder, cinnamon (if using), baking soda, and salt.

3. In a medium bowl, whisk the eggs. Add the yogurt, buttermilk, melted butter, and vanilla and whisk until combined.

4. Stir the wet ingredients into the dry ingredients and mix until just combined. Do not overmix. The batter will be slightly lumpy.

5. Heat a small amount of vegetable oil on a griddle or in a large frying pan over medium heat. Using a ladle or measuring cup, for each pancake scoop about ⅓ cup (75 mL) of batter into the pan. Cook until bubbles appear on the surface of the pancakes, 3 to 4 minutes; peek at the underside to make sure it is nicely browned before flipping. Flip and continue to cook until golden brown on the bottom, another 3 to 4 minutes. Transfer the pancakes to the baking sheet and keep warm in the oven while you cook the remaining pancakes.

6. Serve the pancakes with a dollop of whipped cream or Chantilly Cream and top with syrup and berries.

Vegan: Use a store-bought egg replacer or Flax Eggs (page 317) instead of eggs. Use non-dairy yogurt. Make the vegan option of the Buttermilk (page 317). Use vegan butter. Serve with coconut whipped cream.

Dairy-Free: Use non-dairy yogurt. Make the vegan option of the Buttermilk (page 317). Use vegan butter. Serve with coconut whipped cream.

Gluten-Free: Use a 1:1 gluten-free flour blend.

ALMOND BAKED FRENCH TOAST

Vegetarian • Dairy-Free Option • Gluten-Free Option • Nut-Free Option

Serves 8

TIME	
Prep:	15 MINUTES
Cook:	50 MINUTES
Total:	65 MINUTES

French Toast

8 eggs

1 cup (250 mL) 2% milk

½ cup (125 mL) pure maple syrup

1 tablespoon (15 mL) pure vanilla extract

1 teaspoon (5 mL) pure almond extract

1 day-old soft French loaf, cut into ½-inch (1 cm) cubes

Almond Filling

1½ cups (375 mL) sliced almonds, divided

½ cup (125 mL) sugar

¼ teaspoon (1 mL) salt

¼ cup (60 mL) butter, room temperature

1 egg

For serving

Icing sugar or pure maple syrup

Greek yogurt or whipped cream

Fresh berries

PREP AHEAD

The French toast can be prepped ahead through step 5, but don't bake. Cover and refrigerate for at least 8 hours or overnight. Bake, uncovered, for an easy breakfast or brunch.

STORAGE

Store cooled baked French toast, covered, in the fridge for up to 3 days.

Treats like French toast are often reserved for the weekends or special occasions, but not with this baked French toast stuffed with a delicious almond filling. This hands-off, prep-ahead twist on a classic tastes like an almond croissant—and makes any day feel French toast worthy. Plus, no more standing at the stove flipping individual slices for a bigger crowd. Just pop this dish in the oven and bake.

1. **Make the French Toast:** Preheat the oven to 350°F (180°C) and grease a 13 × 9-inch (3.5 L) baking dish.

2. In a medium bowl, whisk the eggs until smooth. Add the milk, maple syrup, vanilla, and almond extract and whisk until well combined.

3. Place the bread cubes in a large bowl. Pour the wet ingredients over the bread and stir to coat. Transfer the mixture to the prepared baking dish.

4. **Make the Almond Filling:** In a small food processor, combine 1 cup (250 mL) of the sliced almonds with the sugar and salt and pulse until the texture of coarse crumbs. Add the butter and egg and pulse until well combined.

5. Gently and evenly spread the almond filling over the bread mixture. Sprinkle with the remaining ½ cup (125 mL) sliced almonds. Bake until the top is golden brown, 50 to 60 minutes.

6. Dust with icing sugar or drizzle with maple syrup. Serve warm with Greek yogurt and fresh berries.

Dairy-Free: Use a non-dairy milk and vegan butter. Serve with non-dairy yogurt or coconut whipped cream.

Gluten-Free: Use gluten-free bread.

Nut-Free: Omit the almond filling and sliced almonds.

MAKE AHEAD

RASPBERRY LEMON OVERNIGHT OATS

Vegan Option • *Vegetarian* • *Dairy-Free Option* • *Gluten-Free Option* • *Nut-Free*

Serves 4

TIME | *Prep:* 5 MINUTES, PLUS CHILLING TIME

- 3 cups (750 mL) old-fashioned rolled oats
- 3 cups (750 mL) 2% milk
- 2 tablespoons (30 mL) chia seeds, plus more for garnish
- 2 tablespoons (30 mL) hemp hearts
- 2 tablespoons (30 mL) pure maple syrup
- 1 teaspoon (5 mL) pure vanilla extract
- 1 teaspoon (5 mL) lemon zest
- 1 teaspoon (5 mL) fresh lemon juice
- Pinch of salt
- 1 cup (250 mL) fresh or frozen raspberries, plus more for serving
- 1 cup (250 mL) vanilla Greek yogurt, for serving

STORAGE
Store the overnight oats, without toppings, covered, in the fridge for up to 4 days.

Lemons and raspberries are a match made in heaven—their flavours complement each other so well! These overnight oats are creamy, zesty, and satisfying. On Sundays, you'll often find me preparing several mason jars of overnight oats for the week. I have always loved overnight oats—they are the ideal prep-ahead, nutritionally balanced, grab-and-go breakfast or snack, which helps when your life is moving at the speed of light.

1. In a medium bowl, stir together the oats, milk, chia seeds, hemp hearts, maple syrup, vanilla, lemon zest, lemon juice, and salt until well combined. Fold in the raspberries.
2. Evenly divide the mixture among four 1-cup (250 mL) jars with lids or resealable containers. Cover and chill in the fridge for at least 4 hours or overnight.
3. When ready to serve, top the overnight oats with yogurt, raspberries, and a sprinkle of chia seeds if desired.

Vegan and Dairy-Free: Use non-dairy milk and non-dairy yogurt.

Gluten-Free: Use certified gluten-free oats.

MAKE AHEAD

MOCHA OVERNIGHT OATS

Vegan Option · *Vegetarian* · *Dairy-Free Option* · *Gluten-Free Option* · *Nut-Free Option*

Serves 4

TIME — *Prep:* 5 MINUTES, PLUS CHILLING TIME

- 2 cups (500 mL) old-fashioned rolled oats
- 2 cups (500 mL) 2% milk
- ¼ cup (60 mL) smooth natural almond butter, plus more for serving
- ¼ cup (60 mL) toasted chopped raw almonds, plus more for serving
- ¼ cup (60 mL) mini chocolate chips or cacao nibs, plus more for serving
- 3 tablespoons (45 mL) cocoa powder
- 2 tablespoons (30 mL) hemp hearts
- 2 tablespoons (30 mL) pure maple syrup (or to taste)
- 1 tablespoon (15 mL) chia seeds
- 1 tablespoon (15 mL) instant espresso powder
- 1 teaspoon (5 mL) pure vanilla extract
- Pinch of salt

STORAGE
Store the overnight oats, covered, in the fridge for up to 4 days.

When you need breakfast and coffee but know you'll be short on time, make these overnight oats. These Mocha Overnight Oats taste like cookie dough with a hint of coffee, and are a dream come true for coffee lovers. Prep a batch for the busy week ahead and enjoy a simpler morning, knowing these satisfying oats are waiting for you in the fridge.

1. In a medium bowl, stir together the oats, milk, almond butter, almonds, chocolate chips, cocoa powder, hemp hearts, maple syrup, chia seeds, espresso powder, vanilla, and salt until well combined.

2. Evenly divide the mixture among four 1-cup (250 mL) jars with lids or resealable containers. Cover and chill in the fridge for at least 4 hours or overnight.

3. When ready to serve, top the overnight oats with a drizzle of almond butter, chopped almonds, and chocolate chips if desired.

Vegan and Dairy-Free: Use non-dairy milk and dairy-free chocolate.

Gluten-Free: Use certified gluten-free rolled oats.

Nut-Free: Use a seed butter instead of the almond butter. Omit the almonds.

PEANUT BUTTER AND JAM BREAKFAST COOKIES

Vegan Option • Vegetarian • Dairy-Free Option • Gluten-Free Option • Nut-Free Option

Makes 12 large or 24 small cookies

TIME
Prep: 10 MINUTES
Cook: 20 MINUTES
Total: 30 MINUTES

- 2 eggs
- 1 cup (250 mL) mashed ripe banana
- 1 cup (250 mL) smooth natural peanut butter
- ¾ cup (175 mL) pure maple syrup
- ½ cup (125 mL) butter, melted
- 2 teaspoons (10 mL) pure vanilla extract
- 2 cups (500 mL) old-fashioned rolled oats
- 1 cup (250 mL) all-purpose flour
- ½ cup (125 mL) finely chopped salted roasted peanuts
- ¼ cup (60 mL) hemp hearts
- 2 tablespoons (30 mL) chia seeds
- 1 teaspoon (5 mL) cinnamon
- 1 teaspoon (5 mL) baking powder
- ¼ teaspoon (1 mL) salt
- ½ cup (125 mL) jam

STORAGE
Store cooled cookies in a resealable container at room temperature for up to 1 week or in the freezer for up to 3 months.

Three words: Cookies. For. Breakfast. Move over, peanut butter and jelly on toast! These breakfast cookies bring all the nostalgia of the classic combo, but in a better-for-you thumbprint version. They're crunchy and full of healthy ingredients like banana, peanut butter, hemp hearts, and chia seeds. Use your favourite jam in the centre (mine is raspberry).

1. Position the racks in the upper and lower thirds of the oven and preheat to 350°F (180°C). Line 2 baking sheets with parchment paper.

2. In a medium bowl, whisk the eggs. Stir in the mashed banana, peanut butter, maple syrup, melted butter, and vanilla until combined.

3. In a large bowl, stir together the oats, flour, peanuts, hemp hearts, chia seeds, cinnamon, baking powder, and salt.

4. Pour the wet ingredients into the dry ingredients and mix with a spoon or spatula until well combined.

5. Using an ice-cream scoop or large spoon, scoop 6 large (or 12 small) mounds of cookie dough onto each baking sheet, leaving about 1 inch (2.5 cm) between cookies. Using your hand, flatten the cookies until ½ inch (1 cm) thick. With your thumb, press a 1-inch (2.5 cm) indentation in the centre of each cookie. Fill each indentation with a teaspoon of jam.

6. Bake until light golden on the bottom, 18 to 20 minutes, rotating the pans halfway through. Let the cookies cool slightly on the pans, then transfer them to a rack to cool completely.

Vegan: Use a store-bought egg replacer or Flax Eggs (page 317) instead of eggs. Use vegan butter.

Dairy-Free: Use vegan butter.

Gluten-Free: Use a 1:1 gluten-free flour blend. Use certified gluten-free oats.

Nut-Free: Use seed butter instead of peanut butter and sunflower seeds instead of peanuts.

MAKE AHEAD | FREEZER-FRIENDLY

CHOCOLATE HAZELNUT BREAKFAST COOKIES

Vegan Option • Vegetarian • Dairy-Free Option • Gluten-Free Option • Nut-Free Option

Makes 12 large or 24 small cookies

TIME
Prep: 10 MINUTES
Cook: 20 MINUTES
Total: 30 MINUTES

- 2 eggs
- 1 cup (250 mL) mashed ripe banana
- 1 cup (250 mL) smooth natural hazelnut butter
- 1 cup (250 mL) pure maple syrup
- ½ cup (125 mL) butter, melted
- 2 teaspoons (10 mL) pure vanilla extract
- 2 cups (500 mL) old-fashioned rolled oats
- 1 cup (250 mL) all-purpose flour
- 1 cup (250 mL) finely chopped toasted hazelnuts
- ½ cup (125 mL) mini semi-sweet chocolate chips
- ¼ cup (60 mL) hemp hearts
- 2 tablespoons (30 mL) chia seeds
- 1 teaspoon (5 mL) cinnamon
- 1 teaspoon (5 mL) baking powder
- ¼ teaspoon (1 mL) salt

STORAGE
Store cooled cookies in a resealable container at room temperature for up to 1 week or in the freezer for up to 3 months.

Who doesn't love Nutella? A nod to my childhood, these breakfast cookies make an excellent quick breakfast or snack. They're decadent but wholesome, made with bananas, hazelnuts, rolled oats, hemp hearts, and chia seeds. This is the type of cookie you can feel extra good about loving so much! You can find hazelnut butter at most bulk food stores, at your local natural grocery shop, or online.

1. Position the racks in the upper and lower thirds of the oven and preheat to 350°F (180°C). Line 2 baking sheets with parchment paper.

2. In a medium bowl, whisk the eggs. Stir in the mashed banana, hazelnut butter, maple syrup, melted butter, and vanilla until combined.

3. In a large bowl, stir together the oats, flour, hazelnuts, chocolate chips, hemp hearts, chia seeds, cinnamon, baking powder, and salt.

4. Pour the wet ingredients into the dry ingredients and mix until well combined.

5. Using an ice-cream scoop or large spoon, scoop 6 large or 12 small mounds of cookie dough onto each lined baking sheet, leaving about 2 inches (5 cm) between cookies. Using your hand, flatten the cookies until about ¾ inch (2 cm) thick. Bake until golden brown on the bottom, 18 to 20 minutes, rotating the pans halfway through. Let the cookies cool slightly on the pans, then transfer them to a rack to cool completely.

Vegan: Use a store-bought egg replacer or Flax Eggs (page 317) instead of eggs. Use vegan butter and dairy-free chocolate.

Dairy-Free: Use vegan butter and dairy-free chocolate.

Gluten-Free: Use a 1:1 gluten-free flour blend. Use certified gluten-free oats.

Nut-Free: Use a seed butter instead of hazelnut butter. Omit the hazelnuts.

MAKE AHEAD | FREEZER-FRIENDLY

TROPICAL BREAKFAST COOKIES

Vegan Option • Vegetarian • Dairy-Free • Gluten-Free Option • Nut-Free Option

Makes 12 large or 24 small cookies

TIME
Prep: 10 MINUTES
Cook: 20 MINUTES
Total: 30 MINUTES

2 eggs
1 cup (250 mL) mashed ripe banana
1 cup (250 mL) drained crushed pineapple
1 cup (250 mL) smooth cashew butter
¾ cup (175 mL) pure maple syrup
½ cup (125 mL) coconut oil, melted
2 teaspoons (10 mL) pure vanilla extract
½ teaspoon (2 mL) almond extract
2 cups (500 mL) old-fashioned rolled oats
1 cup (250 mL) all-purpose flour
1 cup (250 mL) sweetened shredded coconut, toasted
¼ cup (60 mL) hemp hearts
2 tablespoons (30 mL) chia seeds
1 teaspoon (5 mL) baking powder
¼ teaspoon (1 mL) salt

STORAGE
Store cooled cookies in a resealable container at room temperature for up to 1 week or in the freezer for up to 3 months.

These breakfast cookies are like a little vacation in every bite. I first made them on a chilly morning while dreaming of sun-soaked beaches—and let me tell you, they delivered! Soft, naturally sweet, and just the right amount of chewy, they're everything I want in a grab-and-go breakfast.

1. Position the racks in the upper and lower thirds of the oven and preheat to 350°F (180°C). Line 2 baking sheets with parchment paper.

2. In a medium bowl, whisk the eggs. Stir in the banana, pineapple, cashew butter, maple syrup, melted coconut oil, vanilla, and almond extract until smooth.

3. In a large bowl, stir together the oats, flour, coconut, hemp hearts, chia seeds, baking powder, and salt.

4. Pour the wet ingredients into the dry ingredients and mix until well combined.

5. Using an ice-cream scoop or large spoon, scoop about 6 large or 12 small mounds of cookie dough onto each prepared baking sheet, leaving about 2 inches (5 cm) between cookies. Using your hand, flatten the cookies until about ¾ inch (2 cm) thick. Bake until golden brown around the edges, about 20 minutes, rotating the pans halfway through. Let the cookies cool slightly on the pans, then transfer them to a rack to cool completely.

Vegan: Use a store-bought egg replacer or Flax Eggs (page 317) instead of eggs.

Gluten-Free: Use a 1:1 gluten-free flour blend.

Nut-Free: Use a seed butter instead of the cashew butter and omit the almond extract.

FRUIT SALAD WITH COCONUT LIME YOGURT DRESSING

Vegan Option · Vegetarian · Dairy-Free Option · Gluten-Free · Nut-Free

Serves 4

TIME — *Prep:* 10 MINUTES

Coconut Lime Yogurt Dressing

1 cup (250 mL) coconut-flavoured Greek yogurt

½ teaspoon (2 mL) lime zest

2 tablespoons (30 mL) fresh lime juice

1 tablespoon (15 mL) pure maple syrup

½ teaspoon (2 mL) poppy seeds (optional)

For serving

6 cups (1.5 L) mixed fruit (kiwi, strawberries, grapes, and melon work well)

Toasted sweetened shredded coconut

Granola or Protein Crunch Salad Topper (without the cayenne, page 311) (optional)

PREP AHEAD
The dressing and the fruit can be prepared up to 3 days in advance and stored in separate resealable containers in the fridge.

Meal-prepping a fruit salad is a game-changer for effortless, healthy eating throughout the week. The secret? Choosing fruits that stay fresh and crisp, like melons and whole grapes. But the real star of this show is the Coconut Lime Yogurt Dressing—a creamy, tangy, and refreshing twist that takes your daily fruit to the next level. Top with your favourite granola or my Protein Crunch Salad Topper (made without the cayenne, page 311) for a well-rounded, satisfying breakfast. With easy prep, the salad and dressing make a vibrant, nutritious snack or side dish that's ready whenever you need it.

1. **Make the Coconut Lime Yogurt Dressing:** In a small bowl, whisk together the yogurt, lime zest, lime juice, maple syrup, and poppy seeds, if using. Refrigerate until ready to use.

2. When ready to enjoy, serve bowls of the mixed fruit topped with a drizzle of the Coconut Lime Yogurt Dressing and a sprinkle of toasted coconut and granola, if using.

Vegan and Dairy-Free: Use non-dairy yogurt.

MAKE AHEAD | FREEZER-FRIENDLY

APPLE CINNAMON CREAMY STEEL-CUT OATS

Vegan Option • Vegetarian • Dairy-Free Option • Gluten-Free Option • Nut-Free

Serves 8

TIME

Prep: 10 MINUTES
Cook: 25 MINUTES (FOR STOVETOP METHOD)
Total: 35 MINUTES

2 tablespoons (30 mL) butter or coconut oil

2 cups (500 mL) steel-cut oats

4 or 6 cups (1 or 1.5 L) water

2 cups (500 mL) 2% milk

¼ cup (60 mL) hemp hearts

3 tablespoons (45 mL) flaxseeds (optional)

1 teaspoon (5 mL) cinnamon

1 teaspoon (5 mL) pure vanilla extract

¼ teaspoon (1 mL) salt

2 cups (500 mL) diced peeled apples

½ cup (125 mL) raisins (optional)

STORAGE
Store the cooled cooked oats in a resealable container and refrigerate for up to 5 days, or portion and freeze for up to 2 months. To freeze cooked oats, use resealable meal-prep containers or portion them into a lightly greased muffin tin (a jumbo silicone one works best). Once solid, transfer the portions to a large resealable bag and freeze. When ready to use, let the frozen portions sit on the counter for 10 minutes, then microwave with a splash of milk for about 4 minutes, stirring halfway through and adding more milk if needed.

My oldest son, Charlie, has always loved this combination to start his mornings. The apples, raisins, and cinnamon are like a hug in a bowl, something we can all use. As a mom and dietitian, I love that steel-cut oats are a nutritional breakfast filled with fibre for a healthy start to the day. And flaxseeds and hemp hearts are nutritional powerhouses, packed with omega-3 fats, protein, and fibre. (You can omit the flaxseed if the appearance or texture is not appealing to the little ones.) Toasting the oats first in the butter or coconut oil is optional but really enhances their flavour. This is a great way to use your slow cooker.

Stovetop Instructions

1. Melt the butter in a large, heavy pot over medium heat. Add the steel-cut oats and cook, stirring occasionally, until fragrant and golden, about 2 minutes. Add 4 cups (1 L) water, milk, hemp hearts, flaxseeds (if using), cinnamon, vanilla, and salt. Add the apples and raisins (if using) and stir to combine.

2. Bring to a simmer, reduce the heat to low, and cook, uncovered and stirring occasionally, until the oats are soft, 25 to 30 minutes.

Slow Cooker Instructions

1. To a slow cooker, add the butter, steel-cut oats, 6 cups (1.5 L) water, milk, hemp hearts, flaxseeds (if using), cinnamon, vanilla, and salt. Add the apples and raisins (if using) and stir to combine.

2. Cover and cook on low for 6 to 8 hours, until creamy and the oats are soft.

Vegan and Dairy-Free: Use coconut oil and non-dairy milk.

Gluten-Free: Use certified gluten-free oats.

MAKE AHEAD | FREEZER-FRIENDLY

PEACH CRUMBLE BREAKFAST BARS

Vegan Option • Vegetarian • Dairy-Free Option • Gluten-Free

Makes 24 bars

TIME	
Prep:	20 MINUTES
Cook:	55 MINUTES
Total:	75 MINUTES

Base

2 cups (500 mL) old-fashioned rolled oats

1 cup (250 mL) raw pecans

¾ cup (175 mL) all-purpose flour

¾ cup (175 mL) pure maple syrup

½ cup (125 mL) smooth natural almond butter

½ cup (125 mL) butter, melted

¼ cup (60 mL) hemp hearts

1 teaspoon (5 mL) cinnamon

1 teaspoon (5 mL) pure vanilla extract

Pinch of salt

Peach Filling

10 cups (2.5 L) frozen sliced peaches (two 600 g packages)

⅔ cup (150 mL) lightly packed brown sugar

2 tablespoons (30 mL) cornstarch

2 tablespoons (30 mL) fresh lemon juice

1 teaspoon (5 mL) cinnamon

Pecan Oat Crumble

½ cup (125 mL) old-fashioned rolled oats

½ cup (125 mL) finely chopped pecans

¼ cup (60 mL) all-purpose flour

¼ cup (60 mL) lightly packed brown sugar

¼ cup (60 mL) butter, melted

½ teaspoon (2 mL) cinnamon

These peachy breakfast bars are like having a slice of old-fashioned peach pie, only healthier and more portable. Who doesn't want to start their morning with that? As an Okanagan gal, I have a special place in my heart for peaches. They are juicy and sweet, and work so well in baking, especially when paired with almond, vanilla, and cinnamon flavours. With a buttery oat and creamy almond butter base, sweet peach filling, and crispy pecan and oat crumble topping, there are lots of reasons to love this recipe. Plus, it fills your home with the most amazing aroma. I often top these bars with a generous dollop of Greek yogurt for an extra boost of protein and a more satisfying, filling breakfast.

1. **Make the Base:** Preheat the oven to 350°F (180°C) and line a 13 × 9-inch (3.5 L) baking pan with parchment paper, leaving extra overhang on the sides to make it easier to remove the bars.

2. In a food processor, combine the oats, pecans, flour, maple syrup, almond butter, melted butter, hemp hearts, cinnamon, vanilla, and salt. Process until the mixture is fine and sticks together. The mixture should resemble cookie dough. Firmly and evenly press the mixture into the bottom of the prepared pan. Bake for 10 minutes, then remove from the oven.

3. **Meanwhile, make the Peach Filling:** In a large pot, stir together the peaches, brown sugar, cornstarch, lemon juice, and cinnamon until combined. Cook over medium-low heat, stirring occasionally, until the peaches are soft, about 15 minutes. Remove from the heat. Using a potato masher, lightly mash the mixture.

4. **Make the Pecan Oat Crumble.** In a medium bowl, stir together the oats, chopped pecans, flour, brown sugar, melted butter, and cinnamon to combine.

5. Spread the peach filling evenly over the prepared base. Evenly sprinkle the pecan oat crumble over the filling. Bake for 45 to 50 minutes or until the edges are golden brown. Cool completely before cutting into bars.

Vegan and Dairy-Free: Use vegan butter.

STORAGE
Store cooled bars in a resealable container in the fridge for up to 1 week or in the freezer for up to 3 months.

Easy BAKING

How to Freeze Dough

I love to bake bread and have been asked what feels like a million times over the years if the dough can be frozen. The answer is yes! Here is how you freeze a yeast dough to bake at a later date. This works for bread dough such as my Milk and Honey Bread (page 89), No-Fail Focaccia Dough (page 90), and any other yeast dough recipe.

Step 1: Prepare the dough through the first rise.

Step 2: Deflate the dough and portion it out. Form each piece into a ball and place on a baking sheet lined with parchment paper. Freeze, uncovered, until frozen, about 1 hour.

Step 3: Tightly wrap each frozen ball of dough with plastic wrap and transfer to a resealable bag. Squeeze the air out of the bag as you seal it, then freeze for up to 1 month. To thaw the dough, unwrap it and place in a lightly greased medium bowl, cover tightly with plastic wrap, and place in a warm, draft-free place until doubled in size, about 4 hours. Use as directed in the recipe.

Tip

The longer the dough stays frozen, the harder it will be to rise, since some of the yeast may die over time. I suggest storing the frozen dough in the freezer for no longer than 1 month.

PREP AHEAD | MAKE AHEAD | FREEZER-FRIENDLY

MULTIGRAIN MILK AND HONEY BREAD

Vegan Option • Vegetarian • Dairy-Free Option • Nut-Free

Makes 2 small loaves

TIME
Prep: 10 MINUTES, PLUS 3 HOURS RISING
Cook: 45 MINUTES
Total: 55 MINUTES

- 1 cup (250 mL) lukewarm 2% milk
- ⅓ cup (75 mL) lukewarm water
- ¼ cup (60 mL) pure liquid honey or sugar
- 2¼ teaspoons (12 mL) active dry yeast
- ½ cup (125 mL) old-fashioned rolled oats
- ¼ cup (60 mL) sunflower seeds
- 3 tablespoons (45 mL) butter, melted
- 1 egg, whisked
- 1½ to 2 cups (375 to 500 mL) all-purpose flour, plus more for dusting
- 1 cup (250 mL) whole wheat flour
- 1½ teaspoons (7 mL) salt

There's something so comforting about the aroma of freshly baked bread filling the kitchen—and this Multigrain Milk and Honey Bread is no exception. Made with wholesome oats and seeds, milk, and just the right touch of honey, this bread is soft and nourishing. It's perfect for everything from morning toast to your favourite sandwiches. Whether you're an experienced baker or just dipping your toes into bread making, this simple recipe will have you coming back for slice after slice.

1. **Make the Dough:** In a large bowl, whisk together the milk, water, and honey. Sprinkle in the yeast and stir to combine. Let sit for about 10 minutes, until the yeast activates and foams up.

2. Stir in the oats, sunflower seeds, melted butter, and egg. Let it sit for 5 minutes.

3. Add 1 cup (250 mL) of the all-purpose flour, the whole wheat flour, and salt. Stir with a wooden spoon until stirring gets too difficult.

4. Transfer the dough to a lightly floured work surface. Knead the dough until smooth and elastic, about 5 minutes, adding more flour, ¼ cup (60 mL) at a time, as needed to prevent it from sticking to your hands. Form the dough into a smooth ball. Place the dough in a greased medium bowl, cover with plastic wrap or a damp kitchen towel, and let it sit in a warm, draft-free place until doubled in size, about 2 hours.

5. Grease two 8 × 4-inch (1.5 L) loaf pans.

6. Gently deflate the dough by pushing it down with your hands. Tip the dough out onto a lightly floured work surface and divide it into 2 equal portions. With floured hands, shape each piece of dough into a flat disc, then fold it into a log, tucking in the ends and pinching the seams to seal. Place the loaves in the prepared loaf pans, seam-side down, cover loosely with plastic wrap or a damp kitchen towel, and let rise in a warm, draft-free place until doubled in size, about 1 hour.

Recipe and ingredients continue . . .

Egg Wash

1 egg

1 tablespoon (15 mL) water

Topping

2 tablespoons (30 mL) old-fashioned rolled oats

2 teaspoons (10 mL) sunflower seeds

1 teaspoon (5 mL) sesame seeds

1 teaspoon (5 mL) poppy seeds

PREP AHEAD

The dough can be prepared ahead through step 6, but instead of rising the dough at room temperature, cover with plastic wrap and place in the fridge to rise for at least 8 hours or overnight. Remove the dough from the fridge and let sit, covered, in a warm, draft-free place until doubled in size, about 1 hour. Uncover and bake as directed. The dough can be made ahead and frozen for up to 1 month; see How to Freeze Dough (page 84).

STORAGE

Store cooled bread in a resealable bag at room temperature for up to 3 days or in the freezer for up to 3 months.

7. Thirty minutes before you are ready to bake, preheat the oven to 350°F (180°C).

8. **Meanwhile, make the Egg Wash:** In a small bowl, whisk together the egg and water.

9. **Mix the Toppings:** In a small bowl, stir together the oats, sunflower seeds, sesame seeds, and poppy seeds.

10. Using a pastry brush, brush the tops of the loaves with the egg wash. Sprinkle the loaves evenly with the topping mixture.

11. Bake the loaves until they are deep golden brown, about 45 minutes. Carefully turn the loaves out of the pans onto a rack and allow to cool for at least 10 minutes.

Vegan: Use non-dairy milk, vegan butter, and sugar instead of honey. Omit the egg and egg wash.

Dairy-Free: Use non-dairy milk and vegan butter.

PREP AHEAD | MAKE AHEAD | FREEZER-FRIENDLY

MILK AND HONEY BREAD

Vegan Option · *Vegetarian* · *Dairy-Free Option* · *Nut-Free*

Makes 2 small loaves

TIME
Prep: 10 MINUTES, PLUS 3 HOURS RISING
Cook: 30 MINUTES
Total: 40 MINUTES

1 cup (250 mL) lukewarm 2% milk

⅓ cup (75 mL) lukewarm water

¼ cup (60 mL) pure liquid honey or sugar

2¼ teaspoons (12 mL) active dry yeast

3 tablespoons (45 mL) butter, melted

1 egg, whisked

2¾ to 3¼ cups (675 to 810 mL) all-purpose flour, plus more for dusting

1½ teaspoons (7 mL) salt

Egg Wash

1 egg

1 tablespoon (15 mL) water

PREP AHEAD
The dough can be prepared ahead through step 5, but instead of rising the dough at room temperature, cover with plastic wrap and place in the fridge to rise for at least 8 hours or overnight. Remove the dough from the fridge and let sit, covered, in a warm, draft-free place until doubled in size, about 1 hour. Uncover and bake as directed. The dough can be made ahead and frozen for up to 1 month; see How to Freeze Dough (page 84).

STORAGE
Store cooled bread in a resealable bag at room temperature for up to 3 days or in the freezer for up to 3 months.

This is an uncomplicated, slightly sweet spongy loaf with a perfectly golden crust that is so satisfying to make. It slices beautifully, and freezes like a dream. It's perfect for sandwiches, a simple slice of toast with butter and jam, or served on the side of a steaming bowl of soup.

1. **Make the Dough:** In a large bowl, whisk together the milk, water, and honey. Sprinkle in the yeast and stir to combine. Let sit for about 10 minutes, until the yeast activates and foams up.

2. Stir the melted butter and egg into the yeast mixture. Add 2 cups (500 mL) of the flour and the salt. Stir with a wooden spoon until stirring gets too difficult.

3. Transfer the dough to a lightly floured work surface. Knead the dough until smooth and elastic, about 5 minutes, adding more flour, ¼ cup (60 mL) at a time, as needed to prevent it from sticking to your hands. Form the dough into a smooth ball. Place the dough in a greased medium bowl, cover with plastic wrap or a damp kitchen towel, and let it sit in a warm, draft-free place until doubled in size, about 2 hours.

4. Grease two 8 × 4-inch (1.5 L) loaf pans.

5. Gently deflate the dough by pushing it down with your hands. Tip the dough out onto a lightly floured work surface and divide it into 2 equal portions. With floured hands, shape each piece of dough into a flat disc, then fold it into a log, tucking in the ends and pinching the seams to seal. Place the loaves in the prepared loaf pans, seam-side down, cover loosely with plastic wrap or a damp kitchen towel, and let rise in a warm, draft-free place until doubled in size, about 1 hour.

6. Thirty minutes before you are ready to bake, preheat the oven to 350°F (180°C).

7. **Meanwhile, make the Egg Wash:** In a small bowl, whisk together the egg and water. Using a pastry brush, brush the egg wash onto the tops of the loaves.

8. Bake the loaves until they are deep golden brown, 30 to 35 minutes. Carefully turn the loaves out of the pans onto a rack and allow to cool for at least 10 minutes before slicing.

Vegan: Use non-dairy milk, vegan butter, and sugar instead of honey. Omit the egg and egg wash.

Dairy-Free: Use non-dairy milk and vegan butter.

PREP AHEAD | MAKE AHEAD | FREEZER-FRIENDLY

NO-FAIL FOCACCIA DOUGH

Vegan · Vegetarian · Dairy-Free · Nut-Free

TIME *Prep:* 15 MINUTES, PLUS 2 HOURS RISING

- 1½ cups (375 mL) lukewarm water
- 1 tablespoon (15 mL) sugar
- 1 tablespoon (15 mL) active dry yeast
- ¼ cup (60 mL) extra-virgin olive oil, plus more for the pan and drizzling
- 1½ teaspoons (7 mL) salt
- 3¼ to 3½ cups (810 to 875 mL) all-purpose flour, plus more for dusting

PREP AHEAD
The dough can be prepared ahead through step 3, but instead of rising the dough at room temperature, cover with plastic wrap and place in the fridge to rise for at least 8 hours or overnight. Remove the dough from the fridge and let sit, covered, in a warm, draft-free place until doubled in size, about 1 hour. Proceed with making your chosen focaccia recipe.

STORAGE
Prepare the dough through step 4, deflating the dough (do not proceed to making the focaccia). Tightly wrap the dough in plastic wrap and place in a resealable bag. Store in the freezer for up to 1 month. To thaw the dough, unwrap it and place in large greased bowl, cover tightly with plastic wrap, and let sit in a warm, draft-free place until doubled in size, about 4 hours. Proceed with making your chosen focaccia recipe.

Nothing compares to homemade focaccia, and this no-fail dough recipe is your ticket to Italian bakery-style bread at home—soft and fluffy on the inside with a golden, lightly crisp exterior. Made with a few simple ingredients, this versatile dough can be made into a Focaccia Loaf (page 93)—my spin on a traditional focaccia—or transformed into Focaccia Muffins (page 94), Focaccia Mini Pizzas (page 97), Focaccia Cheese Buns (page 101), or a sweet shareable treat, Focaccia Monkey Bread (page 102).

1. In a large bowl, whisk together the water and sugar to dissolve the sugar. Sprinkle in the yeast and stir to combine. Let it sit for about 10 minutes, until the yeast activates and foams up.

2. Stir the olive oil and salt into the yeast mixture. Add 3 cups (750 mL) of the flour. Stir with a wooden spoon until stirring gets too difficult.

3. Transfer the dough to a well-floured work surface. Knead the dough until smooth and elastic, about 5 minutes, adding more flour as needed to prevent the dough from sticking to your hands. Form the dough into a smooth ball. Place the dough in a medium bowl generously greased with olive oil, cover with plastic wrap, and let it sit in a warm, draft-free place until doubled in size, about 2 hours.

4. Gently deflate the dough by pushing it down with your hands. Proceed with making your chosen focaccia recipe.

PREP AHEAD | MAKE AHEAD | FREEZER-FRIENDLY

FOCACCIA LOAF

Vegan • Vegetarian • Dairy-Free • Nut-Free

Makes 2 loaves

TIME

Prep: 5 MINUTES (NOT INCLUDING MAKING THE NO-FAIL FOCACCIA DOUGH), PLUS 1½ HOURS RISING

Cook: 20 MINUTES

Total: 25 MINUTES

1 batch No-Fail Focaccia Dough (page 90)

Extra-virgin olive oil

1 to 2 teaspoons (5 to 10 mL) flaky sea salt

2 tablespoons (30 mL) chopped fresh rosemary

PREP AHEAD
The No-Fail Focaccia Dough can be made ahead and frozen for up to 1 month; see How to Freeze Dough (page 84).

STORAGE
Store cooled bread in a resealable plastic bag at room temperature for up to 3 days or in the freezer for up to 1 month.

Golden, airy, and irresistibly crisp on the outside, focaccia is a simple yet flavourful bread that pairs beautifully with soups and salads and is a great base for sandwiches. Whether you're a seasoned baker or trying homemade bread for the first time, this easy focaccia loaf recipe delivers bakery-quality results every time!

1. Generously grease two 8 × 4-inch (1.5 L) loaf pans with olive oil.

2. Place the No-Fail Focaccia Dough on a lightly floured work surface and divide it into 2 equal pieces. Shape each piece of dough into a 7-inch (18 cm) log and place in the prepared loaf pans, tucking the ends underneath. Cover with plastic wrap and let sit in a warm, draft-free place until doubled in size, about 1½ hours.

3. Using your fingertips, gently poke indentations across the surface of the loaves in a random pattern. Drizzle the loaves with olive oil and sprinkle with flaky sea salt and rosemary. Cover loosely with plastic wrap and let sit in a warm, draft-free place until they have slightly risen, about 30 minutes.

4. Meanwhile, preheat the oven to 425°F (220°C).

5. Bake the focaccia until it is golden brown, about 20 minutes. Best served warm.

FOCACCIA MUFFINS

Vegan · Vegetarian · Dairy-Free · Nut-Free

Makes 12 muffins

TIME

Prep: 10 MINUTES (NOT INCLUDING MAKING THE NO-FAIL FOCACCIA DOUGH), PLUS 1½ HOURS RISING

Cook: 20 MINUTES

Total: 30 MINUTES

1 batch No-Fail Focaccia Dough (page 90)

Extra-virgin olive oil

1 to 2 teaspoons (5 to 10 mL) flaky sea salt

2 tablespoons (30 mL) chopped fresh rosemary

PREP AHEAD

The dough can be prepared ahead through step 2, but instead of rising the dough at room temperature, cover with plastic wrap and place in the fridge to rise for at least 8 hours or overnight. Remove the dough from the fridge and let sit, covered, in a warm, draft-free place until doubled in size, about 1 hour. Uncover and bake as directed. The No-Fail Focaccia Dough can be made ahead and frozen for up to 1 month; see How to Freeze Dough (page 84).

STORAGE

Store cooled muffins in a resealable container at room temperature for up to 3 days or in the freezer for up to 2 months. Reheat in the microwave or on a baking sheet lined with parchment paper in the oven at 300°F (150°C) until warmed through, 8 to 10 minutes.

Baked to golden perfection with olive oil, rosemary, flaky salt, and just the right amount of crunch, these muffins are like little pockets of single-serve rustic charm. Whether you're serving them alongside a cozy soup such as Roasted Veggie Tortellini Soup (page 151) or Lemon Chicken Orzo Soup (page 146), baking a batch to win someone's heart, adding flair to a charcuterie board, or just sneaking one as a midday snack, these Focaccia Muffins prove that big flavour can come in small packages.

1. Generously grease a 12-cup muffin tin with olive oil.

2. Tip the dough out onto a lightly floured work surface and divide it into 12 equal portions, about 2½ ounces (70 g) each. Shape the dough pieces into balls, tucking the edges under and pinching the bottom to make the tops smooth. Place the buns in the prepared muffin tin, cover loosely with plastic wrap, and let sit in a warm, draft-free place until doubled in size, about 1½ hours.

3. Thirty minutes before you are ready to bake, preheat the oven to 425°F (220°C).

4. Using your fingertips, gently poke 3 holes into the surface of each muffin. Top each muffin with a drizzle of olive oil. Sprinkle with the flaky sea salt and rosemary.

5. Bake the muffins until they are golden brown, about 15 minutes. Carefully turn the muffins out of the tin onto a rack and allow to cool slightly before serving warm.

PREP AHEAD | MAKE AHEAD | FREEZER-FRIENDLY

FOCACCIA MINI PIZZAS

Vegan Option • Vegetarian • Dairy-Free Option • Nut-Free

Makes 8 individual pizzas

TIME

Prep: 20 MINUTES (NOT INCLUDING MAKING THE NO-FAIL FOCACCIA DOUGH)

Cook: 10 MINUTES

Total: 30 MINUTES

1 batch No-Fail Focaccia Dough (page 90)

All-purpose flour, for dusting

Extra-virgin olive oil, for brushing

Toppings (see page 98 for my favourite combinations)

PREP AHEAD

The No-Fail Focaccia Dough can be made ahead and frozen for up to 1 month; see How to Freeze Dough (page 84).

STORAGE

Store cooled cooked pizzas in a resealable container in the fridge for up to 3 days or in the freezer for up to 1 month. If frozen, thaw in the fridge overnight, then reheat in the oven or in an air fryer until warmed through and the cheese bubbles.

Pizza nights will never be the same when you make these focaccia mini pizzas. The focaccia provides the most incredible base for mini pizzas. For a fun family dinner, set out all the toppings and have each person create their own pizzetta. Do not overload the toppings, or the pizza bottom will be too soft. My SOS Spaghetti Sauce (page 312) makes a fabulous homemade pizza sauce.

1. Tip the dough out onto a lightly floured work surface and divide it into 8 equal portions. Shape the dough pieces into smooth balls, tucking the edges under and pinching the bottom to make the tops smooth. Let rest, uncovered, for about 15 minutes while the oven preheats.

2. Preheat the oven to 500°F (260°C) and line a baking sheet with parchment paper.

3. Working with one dough ball at a time, dust the dough with flour. Using floured hands, stretch the dough into a 10-inch (25 cm) circle (it doesn't have to be exact) and place on the baking sheet. You should be able to fit 2 or 3 mini pizzas on the pan.

4. Lightly brush the edges of the pizzas with olive oil. Evenly spread a thin layer of sauce of choice over the dough, leaving about a ½-inch (1 cm) border of exposed dough around the edge. Scatter toppings of choice on the pizza, being careful not to overload it, and finish with a sprinkling of cheese. Bake until the crust is golden brown and the cheese bubbles, about 10 minutes. Serve hot.

Vegan: Use vegan cheese and vegan pizza toppings.

Dairy-Free: Use vegan cheese.

Favourite Topping Combinations

SPICY HAWAIIAN

Pizza sauce or SOS Spaghetti Sauce (page 312), ham, pineapple, banana peppers, and mozzarella

BARBECUE CHICKEN

Barbecue sauce, shredded rotisserie chicken, red onion, green peppers, pineapple (optional), and mozzarella

PESTO SHRIMP

Pesto, cooked peeled and deveined shrimp, sun-dried tomatoes, feta, and mozzarella

CHICKEN ALFREDO

Alfredo sauce, shredded rotisserie chicken, spinach, mozzarella, Parmesan

HOT HONEY PEPPERONI

Pizza sauce or SOS Spaghetti Sauce (page 312), pepperoni, mozzarella, and drizzle cooked pizza with hot honey before serving

FOCACCIA CHEESE BUNS

Vegan Option · Vegetarian · Dairy-Free Option · Nut-Free

Makes 12 buns

TIME

Prep: 15 MINUTES (NOT INCLUDING THE NO-FAIL FOCACCIA DOUGH), PLUS 1½ HOURS RISING

Cook: 20 MINUTES

Total: 35 MINUTES

1 batch No-Fail Focaccia Dough (page 90)

2 cups (500 mL) grated old cheddar cheese, divided

PREP AHEAD

The dough can be prepared ahead through step 4, but instead of rising the dough at room temperature, cover with plastic wrap and place in the fridge to rise for at least 8 hours or overnight. Remove the dough from the fridge and let sit, covered, in a warm, draft-free place until doubled in size, about 1 hour. Uncover and bake as directed. The dough can be made ahead and frozen for up to 1 month; see How to Freeze Dough (page 84).

STORAGE

Store cooled buns in a resealable container at room temperature for up to 3 days or in the freezer for up to 1 month. Reheat in the microwave or on a baking sheet lined with parchment paper in the oven at 300°F (150°C) until warmed through, 8 to 10 minutes.

There used to be a little family-run bakery across the street from my elementary school, and all the kids would take turns covering for each other to sneak away at recess to buy doughnuts and cheese buns. These Focaccia Cheese Buns remind me of those cheese buns from my childhood—minus the adrenaline hit from being naughty. Crispy bits of cheese bake into the golden bottoms of these fluffy, rustic buns. For a dinner bun style, bake them in a 13 × 9-inch (3.5 L) pan, or for flatter, burger-worthy buns, bake in a 15 × 10-inch (38 × 25 cm) baking sheet. Brush warm buns with melted garlic butter before serving for added flavour if desired.

1. Grease a 13 × 9-inch (3.5 L) pan with olive oil for tall dinner-style buns or a 15 × 10-inch (38 × 25 cm) baking sheet for burger-style buns.

2. Scrape the dough onto a lightly floured work surface. Using floured hands, stretch the dough into a 20 × 12-inch (50 × 30 cm) rectangle (it doesn't need to be exact) with a long side facing you.

3. Evenly sprinkle 1½ cups (375 mL) of the cheese lengthwise across the top half of the dough. Fold the dough up and over the cheese and knead until the cheese is incorporated (set aside any cheese that falls out).

4. Divide the dough into 12 equal portions (about 2½ ounces/70 g each). Using floured hands, shape the dough pieces into balls, tucking the edges under and pinching the bottom to make the tops smooth. Evenly space the buns in the prepared baking pan or baking sheet. Sprinkle the buns with the remaining cheese (plus any that fell out during kneading). Cover with plastic wrap and let sit in a warm, draft-free place until doubled in size, about 1½ hours.

5. Thirty minutes before you are ready to bake, preheat the oven to 375°F (190°C).

6. Bake until golden brown on the tops and bottoms, about 20 minutes. Transfer the buns to a rack and allow to cool slightly before serving warm.

Vegan and Dairy-Free: Use vegan cheese.

Re-Fraiche

Make croutons with leftover buns. Cut the buns into bite-size pieces. Scatter the croutons on a baking sheet lined with parchment paper and drizzle with olive oil. Bake in a 350°F (180°C) oven until golden brown, about 10 minutes, tossing halfway through.

FOCACCIA MONKEY BREAD

Vegan Option • Vegetarian • Dairy-Free Option • Nut-Free

Serves 12

TIME

Prep: 15 MINUTES (NOT INCLUDING THE NO-FAIL FOCACCIA DOUGH), PLUS 2 HOURS RISING

Cook: 35 MINUTES

Total: 50 MINUTES

1 batch No-Fail Focaccia Dough (page 90)

½ cup (125 mL) butter, melted

1 teaspoon (5 mL) pure vanilla extract

1 cup (250 mL) lightly packed brown sugar

1 tablespoon (15 mL) cinnamon

PREP AHEAD

The dough can be prepared ahead through step 3, but instead of rising the dough at room temperature, cover tightly with plastic wrap and place in the fridge to rise for at least 8 hours or overnight. Remove the dough from the fridge and let sit, covered, in a warm, draft-free place until doubled in size, about 1 hour. Uncover and bake as directed. The No-Fail Focaccia Dough can be made ahead and frozen for up to 1 month; see How to Freeze Dough (page 84).

STORAGE

Store cooled bread, covered, at room temperature for up to 2 days or in the fridge for up to 4 days. Place the Focaccia Monkey Bread in an oven-safe dish lined with parchment paper, cover loosely with foil and heat in a 300°F (150°C) oven for 10 to 15 minutes, until warmed through.

Pull-apart bread just got a serious upgrade. This sweet Focaccia Monkey Bread combines the pillowy softness of focaccia with the gooey, snackable charm of classic monkey bread—it's the kind of thing you set on the table and suddenly everyone's "just having one more piece." Each bite is coated in a buttery cinnamon sugar glaze that caramelizes into golden perfection, with soft fluffy bits of dough and just the right amount of indulgence. Serve this warm for brunch or dessert.

1. Grease a 10-cup (2.5 L) Bundt pan with nonstick cooking spray.

2. Using a pair of scissors or a sharp knife, cut the dough into 1-inch (2.5 cm) pieces. Place the dough pieces on a lightly floured work surface.

3. In a large bowl, stir together the melted butter and vanilla. Stir in the brown sugar and cinnamon. One or two at a time, add the pieces of dough to the sugar mixture, lightly tossing as you add them to prevent them from sticking together. Arrange the dough pieces evenly in the Bundt pan and cover with plastic wrap. Let sit in a warm, draft-free place until doubled in size, about 1 hour.

4. Thirty minutes before you are ready to bake, preheat the oven to 350°F (180°C).

5. Bake until golden brown, about 35 minutes. Cool in the pan for about 5 minutes, then invert onto a large plate or cake stand. Serve warm.

Vegan and Dairy-Free: Use vegan butter.

PREP AHEAD

POPOVERS

Vegetarian • Nut-Free

Makes 12 popovers

TIME	
	Prep: 5 MINUTES, PLUS 30 MINUTES TO REST
	Cook: 25 MINUTES
	Total: 30 MINUTES

4 large eggs, room temperature

1 cup (250 mL) 2% milk, room temperature

1¼ cups (300 mL) all-purpose flour

2 tablespoons (30 mL) butter, melted

½ teaspoon (2 mL) salt

Canola oil or avocado oil, for greasing the pan

PREP AHEAD

The batter can be prepared through step 1, without resting, up to 1 day ahead. Store in a resealable container in the fridge. Bring the batter to room temperature, then stir gently before pouring into the hot muffin tins.

STORAGE

Popovers are best served hot out of the oven. However, you can store leftovers in a resealable container in the fridge for up to 3 days or in the freezer for up to 1 month. Reheat on a baking sheet in a 350°F (180°C) oven until warmed and crispy on the outside, about 5 minutes (10 minutes from frozen).

Few things are more fun to eat than popovers. My son Max asks me to make these for him weekly. This English-inspired recipe gives you the perfect light and airy popovers. With a crispy exterior and pillowy interior, these are perfect for mopping up gravy or those last puddles of soup in a bowl. Serve hot alongside your favourite soup or to accompany my Pot Roast (page 231). Don't forget the gravy!

To guarantee popover perfection, have your ingredients at room temperature. Be sure to let your batter rest, and make sure the oil in the pan is sizzling hot before pouring in the batter. While this recipe works well when made in a muffin tin (which most of us have), if you have a proper popover pan, that will yield the best results.

1. In a high-speed blender, combine the eggs, milk, flour, melted butter, and salt. Blend until smooth, about 1 minute. Set aside to rest at room temperature for about 30 minutes.

2. Preheat the oven to 450°F (230°C).

3. Add a generous drizzle of canola oil to cover the bottoms of the wells of a nonstick 12-cup popover pan or the cups of a muffin tin. Place the pan in the oven until hot, about 10 minutes.

4. Carefully remove the pan from the oven and close the oven door to retain the heat. Carefully pour the batter into the wells until about two-thirds full (the batter should sizzle) and immediately transfer to the oven.

5. Bake for 15 minutes. Reduce the oven temperature to 350°F (180°C) and continue to bake, without opening the door, until the popovers have risen tall and are golden brown, about 10 minutes. Immediately, carefully tip the popovers out of the pan and serve hot. For the crispiest popovers, use a paring knife to cut a small slit in the top or side of each to release the steam.

SOUR CREAM AND ONION BISCUITS

Vegan Option · Vegetarian · Dairy-Free Option · Gluten-Free Option · Nut-Free

Makes 8 biscuits

TIME
Prep: 10 MINUTES
Cook: 20 MINUTES
Total: 30 MINUTES

- 2 cups (500 mL) all-purpose flour
- 4 teaspoons (20 mL) baking powder
- 1 teaspoon (5 mL) sugar
- 1 teaspoon (5 mL) salt
- ½ teaspoon (2 mL) dried dill
- ½ teaspoon (2 mL) onion powder
- ½ teaspoon (2 mL) garlic powder
- ¼ teaspoon (1 mL) pepper
- ½ cup (125 mL) cold butter, cut into ½-inch (1 cm) cubes
- 4 green onions (white and light green parts only), sliced
- 1 egg, whisked
- 1 cup (250 mL) sour cream or plain full-fat Greek yogurt
- 2 tablespoons (30 mL) 2% milk
- Melted butter (optional)
- Flaky sea salt (optional)

PREP AHEAD
The biscuits can be prepared through step 5 up to 1 day ahead. Cover tightly with plastic wrap and store in the fridge. Uncover and bake as directed.

STORAGE
Store cooled biscuits in a resealable container in the fridge for up to 4 days or in the freezer for up to 1 month. Reheat in a toaster oven or toaster, split in half if needed.

The nostalgic flavours of sour cream and onion take me straight back to childhood—though back then, they usually came in the form of potato chips. I knew this epic combination would shine through in these warm, moist biscuits. Perfectly cozy and full of flavour, they're the ultimate sidekick to a steaming bowl of soup or a game-changer for make-ahead breakfast sandwiches. Consider this your cue to make a batch of my Sheet-Pan Eggs (page 57).

1. Preheat the oven to 425°F (220°C) and line a baking sheet with parchment paper.

2. In a large bowl, whisk together the flour, baking powder, sugar, salt, dill, onion powder, garlic powder, and pepper. Add the butter, and using your fingers or a pastry blender, break apart until the size of small peas. Stir in the green onions.

3. In a medium bowl, whisk together the egg, sour cream, and milk.

4. Add the wet ingredients to the dry ingredients and, using a fork, mix until shaggy clumps form. Fold the dough over itself a couple of times until it comes together.

5. Transfer the dough to a lightly floured work surface and press any loose bits together. Pat the dough into a 10-inch (25 cm) circle or square (it doesn't have to be perfect). Using a 2.5-inch (6.5 cm) biscuit cutter (or a similar size) or a sharp knife, cut the dough into 8 biscuits. Transfer the biscuits to the prepared baking sheet.

6. Bake until golden brown on the bottom, about 18 minutes. Brush the warm biscuits with melted butter and sprinkle with flaky sea salt if desired. Serve warm.

Vegan: Use vegan butter, vegan sour cream, and non-dairy milk. Omit the egg.

Dairy-Free: Use vegan butter, vegan sour cream, and non-dairy milk.

Gluten-Free: Use a 1:1 gluten-free flour blend.

Re-Fraiche

- Transform these biscuits into breakfast sandwiches using Sheet-Pan Eggs (page 57) and your favourite toppings.

- Make croutons for soup out of leftover biscuits. Cut the biscuits into cubes and place them on a baking sheet lined with parchment paper. Drizzle lightly with olive oil and toss to combine. Bake in a 350°F (180°C) oven until golden brown, about 15 minutes, tossing halfway through.

GREEK YOGURT BISCUITS

Vegan Option • Vegetarian • Dairy-Free Option • Gluten-Free Option • Nut-Free

Makes 8 biscuits

TIME	
Prep:	10 MINUTES
Cook:	20 MINUTES
Total:	30 MINUTES

2 cups (500 mL) all-purpose flour

4 teaspoons (20 mL) baking powder

1 teaspoon (5 mL) sugar

1 teaspoon (5 mL) salt

½ cup (125 mL) cold butter, cut into ½-inch (1 cm) cubes

1 egg

1 cup (250 mL) plain full-fat Greek yogurt

2 tablespoons (30 mL) 2% milk

Topping for Sweet Biscuits (optional)

Table (18%) cream or heavy (35%) cream

Coarse sugar

Re-Fraiche

• Transform unsweetened biscuits into breakfast sandwiches using Sheet-Pan Eggs (page 57) and your favourite toppings.

• Make into shortcakes by following the instructions for the sweet biscuits and serving with dollops of Chantilly Cream (page 333) and berries.

• Make croutons for soup out of leftover biscuits. Cut the biscuits into cubes and place on a baking sheet lined with parchment paper. Drizzle lightly with olive oil and toss to combine. Bake in a 350°F (180°C) oven until golden brown, about 15 minutes, tossing halfway through.

These biscuits are irresistibly moist, with a boost of protein thanks to the Greek yogurt. Serve with a generous spread of butter or jam, dunk them in a hearty soup like Curried Coconut Squash Soup (page 145), or use them to make an epic breakfast sandwich with Sheet-Pan Eggs (page 57) and Apple Chicken Sausage Patties (page 48).

1. Preheat the oven to 425°F (220°C) and line a baking sheet with parchment paper.

2. In a large bowl, whisk together the flour, baking powder, sugar, and salt. Add the butter, and using your fingers or a pastry blender, break apart the butter until the size of small peas.

3. In a medium bowl, whisk together the egg, yogurt, and milk.

4. Add the wet ingredients to the dry ingredients and, using a fork, mix until shaggy clumps form. Fold the dough over itself a couple of times until it comes together.

5. Transfer the dough to a lightly floured surface and press any loose bits together. Pat the dough into a 10-inch (25 cm) circle or square (it doesn't have to be perfect). Using a 2.5-inch (6.5 cm) biscuit cutter (or a similar size) or a sharp knife, cut the dough into 8 biscuits. Transfer the biscuits to the prepared baking sheet.

6. For sweet biscuits (if making), brush the tops with cream and sprinkle with coarse sugar.

7. Bake until golden brown on the top and bottom, about 18 minutes. Serve warm.

Vegan: Use vegan butter, non-dairy yogurt, and non-dairy milk. Omit the egg. Omit the cream.

Dairy-Free: Use vegan butter, non-dairy yogurt, and non-dairy milk. Omit the cream.

Gluten-Free: Use a 1:1 gluten-free flour blend.

PREP AHEAD
The biscuits can be prepared through step 5 up to 1 day ahead. Cover tightly with plastic wrap and refrigerate. Uncover and bake as directed.

STORAGE
Store cooled biscuits in a resealable container in the fridge for up to 4 days or in the freezer for up to 1 month. Reheat in a toaster oven or toaster, split in half if needed.

MAKE AHEAD | FREEZER-FRIENDLY

HAM AND CHEESE MUFFINS

Vegan Option · Vegetarian Option · Dairy-Free Option · Gluten-Free Option · Nut-Free

Makes 12 large muffins

TIME
Prep: 10 MINUTES
Cook: 25 MINUTES
Total: 35 MINUTES

- 2 cups (500 mL) all-purpose flour
- 1 tablespoon (15 mL) sugar
- 2 teaspoons (10 mL) baking powder
- 1 teaspoon (5 mL) baking soda
- 1 teaspoon (5 mL) garlic powder
- ½ teaspoon (2 mL) onion powder
- ½ teaspoon (2 mL) salt
- 3 eggs
- 1¼ cups (300 mL) buttermilk
- ½ cup (125 mL) butter, melted
- 1 cup (250 mL) lightly packed grated old cheddar cheese
- 1 cup (250 mL) diced ham
- ¼ cup (60 mL) grated Parmesan cheese

STORAGE
Store cooled muffins in a resealable container in the fridge for up to 4 days or in the freezer for up to 2 months.

In my house, I always need to make a double batch of these Ham and Cheese Muffins. With two growing boys at home, these moist, savoury muffins tend to disappear fast, which I love! They freeze beautifully and are totally lunchbox approved. Serve hot out of the oven with some butter or dunk them in a steaming bowl of soup like Pierogi Soup (page 156); they are a ten-out-of-ten! If you don't have buttermilk, make your own (see page 317).

1. Preheat the oven to 350°F (180°C) and line a muffin tin with paper liners or spray with nonstick cooking spray.

2. In a large bowl, whisk together the flour, sugar, baking powder, baking soda, garlic powder, onion powder, and salt.

3. In a medium bowl, whisk the eggs. Stir in the buttermilk and melted butter.

4. Add the wet ingredients to the dry ingredients and stir until just incorporated. The batter will be thick. Fold in the cheddar cheese, ham, and Parmesan.

5. Divide the batter among the muffin cups. Bake until the muffins are golden brown on top and a wooden skewer inserted into the centre comes out clean, about 25 minutes.

Vegan: Use a store-bought egg replacer or Flax Eggs (page 317) instead of eggs. Make the vegan option of the Buttermilk (page 317). Use vegan butter and vegan cheese. Use roasted cubed butternut squash instead of ham or omit the ham. Use vegan parm.

Vegetarian: Use roasted cubed butternut squash instead of ham or omit the ham.

Dairy-Free: Make the vegan option of the Buttermilk (page 317). Use vegan butter, vegan cheese, and vegan parm.

Gluten-Free: Use a 1:1 gluten-free flour blend.

EKCO

APPLE RAISIN BRAN MUFFINS

Vegan Option · *Vegetarian* · *Dairy-Free Option* · *Nut-Free*

Makes 12 large muffins

TIME
Prep: 10 MINUTES
Cook: 20 MINUTES
Total: 30 MINUTES

- 2 cups (500 mL) wheat bran
- 1 cup (250 mL) oat bran
- 1 cup (250 mL) all-purpose flour
- 2 teaspoons (10 mL) baking soda
- 1 teaspoon (5 mL) baking powder
- 1 teaspoon (5 mL) cinnamon
- ¼ teaspoon (1 mL) salt
- 2 eggs
- 2 cups (500 mL) grated peeled apple
- ½ cup (125 mL) 2% milk
- ½ cup (125 mL) canola oil or avocado oil
- ½ cup (125 mL) pure liquid honey
- ⅓ cup (75 mL) fancy molasses
- 1 teaspoon (5 mL) pure vanilla extract
- 1 cup (250 mL) raisins or blueberries

PREP AHEAD
The muffin batter can be prepared through step 4 up to 5 days ahead. Store in a resealable container in the fridge.

STORAGE
Store cooled muffins in a resealable container at room temperature for up to 4 days or in the freezer for up to 2 months.

The most underrated nutrient must be fibre, and this recipe delivers. There's something timeless about a good bran muffin—hearty, wholesome, and just the right amount of sweet. This recipe is a nod to the classics but with a nourishing twist of grated apple for extra moisture and vitamins. Packed with fibre and made with simple, real ingredients, they're a satisfying way to start your day or fuel a busy afternoon. As a dietitian, I love that they support digestion and keep you feeling full longer—proof that nutritious and delicious can absolutely go hand in hand. Whether you enjoy them warm from the oven or tucked into a lunchbox, this is one recipe you'll come back to again and again.

1. Preheat the oven to 350°F (180°C) and grease a muffin tin or line with paper liners.
2. In a large bowl, stir together the wheat bran, oat bran, flour, baking soda, baking powder, cinnamon, and salt.
3. In a medium bowl, whisk the eggs well. Add the grated apple, milk, oil, honey, molasses, and vanilla and whisk to combine.
4. Fold the wet ingredients into the dry ingredients and mix with a rubber spatula until just incorporated. Fold in the raisins.
5. Fill the muffin cups about three-quarters full with batter. Bake until a wooden skewer inserted into the centre of the muffins comes out clean, about 20 minutes. Let cool slightly in the tin. Serve warm or transfer to a rack and cool completely before storing.

Vegan: Use a store-bought egg replacer or Flax Eggs (page 317) instead of eggs. Use non-dairy milk. Use pure maple syrup instead of honey.

Dairy-Free: Use non-dairy milk.

BAKERY-STYLE BLUEBERRY MUFFINS

Vegan Option · Vegetarian · Dairy-Free Option · Gluten-Free Option · Nut-Free

Makes 12 large muffins

TIME
Prep: 10 MINUTES
Cook: 20 MINUTES
Total: 30 MINUTES

- 2 eggs
- 1 cup (250 mL) plain 2% Greek yogurt
- ½ cup (125 mL) butter, melted
- 2 teaspoons (10 mL) lemon zest
- 2 tablespoons (30 mL) fresh lemon juice
- 2 teaspoons (10 mL) pure vanilla extract
- 2 cups (500 mL) + 1 tablespoon (15 mL) all-purpose flour, divided
- ¾ cup (175 mL) sugar
- 1 tablespoon (15 mL) baking powder
- 1 teaspoon (5 mL) baking soda
- ¼ teaspoon (1 mL) salt
- 2 cups (500 mL) fresh or frozen blueberries
- 2 tablespoons (30 mL) coarse sugar

STORAGE
Store cooled muffins in a resealable container at room temperature for up to 3 days, in the fridge for up to 4 days, or in the freezer for up to 2 months.

Everyone needs the perfect go-to blueberry muffin recipe. Let this be yours! I make these muffins regularly and like to keep a batch in the freezer for quick snacks and breakfasts. These taste just like a blueberry muffin you would get at your local bakery but are better for you.

1. Preheat the oven to 400°F (200°C) and line a 12-cup muffin tin with paper liners.
2. In a medium bowl, whisk the eggs well. Add the yogurt, melted butter, lemon zest, lemon juice, and vanilla and whisk to combine.
3. In a large bowl, whisk together 2 cups (500 mL) of the flour, sugar, baking powder, baking soda, and salt.
4. In a small bowl, combine the blueberries with the remaining 1 tablespoon (15 mL) flour and toss to coat.
5. Fold the wet ingredients into the dry ingredients and mix until just incorporated. The batter will be thick. Fold in the blueberries.
6. Divide the batter among the muffin cups. Top each muffin with a sprinkle of coarse sugar. Bake the muffins until they are golden brown and a wooden skewer inserted into the centre comes out clean, about 20 minutes. Transfer the muffins to a rack and cool completely.

Vegan: Use a store-bought egg replacer or Flax Eggs (page 317) instead of eggs. Use non-dairy yogurt and vegan butter.

Dairy-Free: Use non-dairy yogurt and vegan butter.

Gluten-Free: Use a 1:1 gluten-free flour blend.

Simple SALADS

HERBY GREEN SALAD

Vegan Option • Vegetarian • Dairy-Free Option • Gluten-Free Option • Nut-Free

Serves 6 to 8

TIME | *Prep:* 20 MINUTES

Herby Green Salad

5 cups (1.25 L) curly kale, stems removed, sliced

1 heart of romaine lettuce, sliced

1 English cucumber, seeded and cut into half-moons

2 cups (500 mL) cherry tomatoes, cut in half

½ cup (125 mL) crumbled feta cheese

½ cup (125 mL) roughly chopped fresh dill

½ cup (125 mL) roughly chopped fresh basil

⅓ cup (75 mL) diced red onion

1 cup (250 mL) croutons or Pita Croutons (page 322)

⅓ cup (75 mL) raw pumpkin seeds

Tamari Dressing

2 tablespoons (30 mL) apple cider vinegar

1 tablespoon (15 mL) tamari

1 tablespoon (15 mL) nutritional yeast

1 teaspoon (5 mL) Dijon mustard

½ teaspoon (2 mL) pure maple syrup

2 cloves garlic, minced

⅓ cup (75 mL) avocado oil or canola oil

My cousin Jillian served me a version of this salad at an impromptu visit one warm summer evening after we raided her garden. Jillian is such a creative person, and I love this genius combination of basil and dill. I think everyone deserves a salad like this in their lives, especially in the height of summer when produce is at its peak. You can thank Jillian for this one! The tamari dressing is irresistible, but you can use any dressing you wish. Removing the seeds from the cucumber before slicing is optional but helps the salad to keep longer.

1. **Assemble the salad:** In a large bowl, toss together the kale, romaine, cucumber, tomatoes, feta, dill, basil, and red onion.

2. **Make the Tamari Dressing:** In a mason jar with a lid, combine the apple cider vinegar, tamari, nutritional yeast, mustard, maple syrup, and garlic. Seal the jar and shake to combine. Add the avocado oil and shake again until emulsified.

3. When ready to serve, sprinkle the croutons and pumpkin seeds over the salad. Give the Tamari Dressing another few shakes if needed, drizzle it to taste over the salad, and toss to combine.

Vegan and Dairy-Free: Omit the feta cheese or substitute with vegan feta.

Gluten-Free: Use gluten-free tamari. Omit the croutons or substitute with gluten-free croutons.

PREP AHEAD
The Tamari Dressing can be made up to 1 week ahead and stored in a resealable container in the fridge. The Herby Green Salad can be prepped (without the dressing, croutons, or pumpkin seeds) up to 5 days ahead and stored in the fridge.

EVERYTHING BAGEL SALMON SALAD

Dairy-Free Option • Gluten-Free Option • Nut-Free

Serves 4

TIME
Prep: 15 MINUTES
Cook: 10 MINUTES (NOT INCLUDING MAKING THE EVERYTHING BAGEL SALMON)
Total: 25 MINUTES

Tender, flaky salmon is coated in everything bagel seasoning, roasted to perfection, and served over crisp greens with crunchy cucumbers, spicy arugula, and a tangy caper dill dressing to make this protein-packed, satisfying salad. Perfect for lunch or dinner, this recipe brings all the flavours of your favourite bagel shop to you in a light and wholesome way! This is a great way to use leftover Everything Bagel Salmon (page 257), but of course it's worth cooking a fresh batch simply to have this salad.

Everything Bagel Croutons

- 2 everything bagels, cut into bite-size pieces
- 1 tablespoon (15 mL) extra-virgin olive oil
- Pinch of salt

Creamy Caper Dill Dressing

- ¼ cup (60 mL) mayonnaise
- 1 tablespoon (15 mL) fresh lemon juice
- 1 tablespoon (15 mL) white wine vinegar
- 1 tablespoon (15 mL) chopped fresh dill
- 1 tablespoon (15 mL) drained capers
- 1½ teaspoons (7 mL) caper brine
- 1½ teaspoons (7 mL) Dijon mustard
- 1 clove garlic, minced
- Pinch of sugar
- Salt

Everything Bagel Salmon Salad

- 3 cups (750 mL) baby spinach
- 3 cups (750 mL) arugula
- 1 cup (250 mL) sliced mini or English cucumbers
- ¼ cup (60 mL) thinly sliced red onion
- ¼ cup (60 mL) crumbled goat cheese or crumbled Boursin cheese
- ½ batch cooked Everything Bagel Salmon (page 257)

1. **Make the Everything Bagel Croutons:** Preheat the oven to 400°F (200°C) and line a baking sheet with parchment paper.

2. On the baking sheet, toss the bagel pieces with the olive oil and salt and spread out in an even layer. Bake until golden brown, about 10 minutes, tossing halfway through. Set aside.

3. **Make the Creamy Caper Dill Dressing:** In a medium bowl with tall sides, combine the mayonnaise, lemon juice, white wine vinegar, dill, capers, caper brine, mustard, garlic, and sugar. Blend with an immersion blender until smooth. (Alternatively, blend in a small-capacity blender.) Season to taste with salt.

4. **Assemble the Salad:** In a large serving bowl, combine the spinach, arugula, cucumber, red onion, and goat cheese. When ready to serve, slowly pour the Creamy Caper Dill Dressing over the salad, just enough to coat the salad or to taste. Toss to combine. Top the salad with the Everything Bagel Salmon and the Croutons.

Dairy-Free: Omit the cheese or use vegan cream cheese.

Gluten-Free: Use gluten-free bagels.

PREP AHEAD

The Everything Bagel Croutons can be made up to 1 week ahead and stored in a resealable container at room temperature. The Creamy Caper Dill Dressing can be prepped up to 1 week ahead and stored in a resealable container in the fridge. The undressed salad will last up to 3 days stored in a resealable container in the fridge. The salmon can be cooked up to 2 days ahead and stored in a resealable container in the fridge.

SANTA FE PASTA SALAD

Vegan Option · Vegetarian Option · Dairy-Free Option · Gluten-Free Option · Nut-Free

Serves 8

TIME
Prep: 20 MINUTES
Cook: 20 MINUTES
Total: 40 MINUTES

Southwest Dressing

1 cup (250 mL) plain full-fat Greek yogurt

½ cup (125 mL) mayonnaise

¼ cup (60 mL) finely chopped fresh cilantro

2 tablespoons (30 mL) taco seasoning

2 teaspoons (10 mL) onion powder

2 cloves garlic, minced

Juice of 1 lime

1 teaspoon (5 mL) unseasoned rice vinegar

Pinch of sugar

Salt

Chicken

2 boneless, skinless chicken breasts (about 1½ pounds/675 g total)

1 tablespoon (15 mL) taco seasoning

1 tablespoon (15 mL) extra-virgin olive oil

Salad

11 ounces (300 g) pasta (bow tie, rotini, or similar shape)

1 cup (250 mL) thawed frozen or canned corn kernels, drained

1 cup (250 mL) diced red, orange, or yellow sweet peppers

1 cup (250 mL) halved cherry tomatoes

½ cup (125 mL) crumbled feta cheese

½ cup (125 mL) roughly chopped fresh cilantro

¼ cup (30 mL) finely diced red onion or Quick Pickled Red Onions (page 331)

1 avocado, pitted, peeled, and diced

This colourful, crunchy pasta salad is the perfect go-to dish for weekday lunches, make-ahead dinners, summer barbecues, and beyond. It's smoky, sweet, tangy, and hearty, all the things a great meal salad should be. The Southwest Dressing, made with taco seasoning, amplifies the fiesta flavours and is not only a fantastic dressing but also a delicious dip or marinade to tenderize chicken. Both the dressing and the salad can be prepped days ahead.

1. Preheat the oven to 400°F (200°C) and line a 15 × 10-inch (38 × 25 cm) baking sheet with parchment paper.

2. **Make the Southwest Dressing:** In a small bowl, whisk together the yogurt, mayonnaise, cilantro, taco seasoning, onion powder, garlic, lime juice, rice vinegar, and sugar. Season to taste with salt. Cover and refrigerate until ready to use.

3. Bring a large pot of salted water to a boil. Add the pasta and cook until just tender. Drain the pasta and rinse under cold running water. Set aside.

4. **Meanwhile, cook the Chicken:** Season the chicken on both sides with the taco seasoning. Heat the olive oil in a medium frying pan over medium-high heat. Place the chicken in the pan and cook until golden brown, about 3 minutes per side. Transfer the chicken to the prepared baking sheet and bake until the chicken is cooked through and the internal temperature reaches 165°F (74°C) on an instant-read thermometer, about 12 minutes. Set aside to rest for 10 minutes.

5. Cut the chicken into cubes.

6. **Assemble the Salad:** In a large bowl, combine the cooked pasta, cooked chicken, corn, sweet peppers, tomatoes, feta, cilantro, and red onion. When ready to serve, pour the dressing over the salad and toss to combine. Top with the avocado.

Recipe continues . . .

PREP AHEAD
The Southwest Dressing can be made up to 1 week ahead and stored in a resealable container in the fridge. The undressed salad can be made up to 5 days ahead and refrigerated in a resealable container. The chicken can be cooked up to 4 days ahead and refrigerated in a resealable container.

STORAGE
Store the dressed salad in a resealable container in the fridge for up to 3 days.

Vegan: Use non-dairy yogurt and vegan mayonnaise. Instead of chicken, use extra-firm tofu or canned black beans (drained and rinsed). Omit the feta cheese or use vegan feta.

Vegetarian: Instead of chicken, use extra-firm tofu or canned black beans (drained and rinsed).

Dairy-Free: Use non-dairy yogurt.

Gluten-Free: Use gluten-free pasta.

Tips

- To make this lower carb, omit the pasta and add about 6 cups (1.5 L) of chopped kale or romaine lettuce.
- To boost the protein, double the amount of chicken or add 1 package (12 ounces/350 g) extra-firm tofu, cubed, or 1 can (19 ounces/540 mL) of black beans (drained and rinsed).

Southwest Dressing

PREP AHEAD | MAKE AHEAD

CURRY CHICKEN PASTA SALAD

Vegan Option · Vegetarian Option · Dairy-Free Option · Gluten-Free Option · Nut-Free

Serves 8

TIME
Prep: 20 MINUTES
Cook: 20 MINUTES
Total: 40 MINUTES

Curry Chicken

2 boneless, skinless chicken breasts (about 1½ pounds/675 g total)

1 tablespoon (15 mL) curry powder

½ teaspoon (2 mL) salt

2 teaspoons (10 mL) extra-virgin olive oil

Pasta Salad

11 ounces (300 g) pasta (bow tie, rotini, or similar shape)

1 cup (250 mL) diced celery

1 cup (250 mL) diced Ambrosia apple

1 cup (250 mL) diced red, orange, or yellow sweet peppers

½ cup (125 mL) roughly chopped fresh cilantro

½ cup (125 mL) dried cranberries or golden raisins

¼ cup (60 mL) finely diced red onion or Quick Pickled Red Onions (page 331)

Curry Dressing

1 cup (250 mL) plain full-fat Greek yogurt

½ cup (125 mL) mayonnaise

¼ cup (60 mL) finely chopped fresh cilantro

1 to 2 tablespoons (15 to 30 mL) curry powder

2 teaspoons (10 mL) onion powder

2 cloves garlic, minced

Juice of 1 lime

1 teaspoon (5 mL) unseasoned rice vinegar

½ teaspoon (2 mL) sugar

Salt

This Curry Chicken Pasta Salad is bursting with a creamy, perfectly spiced curry dressing, crisp apples, sweet dried cranberries, and crunchy veggies. I love how this salad is as delicious the next day as it is freshly made and swear that it tastes better served as leftovers! Ambrosia apples resist browning, but you may use any apple variety.

1. Preheat the oven to 400°F (200°C) and line a 15 × 10-inch (38 × 25 cm) baking sheet with parchment paper.

2. **Cook the Chicken:** Season the chicken on both sides with the curry powder and salt.

3. Heat the olive oil in a medium frying pan over medium heat. Place the chicken in the pan and cook until golden brown, 3 to 4 minutes per side. Transfer the chicken to the prepared baking sheet and bake until cooked through and the internal temperature reaches 165°F (74°C) on an instant-read thermometer, about 12 minutes. Set aside to rest for 10 minutes. Roughly chop the chicken.

4. **Meanwhile, make the Salad:** Bring a large pot of salted water to a boil. Add the pasta and cook until just tender. Drain the pasta in a colander and rinse under cold running water. Set aside.

5. **Make the Curry Dressing:** In a small bowl, whisk together the yogurt, mayonnaise, cilantro, curry powder, onion powder, garlic, lime juice, rice vinegar, and sugar. Season to taste with salt. Cover and refrigerate until ready to use.

6. **Assemble the Salad:** In a large bowl, combine the cooked pasta, cooked chicken, celery, apple, sweet peppers, cilantro, cranberries, and red onion. Toss with the dressing to taste and serve.

Recipe continues . . .

PREP AHEAD
The chicken and the pasta can be cooked up to 4 days ahead. Store in separate resealable containers in the fridge.

STORAGE
Store the dressed salad in a resealable container in the fridge for up to 5 days.

Vegan: Use extra-firm tofu or canned chickpeas (drained and rinsed) instead of chicken. Use non-dairy yogurt and vegan mayonnaise.

Vegetarian: Use extra-firm tofu or canned chickpeas (drained and rinsed) instead of chicken.

Dairy-Free: Use non-dairy yogurt.

Gluten-Free: Use gluten-free pasta.

Tips

- To make this lower carb, omit the pasta and add about 6 cups (1.5 L) of chopped curly kale or romaine lettuce.
- To boost the protein, double the amount of chicken, or add 1 package (12 ounces/340 g) extra-firm tofu, cubed, or 1 can (19 ounces/540 mL) black beans (drained and rinsed).

Curry Dressing

SUPER TUSCAN SALAD

Vegan Option · Vegetarian Option · Dairy-Free Option · Gluten-Free Option · Nut-Free

Serves 6

TIME *Prep:* 15 MINUTES (NOT INCLUDING MAKING THE CRISPY PANKO)

Mediterranean Dressing

⅓ cup (75 mL) extra-virgin olive oil

3 tablespoons (45 mL) fresh lemon juice

2 tablespoons (30 mL) mayonnaise

2 tablespoons (30 mL) red wine vinegar

1 tablespoon (15 mL) dried oregano or Italian seasoning

2 teaspoons (10 mL) Dijon mustard

1 teaspoon (5 mL) sugar

2 cloves garlic, minced

Salt and pepper

Super Tuscan Salad

2 hearts of romaine lettuce, chopped

1 can (19 ounces/540 mL) chickpeas, drained and rinsed

1 cup (250 mL) halved bocconcini

1 cup (250 mL) halved cherry tomatoes

½ cup (125 mL) chopped marinated artichokes

½ cup (125 mL) pepperoncini, sliced

¼ cup (60 mL) sliced fresh basil

¼ red onion, thinly sliced

3½ ounces (100 g) sliced salami

½ batch Crispy Panko (page 325), for serving

Imagine walking into an Italian deli, picking out all the best ingredients, and chopping them up to create the perfect salad. Meet the Super Tuscan Salad! Crisp romaine lettuce, hearty chickpeas, mini bocconcini, and marinated artichokes. Add sliced pepperoncini, juicy cherry tomatoes, fresh basil, red onion, and a little salami for good measure, top with Crispy Panko (page 325), and toss in a light and zesty Mediterranean Dressing. To boost the protein, top the salad with grilled chicken breast, rotisserie chicken, salmon, or cubed extra-firm tofu.

1. **Make the Mediterranean Dressing:** In a mason jar with a lid, combine the olive oil, lemon juice, mayonnaise, red wine vinegar, oregano, mustard, sugar, and garlic. Seal the jar and shake until the dressing is emulsified. Season to taste with salt and pepper and shake again. Set aside until ready to use.

2. **Assemble the Salad:** Place the romaine in a large salad bowl. Add the chickpeas, bocconcini, tomatoes, artichokes, pepperoncini, basil, red onion, and salami. When ready to serve, shake to emulsify and slowly pour the Mediterranean Dressing over the salad, just enough to coat or to taste. Toss to combine. Top with Crispy Panko.

Vegan: Use vegan mayonnaise. Omit the bocconcini and salami.

Vegetarian: Omit the salami.

Dairy-Free: Omit the bocconcini.

Gluten-Free: Use gluten-free salami. Use gluten-free panko crumbs to make the Crispy Panko.

PREP AHEAD
The Crispy Panko can be made up to 1 month ahead and stored in a resealable container at room temperature. The Mediterranean Dressing can be made up to 1 week ahead and stored in a resealable container in the fridge. The undressed salad, without the Crispy Panko, will last up to 4 days when stored in a resealable container in the fridge.

DILL PICKLE TUNA SALAD

Dairy-Free Option · *Gluten-Free* · *Nut-Free*

Serves 4 to 6

TIME | *Prep:* 15 MINUTES

- 2 cans (6 ounces/170 g each) tuna packed in water, drained
- 1 cup (250 mL) cooked quinoa, cooled
- ½ cup (125 mL) mayonnaise
- ¼ cup (60 mL) plain full-fat Greek yogurt
- 1 cup (250 mL) finely diced celery
- ¼ cup (60 mL) chopped fresh dill
- ¼ cup (60 mL) finely diced Quick Pickled Red Onions (page 331), plus more for serving
- ¼ cup (60 mL) finely diced dill pickles
- 2 tablespoons (30 mL) dill pickle brine
- Salt and pepper

STORAGE
Store the salad in a resealable container in the fridge for up to 4 days.

There's a little natural food shop here in Kelowna called Nature's Fare that makes the best tuna salad sandwich—simple, satisfying, and just a little unexpected. One day, I took a closer look at the ingredient list and spotted a surprise: quinoa. Genius. Adding quinoa gives the tuna salad an extra boost of protein and fibre, making it more filling and more balanced. Inspired, I set out to make my own version at home—and I have to say, this might just be better. Why settle for basic when you can elevate tuna salad with dill pickles, fresh dill, crunchy celery, and a handful of quinoa? One bite and you'll be hooked.

Serve the tuna salad with crackers, tucked into lettuce wraps, or sandwiched between slices of Multigrain Milk and Honey Bread (page 85). I like using white (albacore) tuna for its higher omega-3 content, but light tuna works beautifully too.

1. In a medium bowl, combine the tuna (break up with a fork if needed), quinoa, mayonnaise, yogurt, celery, dill, Quick Pickled Red Onions, dill pickles, and pickle brine. Stir until combined. Season to taste with salt and pepper.

Dairy-Free: Use non-dairy yogurt.

Tip

Serve with crackers, as a sandwich, or with butter lettuce to make lettuce wraps. Make into a tuna melt by spreading on toast, topping with cheese, and broiling.

PREP AHEAD

RANCH COBB SALAD

Vegan Option • Vegetarian Option • Dairy-Free Option • Gluten-Free Option • Nut-Free

Serves 4 to 6

TIME
Prep: 20 MINUTES
Cook: 20 MINUTES
Total: 40 MINUTES

Herb Ranch Dressing

1 cup (250 mL) plain full-fat Greek yogurt

½ cup (125 mL) mayonnaise

2 tablespoons (30 mL) finely chopped fresh flat-leaf parsley

1 tablespoon (15 mL) finely chopped fresh dill

1 tablespoon (15 mL) finely chopped fresh chives

2 teaspoons (10 mL) onion powder

1 teaspoon (5 mL) unseasoned rice vinegar

2 cloves garlic, minced

Juice of 1 lemon

Pinch of sugar

Salt and pepper

Chicken

2 boneless, skinless chicken breasts (about 1½ pounds/675 g total)

2 teaspoons (10 mL) extra-virgin olive oil

There's something undeniably classic about a Cobb salad—when I spot it on a menu, I can't resist. As a dietitian, I love that it checks all the boxes: protein, healthy fats from avocado, and plenty of fibre from fresh veggies. It's the kind of meal that actually satisfies. What brings it all together? My go-to Herb Ranch Dressing. Creamy, flavourful, and endlessly versatile, it's just as perfect drizzled over greens as it is served with crisp veggies for dipping.

For best flavour, marinate the chicken in the dressing overnight before cooking.

1. **Make the Herb Ranch Dressing:** In a small bowl, combine the yogurt, mayonnaise, parsley, dill, chives, onion powder, rice vinegar, garlic, lemon juice, and sugar. Whisk until smooth. Season to taste with salt and pepper. Cover and store in the fridge until ready to use.

2. **Prepare the Chicken:** Place the chicken in a resealable container or plastic bag and add ½ cup (125 mL) of the Herb Ranch Dressing. Seal the container or bag and shake well to coat. Store in the fridge until ready to cook, up to overnight.

3. Preheat the oven to 400°F (200°C) and line a 15 × 10-inch (38 × 25 cm) baking sheet with parchment paper.

4. Heat the olive oil in a frying pan over medium-high heat. Place the chicken breasts in the pan and cook until golden brown, 3 to 4 minutes per side. Transfer the chicken to the prepared baking sheet and bake until cooked through and the internal temperature reaches 165°F (74°C) on an instant-read thermometer, about 12 minutes. Cover with foil and set aside to rest for 10 minutes. Slice or chop the chicken.

Recipe and ingredients continue . . .

Salad

2 hearts of romaine lettuce, chopped

4 hard-boiled eggs, sliced

4 slices cooked bacon, crumbled

1 avocado, pitted, peeled, and diced

1 cup (250 mL) halved cherry tomatoes

2 tablespoons (30 mL) finely diced red onion

¼ cup (60 mL) crumbled feta cheese or blue cheese

½ batch Crispy Panko (page 325), for serving

5. **Assemble the Salad:** Place the romaine in a large serving bowl. Add the cooked chicken, eggs, bacon, avocado, cherry tomatoes, red onion, and feta. Slowly pour the Herb Ranch Dressing over the salad, just enough to coat or to taste. Toss to combine. Top with the Crispy Panko.

Vegan: Omit the chicken, egg, and bacon. Use non-dairy plain yogurt, vegan mayonnaise, and vegan feta.

Vegetarian: Omit the chicken and bacon.

Dairy-Free: Use non-dairy plain yogurt and vegan feta.

Gluten-Free: Use gluten-free panko crumbs to make the Crispy Panko (page 325).

PREP AHEAD

The Crispy Panko can be made up to 1 month ahead and stored in a resealable container at room temperature. The Herb Ranch Dressing can be made up to 4 days ahead and stored in a resealable container in the fridge. The undressed salad, without the Crispy Panko, will last up to 3 days when stored in a resealable container in the fridge.

Tips

- Transform this dish into a pasta salad by omitting the romaine and substituting about 4 cups (1 L) of cooked pasta.
- Make a double batch of Herb Ranch Dressing (or use leftovers) to marinate chicken breasts or thighs. Store the coated chicken in a resealable plastic bag in the freezer for up to 3 months. Thaw in the fridge overnight before cooking.

Herb Ranch Dressing

THAI KALE SALAD WITH SESAME TOFU CROUTONS

Vegan • Vegetarian • Dairy-Free • Gluten-Free Option • Nut-Free Option

Serves 4 to 6

TIME
Prep: 20 MINUTES
Cook: 5 MINUTES
Total: 25 MINUTES

Kale Salad

1 cup (250 mL) quinoa

1 bunch curly kale, stems removed, finely chopped

1 teaspoon (5 mL) extra-virgin olive oil

Salt

3 cups (750 mL) shredded red cabbage

2 cups (500 mL) diced red, orange, or yellow sweet peppers

1½ cups (375 mL) grated peeled carrots

1 cup (250 mL) cooked shelled edamame

1 mango, peeled and diced

½ cup (125 mL) roughly chopped fresh cilantro

¼ cup (60 mL) sliced green onions (white and light green parts only)

¼ cup (60 mL) roughly chopped salted peanuts, for serving

Lime wedges, for garnish

Sesame Peanut Dressing

⅓ cup (75 mL) smooth natural peanut butter

¼ cup (60 mL) low-sodium soy sauce

3 tablespoons (45 mL) pure maple syrup

2 tablespoons (30 mL) sesame oil

2 tablespoons (30 mL) unseasoned rice vinegar

2 tablespoons (30 mL) fresh lime juice

2 teaspoons (10 mL) grated peeled fresh ginger

3 cloves garlic, minced

As a dietitian, I've always believed that colour on your plate is the easiest path to good health. At home, the philosophy shows up in the simplest ways—like this Thai-inspired kale salad, brimming with bright flavours and jewel-toned ingredients that make eating well feel effortless. This addictive, crunchy salad features hearty kale, quinoa, sweet mango, vibrant veggies, fresh herbs, and crispy sesame tofu croutons, all drizzled with one of my all-time favourite dressings, a flavourful sesame peanut dressing. To boost the protein, add cooked salmon, chicken, or shrimp to the salad before serving.

1. **Cook the quinoa:** In a medium saucepan with a lid, combine the quinoa with 2 cups (500 mL) of water and a pinch of salt. Bring to a boil over medium-high heat. Once boiling, reduce the heat to low, cover, and let simmer for about 15 minutes, or until the water is absorbed and the quinoa is tender. Remove from the heat, fluff with a fork, and set aside to cool.

2. **Meanwhile, make the Sesame Peanut Dressing:** In a mason jar with a lid, combine the peanut butter, soy sauce, maple syrup, sesame oil, rice vinegar, lime juice, ginger, and garlic. Seal the jar and shake until smooth. (Alternatively, use a small food processor.) Store in the fridge until ready to use.

3. **Make the Kale Salad:** In a large bowl, combine the kale with the olive oil and a pinch of salt. Massage with your fingers for about 2 minutes to tenderize the kale. Add the cooked quinoa, cabbage, sweet peppers, carrots, edamame, mango, cilantro, and green onions.

Recipe and ingredients continue . . .

Sesame Tofu Croutons

2 packages (12 ounces/350 g each) extra-firm tofu, cut into ½-inch (1 cm) cubes

1 tablespoon (15 mL) extra-virgin olive oil

1 tablespoon (15 mL) sesame seeds

PREP AHEAD

The Sesame Peanut Dressing can be made up to 1 week ahead and stored in a resealable container in the fridge. The undressed salad will last up to 5 days when stored in a resealable container in the fridge. The Sesame Tofu Croutons can be made up to 3 days ahead and stored in a resealable container in the fridge.

4. **Make the Sesame Tofu Croutons:** Press the tofu cubes between 2 sheets of paper towel to remove any extra moisture.

5. Heat the olive oil in a medium frying pan over medium heat. Add the tofu cubes to the pan and fry until light golden on all sides, about 3 minutes in total. Add 2 tablespoons of the Sesame Peanut Dressing and continue to cook for about 1 minute, stirring occasionally to coat the tofu on all sides, until the sauce gets sticky. Remove from the heat, immediately sprinkle with the sesame seeds, and toss to coat on all sides.

6. When ready to serve, toss the salad with the remaining Sesame Peanut Dressing. Top with the chopped peanuts and Sesame Tofu Croutons. Garnish with lime wedges.

Gluten-Free: Use gluten-free soy sauce.

Nut-Free: Use tahini instead of peanut butter. Omit the peanuts.

Re-Fraiche

Use leftover Sesame Peanut Dressing and Sesame Tofu Croutons to make Sesame Tofu Buddha Bowls (see page 22).

STRAWBERRY SUNSHINE SALAD

Vegan Option • *Vegetarian* • *Dairy-Free Option* • *Gluten-Free* • *Nut-Free*

Serves 4 to 6

TIME | *Prep:* 15 MINUTES

Strawberry Dressing

1 cup (250 mL) roughly chopped fresh strawberries

¼ cup (60 mL) extra-virgin olive oil

2 tablespoons (30 mL) mayonnaise

2 tablespoons (30 mL) fresh lemon juice

1 tablespoon (15 mL) white wine vinegar

1 tablespoon (15 mL) pure liquid honey

1 clove garlic, minced

Salt

Salad

8 cups (2 L) lightly packed baby spinach

2 cups (500 mL) cooked quinoa, cooled

1 cup (250 mL) thinly sliced fresh strawberries

¼ cup (60 mL) thinly sliced red onion

⅓ cup (75 mL) crumbled goat cheese

½ English cucumber, cut into half-moons

½ batch Protein Crunch Salad Topper (page 311), for serving

This vibrant salad is sunshine, and it's as delightful to look at as it is to eat. Sweet, juicy strawberries take centre stage on a bed of spinach, quinoa, and creamy goat cheese, all tied together with a spa-worthy strawberry-lemon dressing. Rich in vitamin C, fibre, and plant-based protein, this salad is as nourishing as it is beautiful. The Protein Crunch Salad Topper (page 311) adds the perfect finishing touch, making this a truly satisfying meal. If self-care had a flavour, this salad would be it!

1. **Make the Strawberry Dressing:** Combine the strawberries, olive oil, mayonnaise, lemon juice, white wine vinegar, honey, and garlic in a blender and blend until smooth. Season to taste with salt. Store in a resealable container in the fridge until ready to use.

2. **Make the Salad:** In a large serving bowl, combine the spinach, cooked quinoa, strawberries, red onion, goat cheese, and cucumber. When ready to serve, slowly pour the Strawberry Dressing over the salad, just enough to coat or to taste. Toss to combine. Top with a sprinkle of the Protein Crunch Salad Topper.

Vegan: Use vegan mayonnaise. Use pure maple syrup instead of honey. Omit the cheese or use vegan feta.

Dairy-Free: Omit the cheese or use vegan feta.

PREP AHEAD

The Strawberry Dressing can be made up to 1 week ahead and stored in a resealable container in the fridge. The undressed salad, without the topper, can be prepped up to 4 days ahead and stored in a resealable container in the fridge. The Protein Crunch Salad Topper can be made 1 month ahead and stored in a resealable container at room temperature.

BIG CRUNCHY GREEK KALE SALAD

Vegan Option · Vegetarian · Dairy-Free Option · Gluten-Free Option · Nut-Free

Serves 6 to 8

TIME — *Prep:* 15 MINUTES (NOT INCLUDING MAKING THE PITA CROUTONS)

- 1 bunch curly kale, stems removed, finely chopped
- 1 tablespoon (15 mL) extra-virgin olive oil
- Salt
- 1 can (19 ounces/540 mL) chickpeas, drained and rinsed
- 1 English cucumber, diced
- ¼ red onion, diced
- 2 red, orange or yellow sweet peppers, diced
- ½ cup (125 mL) crumbled feta cheese
- ¼ cup (60 mL) pitted Kalamata olives
- 1 cup (250 mL) halved cherry tomatoes
- 1 batch Mediterranean Dressing (page 129)
- 1 batch Pita Croutons (page 322)

PREP AHEAD
The Mediterranean Dressing can be made up to 1 week ahead and stored in a resealable container in the fridge. The undressed salad, without the Pita Croutons, can be stored in a resealable container in the fridge for up to 5 days.

STORAGE
Store the dressed salad in a resealable container in the fridge for up to 2 days.

Everyone needs a great Greek salad recipe in their back pocket, especially one that holds up well when made ahead. Kale and chickpeas provide hearty texture and nutrition in this version. It's incredibly satisfying on its own, but you can also serve this salad alongside Lemon Dill Chicken (page 193) or Shrimp and Feta Spinach Rice (page 173) for a delicious, balanced, and nourishing meal.

1. In a large bowl, combine the kale with the olive oil and a generous pinch of salt. Massage the kale with your fingers for about 2 minutes to tenderize the kale.

2. Add the chickpeas, cucumber, red onion, sweet peppers, feta, olives, and cherry tomatoes.

3. When ready to serve, add the Mediterranean Dressing to taste and toss well. Sprinkle with the Pita Croutons.

Vegan: Use vegan mayonnaise and vegan feta.

Dairy-Free: Use vegan feta.

Gluten-Free: Use gluten-free pita to make the Pita Croutons (page 322).

STAUB
LA COCOTTE
STAUB

Make-Ahead SOUPS

MAKE AHEAD | FREEZER-FRIENDLY

CURRIED COCONUT SQUASH SOUP

Vegan Option • *Vegetarian Option* • *Dairy-Free Option* • *Nut-Free*

Serves 4 to 6

TIME
Prep: 10 MINUTES
Cook: 30 MINUTES
Total: 40 MINUTES

¼ cup (60 mL) butter or extra-virgin olive oil

2 cups (500 mL) chopped yellow onion

2 cloves garlic, minced

1 tablespoon (15 mL) curry powder

8 cups (2 L) cubed peeled butternut squash (about 2 pounds/900 g)

4 cups (1 L) chicken or vegetable stock, plus more as needed

2 Gala apples, peeled and quartered

1 can (14 ounces/400 mL) full-fat coconut milk

Salt and pepper

STORAGE

Store cooled soup in a resealable container in the fridge for up to 4 days or in the freezer for up to 3 months. (Batch-freezing in jumbo silicone muffin tins makes it easier to thaw individual servings.) If frozen, thaw in the fridge overnight, then reheat on the stovetop or in the microwave until warmed through.

This quick curry soup is nourishing and delicious with only a few simple ingredients. The butternut squash and apple lend sweetness to this vitamin-packed soup with a touch of curry and creamy coconut milk. Do your future self a favour and double the recipe to freeze. Serve this soup hot with warm naan bread or Sour Cream and Onion Biscuits (page 106).

1. In a large pot with a lid, melt the butter over medium heat. Add the onion and cook, stirring occasionally, until soft and translucent, 3 to 4 minutes. Add the garlic and curry powder and cook, stirring, until fragrant, about 1 minute. Stir in the butternut squash, chicken stock, and apples. Bring to a boil, then reduce the heat to low, cover, and cook, stirring occasionally, until the butternut squash and apples are tender, about 25 minutes.

2. Stir in the coconut milk. Using an immersion blender, carefully blend the soup until smooth. Thin with extra chicken stock if needed. Season to taste with salt and pepper. Serve hot.

Vegan: Use olive oil or vegan butter instead of butter. Use vegetable stock.

Vegetarian: Use vegetable stock.

Dairy-Free: Use olive oil instead of butter.

MAKE AHEAD | FREEZER-FRIENDLY | SOS

LEMON CHICKEN ORZO SOUP

Vegan Option · Vegetarian Option · Dairy-Free · Gluten-Free Option · Nut-Free

Serves 6 to 8

TIME
Prep: 10 MINUTES
Cook: 20 MINUTES
Total: 30 MINUTES

- 1 tablespoon (15 mL) all-purpose flour
- 1½ teaspoons (7 mL) Italian seasoning, divided
- 1 teaspoon (5 mL) garlic powder
- ½ teaspoon (2 mL) salt
- ¼ teaspoon (1 mL) pepper
- 2 boneless, skinless chicken breasts (about 1½ pounds/675 g total)
- 2 tablespoons (30 mL) extra-virgin olive oil
- 1 cup (250 mL) diced yellow onion
- 2½ cups (625 mL) diced celery
- 2 cups (500 mL) diced carrots
- 2 cloves garlic, minced
- 10 cups (2.5 L) chicken stock
- 1 cup (250 mL) orzo
- 1 tablespoon (15 mL) finely chopped fresh flat-leaf parsley
- 1 tablespoon (15 mL) finely chopped fresh dill
- 2 teaspoons (10 mL) fresh lemon juice
- Salt and pepper

STORAGE
Store cooled soup in a resealable container in the fridge for up to 4 days or in the freezer for up to 3 months. If frozen, thaw in the fridge overnight, then reheat on the stovetop or in a microwave until warmed through.

If you're looking for a soup that's light yet hearty, healthy, and packed with bright, zesty flavours, this Lemon Chicken Orzo Soup hits all the right notes. With its refreshing herbaceous broth, it strikes the perfect balance of comfort with a bit of zip. If you plan on having leftovers and are making it ahead of time, I recommend cooking the orzo separately and adding it to each bowl to prevent it from soaking up excess liquid.

1. In a medium shallow bowl, stir together the flour, 1 teaspoon (5 mL) of the Italian seasoning, garlic powder, salt, and pepper. Coat the chicken breasts evenly on both sides with the spice mixture.

2. Heat the olive oil in a large, heavy pot over medium heat. Add the chicken and cook until golden brown, 3 to 4 minutes per side. Add the onion and cook, stirring occasionally, until soft and translucent, 3 to 4 minutes. Add the celery, carrots, garlic, and remaining ½ teaspoon (2 mL) Italian seasoning and cook, stirring, until the vegetables are tender, 3 to 4 minutes. Add the chicken stock and bring to a boil.

3. Add the orzo and cook, stirring occasionally, until the orzo is tender, about 10 minutes.

4. Meanwhile, using tongs, remove the chicken from the pot. Use two forks to shred the chicken. Return the shredded chicken to the pot. Stir in the parsley, dill, and lemon juice, and season to taste with salt and pepper. Serve immediately.

Vegan and Vegetarian: Omit the chicken; add the flour and spices with the onion in step 2. Use vegetable stock. Add 1 can (19 ounces/540 mL) of chickpeas (drained and rinsed) with the orzo in step 3.

Gluten-Free: Use a 1:1 gluten-free flour blend. Use gluten-free orzo or another small gluten-free pasta.

BUTTER CHICKEN SOUP

Vegan Option • Vegetarian Option • Dairy-Free Option • Gluten-Free • Nut-Free Option

Serves 6 to 8

TIME
Prep: 10 MINUTES, PLUS 30 MINUTES MARINATING
Cook: 25 MINUTES
Total: 35 MINUTES

Marinade

3 tablespoons (45 mL) garam masala

2 tablespoons (30 mL) sweet paprika

1 tablespoon (15 mL) ground cumin

1 tablespoon (15 mL) ground coriander

1 tablespoon (15 mL) ground turmeric

2 teaspoons (10 mL) chili powder

1 teaspoon (5 mL) salt

8 to 10 boneless, skinless chicken thighs (about 2 pounds/900 g total), cut into bite-size pieces

½ cup (125 mL) plain full-fat Greek yogurt

1 tablespoon (15 mL) fresh lemon juice

5 cloves garlic, minced

2 tablespoons (30 mL) grated peeled fresh ginger

Soup

4 tablespoons (60 mL) butter or extra-virgin olive oil, divided

2 cups (500 mL) chopped yellow onion

2 cans (5.5 ounces/156 mL each) tomato paste

8 cups (2 L) chicken stock

1 can (28 ounces/796 mL) diced tomatoes

2 tablespoons (30 mL) sugar, or to taste

½ cup (125 mL) basmati rice

1 cup (250 mL) heavy (35%) cream, Cashew Cream (page 332), or coconut cream, plus more for garnish

Cilantro, for garnish (optional)

Inspired by the beloved northern Indian dish murgh makhani, this butter chicken soup takes all the rich, aromatic flavours of the classic curry and tucks them into a cozy bowl. Creamy, spiced, and deeply comforting, it's the kind of soup that is perfect for dunking warm chewy naan into. A handful of basmati rice gives it heartiness and texture—just remember to stir it in at the end if you're making the soup ahead, so it doesn't get too thick.

1. **Marinate the Chicken:** In a small bowl, stir together the garam masala, sweet paprika, cumin, coriander, turmeric, chili powder, and salt.

2. Place the chicken in a medium bowl. Add the yogurt, lemon juice, garlic, ginger, and about half of the spice mixture. Stir to completely coat the chicken. Cover and marinate in the fridge for at least 30 minutes or overnight.

3. When ready to make the soup, melt 2 tablespoons (30 mL) of the butter in a large pot with a lid over medium heat. Add the marinated chicken and cook, stirring occasionally, until just cooked through, about 5 minutes. Transfer the chicken to a plate.

4. In the same pot (no need to wipe it) over medium heat, melt the remaining 2 tablespoons (30 mL) butter. Add the onion and cook, stirring occasionally, until soft and translucent, 3 to 4 minutes. Add the remaining spice mixture and tomato paste and cook, stirring occasionally, for another 2 minutes. Remove from the heat. Stir in the chicken stock, diced tomatoes, and sugar. Using an immersion blender, blend until smooth. Return to the heat and bring to a simmer.

5. Add the chicken and rice to the pot, cover, and simmer, stirring occasionally, until the rice is tender, about 15 minutes. Stir in the cream and remove from the heat. Taste and adjust for sugar. Garnish with the cilantro and a drizzle of cream if desired. Serve hot.

Recipe continues . . .

STORAGE

Store cooled soup in a resealable container in the fridge for up to 4 days or in the freezer for up to 2 months. If frozen, thaw in the fridge overnight, then reheat on the stovetop or in the microwave until warmed through.

FREEZER-FRIENDLY

Cook the rice separately and store in a resealable bag in the freezer for up to 3 months. Freeze the soup separately in a resealable container. When ready to serve, thaw the rice and soup in the fridge overnight, then reheat the soup on the stovetop or in a microwave until warmed through. Stir the thawed rice into the soup until heated through before serving.

Vegan: Use olive oil instead of butter. Omit step 2 and use 1 can (19 ounces/540 mL) of chickpeas (drained and rinsed) or 1 package (12 ounces/340 g) extra-firm tofu (drained and cubed) instead of chicken in step 4. Add all the spice mixture in step 4. Use vegetable stock. Use Cashew Cream (page 332) or coconut cream instead of heavy cream.

Vegetarian: Omit step 2 and use 1 can (19 ounces/540 mL) of chickpeas (drained and rinsed) or 1 package (12 ounces/340 g) extra-firm tofu (drained and cubed) instead of chicken in step 4. Add all the spice mixture in step 4. Use vegetable stock.

Dairy-Free: Use olive oil. Use Cashew Cream (page 332) or coconut cream instead of heavy cream.

Nut-Free: Use heavy (35%) cream.

MAKE AHEAD | FREEZER-FRIENDLY

ROASTED VEGGIE TORTELLINI SOUP

Vegan Option • Vegetarian Option • Dairy-Free Option • Gluten-Free Option • Nut-Free

Serves 8

TIME
Prep: 10 MINUTES
Cook: 60 MINUTES
Total: 70 MINUTES

- 2 sweet red peppers, halved and seeds removed
- 4 large tomatoes, halved
- 2 carrots, peeled and chopped into 1-inch (2.5 cm) pieces
- 1 large yellow onion, quartered
- 2 tablespoons (30 mL) extra-virgin olive oil, divided
- 2 teaspoons (10 mL) Italian seasoning, divided
- Pinch of red chili flakes (optional)
- Salt and pepper
- 2 heads garlic
- 6 to 8 cups (1.5 to 2 L) chicken or vegetable stock, divided
- ¼ cup (60 mL) cream cheese, room temperature
- 4 Italian sausages (about 14 ounces/400 g total), casings removed
- 1 can (5.5 ounces/156 mL) tomato paste
- 1 package (12 ounces/350 g) cheese tortellini, refrigerated or frozen
- 2 cups (500 mL) lightly packed roughly chopped spinach
- ¼ cup (60 mL) lightly packed roughly chopped fresh basil
- ½ cup (125 mL) grated Parmesan cheese

I once served this soup to a hungry crowd after a cold day working outside, and it earned the compliment: "This is the best soup I've ever had!" I'll take it! There's something so heartwarming about witnessing that first-bite moment when people love what you've cooked. This soup is hearty with a natural sweetness from roasting the vegetables that lends an impeccable depth of flavour. Serve with crusty bread or warm Focaccia Muffins (page 94) so no drop is left behind.

1. Preheat the oven to 400°F (220°C) and line a large baking sheet with parchment paper.

2. Place the sweet peppers, tomatoes, carrots, and onion on the prepared baking sheet. Drizzle with 1 tablespoon (15 mL) of the olive oil and sprinkle with 1 teaspoon (5 mL) of the Italian seasoning and red chili flakes (if using). Season to taste with salt and pepper. Toss to combine and spread in an even layer. Slice about ¼ inch (5 mm) off the top of each head of garlic to expose the cloves, keeping the heads intact. Drizzle the remaining 1 tablespoon (15 mL) olive oil over the exposed cloves. Wrap each head individually in foil and place on the baking sheet with the veggies. Roast until the vegetables are golden and fork-tender, about 45 minutes. Set aside to cool.

3. When the garlic is cool enough to handle, squeeze the skin to pop out the roasted cloves.

4. In a high-speed blender, combine the roasted vegetables, roasted garlic, 4 cups (1 L) of the chicken stock, and cream cheese. Blend on medium-high speed until smooth, about 1 minute.

Recipe continues . . .

STORAGE
Store cooled soup, without the spinach, basil, and Parmesan, in a resealable container in the fridge for up to 4 days or in the freezer for up to 2 months. If frozen, thaw in the fridge overnight, then reheat on the stovetop or in the microwave until heated through. Stir in the spinach and basil until wilted just before serving. Garnish with the Parmesan.

5. Heat a large, heavy pot with a lid over medium heat. Add the sausage, breaking the meat into smaller pieces with a wooden spoon, until browned, about 5 minutes.

6. Add the remaining 1 teaspoon (5 mL) Italian seasoning and the tomato paste and continue to cook, stirring, for about 2 minutes. Stir in the blended vegetable mixture, 2 cups (500 mL) of the chicken stock, and the tortellini. Bring to a simmer, then cover and cook, stirring occasionally, until the tortellini float to the surface and are tender, 6 to 8 minutes. Add the spinach and basil and continue to cook until the spinach is just wilted, about 3 minutes. Season to taste with salt and pepper; thin with extra chicken stock if needed. Garnish with the Parmesan before serving.

Vegan: Use vegetable stock and vegan cream cheese. Use plant-based Italian sausage, vegan tortellini, and vegan parm.

Vegetarian: Use vegetable stock and plant-based Italian sausage.

Dairy-Free: Use vegan cream cheese, vegan tortellini, and vegan parm.

Gluten-Free: Use gluten-free sausage and tortellini.

MAKE AHEAD | FREEZER-FRIENDLY

BLACK BEAN ENCHILADA SOUP

Vegan Option · Vegetarian Option · Dairy-Free Option · Gluten-Free Option · Nut-Free

Serves 8

TIME
Prep: 15 MINUTES
Cook: 30 MINUTES
Total: 45 MINUTES

- 3 boneless, skinless chicken breasts (about 2 pounds/900 g total)
- 1 tablespoon (15 mL) taco seasoning
- 2 tablespoons (30 mL) extra-virgin olive oil
- 2 cups (500 mL) diced yellow onion
- 1 red, orange, or yellow sweet pepper, diced
- 2 teaspoons (10 mL) ground cumin
- 1 teaspoon (5 mL) smoked paprika
- 4 cloves garlic, minced
- 8 cups (2 L) chicken or vegetable stock
- 2 cans (19 ounces/540 mL each) black beans, drained and rinsed
- 2 cans (10 ounces/283 mL each) enchilada sauce (or make your own; see page 316)
- 2 cups (500 mL) frozen corn kernels
- 1 tablespoon (15 mL) tomato paste
- Salt and pepper

For serving

- Sour cream
- Lime wedges
- Chopped fresh cilantro
- Sliced green onions
- Tortilla strips or chips
- Grated cheddar cheese
- Diced avocado
- Sliced jalapeño peppers

Why not pack the best parts of an enchilada into a cozy one-pot soup? This hearty, fibre-filled soup is made with black beans, warm spices, and a hint of smoky flavour from the smoked paprika. Just as you would dress up enchiladas, have fun with your favourite toppings! The flavours of this soup get even better the next day.

1. Sprinkle both sides of the chicken with the taco seasoning. Heat the olive oil in large, heavy pot over medium heat. Place the chicken in the pot and cook until golden brown, about 3 minutes per side. Stir in the onion and cook, stirring occasionally, until the onion is soft and translucent, 3 to 4 minutes. Stir in the sweet pepper, cumin, smoked paprika, and garlic and continue cooking, stirring occasionally, until the peppers soften and the garlic is fragrant, about 2 minutes.

2. Stir in the chicken stock, black beans, enchilada sauce, corn, and tomato paste and bring to a boil. Reduce the heat to low and cook, stirring occasionally, until the chicken is cooked through and the internal temperature reaches 165°F (74°C) on an instant-read thermometer, about 15 minutes.

3. Using tongs, carefully transfer the chicken to a large bowl. Use two forks to shred the chicken (or see Tip below). Stir the shredded chicken into the soup and season to taste with salt and pepper.

4. Serve hot and garnish with sour cream, lime wedges, cilantro, green onions, tortilla strips, cheese, avocado, and sliced jalapeños if desired.

Vegan: Omit the chicken; add the taco seasoning with the onion in step 2. Use vegetable stock. Serve with vegan sour cream and cheese.

Vegetarian: Omit the chicken; add the taco seasoning with the onion in step 2. Use vegetable stock.

Dairy-Free: Use vegan sour cream and vegan cheese.

Gluten-Free: Use a gluten-free taco seasoning.

STORAGE
Store cooled soup, without garnishes, in a resealable container in the fridge for up to 4 days or in the freezer for up to 3 months. Thaw in the fridge overnight, then reheat on the stovetop or in the microwave until warmed through.

Tip

To quickly and easily shred chicken, in step 3, transfer the cooked chicken to the bowl of a stand mixer fitted with the paddle attachment and mix on low speed for about 30 seconds, until shredded.

PIEROGI SOUP

Vegan Option • Vegetarian Option • Dairy-Free Option • Gluten-Free Option • Nut-Free

Serves 6

TIME
Prep: 10 MINUTES
Cook: 20 MINUTES
Total: 30 MINUTES

2 pounds (900 g) russet potatoes, peeled and cut into ½-inch (1 cm) cubes, divided

½ pound (225 g) thick-cut bacon, diced

1 large yellow onion, roughly chopped

6 cloves garlic, minced

2 tablespoons (30 mL) all-purpose flour

4 cups (1 L) cauliflower florets

6 cups (1.5 L) chicken or vegetable stock

½ cup (125 mL) sour cream, plus more for garnish

½ cup (125 mL) grated cheddar cheese, plus more for garnish (optional)

¼ cup (60 mL) chopped fresh dill, plus more for garnish

Salt and pepper

Sliced green onions or fresh chives, for garnish

STORAGE
Store cooled soup, without garnishes, in a resealable container in the fridge for up to 4 days. Reheat on the stovetop or in the microwave until warmed through.

As a Ukrainian, pierogi flavours for me are the ultimate definition of comfort and nostalgia. Inspired by my beloved Granny Marge, this soul-in-a-bowl soup brings me back to my roots and the love of cooking she passed down to me.

A traditional-tasting meal doesn't have to mean hours of simmering over the stove. Ready in just 30 minutes, this soup is packed with flavour and features hidden cauliflower as an added twist. This recipe is a modern take on the classics, perfect for today's busy lifestyle while still delivering that comforting, nostalgic taste.

1. Add half the potatoes to a small pot of salted water. Bring to a boil and cook until the potatoes are fork-tender, 8 to 10 minutes. Drain and set aside.

2. In a large, heavy pot, cook the bacon over medium-low heat until the fat is mostly rendered and the bacon is slightly crispy, about 6 minutes. Transfer the bacon to a plate lined with paper towel and set aside. Drain off half the bacon fat from the pot.

3. Return the pot to medium heat. Add the onion and cook, stirring occasionally, until soft and translucent, 3 to 4 minutes. Add the garlic, sprinkle in the flour, and cook, stirring constantly, until nutty and fragrant, 1 to 2 minutes. Add the remaining uncooked potatoes, cauliflower, and chicken stock and bring to a boil. Reduce the heat to medium-low and cook, stirring occasionally, until the potatoes are fork-tender, about 10 minutes.

4. Stir in the sour cream. Using an immersion blender, blend the soup until smooth and creamy, about 1 minute. Stir in the reserved cooked potatoes, cheese, and dill. Season to taste with salt and pepper.

5. Serve the soup hot with a sprinkle of cheese, green onions, dill, and reserved crispy bacon on top.

Vegan: Omit the bacon and use 2 tablespoons (30 mL) olive oil. Use vegetable stock. Use vegan sour cream and vegan cheese. Add ¼ cup (60 mL) nutritional yeast for flavour.

Vegetarian: Omit the bacon and use 2 tablespoons (30 mL) olive oil. Use vegetable stock. Add ¼ cup (60 mL) nutritional yeast for flavour.

Dairy-Free: Use vegan sour cream and vegan cheese.

Gluten-Free: Use gluten-free bacon. Use a 1:1 gluten-free flour blend.

GYOZA SOUP

Vegan Option · *Vegetarian Option* · *Dairy-Free* · *Gluten-Free Option* · *Nut-Free*

Serves 6 to 8

TIME
Prep: 10 MINUTES
Cook: 10 MINUTES
Total: 20 MINUTES

2 tablespoons (30 mL) sesame oil

2 tablespoons (30 mL) grated peeled fresh ginger

1 tablespoon (15 mL) minced garlic (about 5 cloves)

2 cups (500 mL) thinly sliced cremini mushrooms

8 cups (2 L) chicken or vegetable stock

2 tablespoons (30 mL) soy sauce

2 teaspoons (10 mL) fish sauce

1 pound (450 g) precooked fresh or frozen gyoza (potstickers)

2 cups (500 mL) broccoli florets

2 cups (500 mL) thinly sliced baby bok choy

1 cup (250 mL) thinly sliced peeled carrots

1 cup (250 mL) snow peas, cut in half

½ cup (125 mL) sliced green onions (white and light green parts only)

Sesame seeds, for garnish (optional)

STORAGE
Store cooled soup in a resealable container in the fridge for up to 4 days.

The idea for this gyoza soup came from Shayna, one of our all-star Team Fraîche members. The flavourful gingery broth is loaded with vegetables and is on the table in 20 minutes. The shortcut? Precooked fresh or frozen gyoza (potstickers). This is the perfect go-to meal when you're craving comfort in a hurry. To boost the protein, add uncooked peeled and deveined shrimp with the gyoza and cook until the shrimp are cooked through.

1. Heat the sesame oil in a large pot with a lid over medium heat. Add the ginger and garlic and cook, stirring, until fragrant, about 1 minute. Add the mushrooms and cook, stirring occasionally, until the mushrooms are softened, about 3 minutes. Stir in the chicken stock, soy sauce, and fish sauce. Bring to a simmer, then reduce the heat to low.

2. Add the gyoza, broccoli, bok choy, carrots, and snow peas, cover, and simmer until the veggies are *just* cooked and the gyozas float to the surface, 3 to 4 minutes for fresh gyoza and 5 to 6 minutes for frozen.

3. Stir in the green onions and garnish with sesame seeds if desired. Serve hot.

Vegan and Vegetarian: Use vegetable stock. Omit the fish sauce. Use vegetable gyoza.

Gluten-Free: Use gluten-free gyoza.

No-Fuss CASSEROLES

SWEET AND SOUR CHICKEN CASSEROLE

Vegan Option · *Vegetarian Option* · *Dairy-Free* · *Gluten-Free Option* · *Nut-Free Option*

Serves 4 to 6

TIME
Prep: 10 MINUTES
Cook: 45 MINUTES
Total: 55 MINUTES

2 cups (500 mL) rice (I use jasmine)

Sweet and Sour Sauce

½ cup (125 mL) ketchup

¼ cup (60 mL) pineapple juice (from canned pineapple below)

¼ cup (60 mL) unseasoned rice vinegar

¼ cup (60 mL) pure liquid honey

2 tablespoons (30 mL) soy sauce

2 cloves garlic, minced

Chicken

4 boneless, skinless chicken breasts (about 3 pounds/1.35 kg total), cubed

2 tablespoons (30 mL) cornstarch

1 can (14 ounces/398 mL) pineapple chunks, drained (reserve juice for sauce)

1 cup (250 mL) finely diced yellow onion

1 red, orange, or yellow sweet pepper, cut into 1-inch (2.5 cm) pieces

1 green sweet pepper, cut into 1-inch (2.5 cm) pieces

For serving

3 green onions (white and light green parts only), thinly sliced

Sesame seeds

Red chili flakes (optional)

½ cup (125 mL) roasted cashews (optional)

My brother Terry loves sweet and sour chicken. We grew up ordering it at our favourite Chinese restaurant, the Golden Palace, in Peace River, Alberta. We will never forget Frank and Sam's sweet and sour chicken balls—deep-fried to perfection. This lightened-up casserole version takes us right back to our childhood. The cashews aren't traditionally added but they give some crunch and extra protein to the dish that I love.

1. Preheat the oven to 425°F (220°C).
2. Cook the rice according to package directions. Keep warm.
3. **Meanwhile, make the Sweet and Sour Sauce:** In a small bowl, whisk together the ketchup, pineapple juice, rice vinegar, honey, soy sauce, and garlic.
4. **Assemble and Bake:** In a 9-inch (2.5 L) square baking dish, mix together the chicken and cornstarch to coat. Stir in the Sweet and Sour Sauce, pineapple chunks, and onion. Cover tightly with a lid or foil and bake for 25 minutes.
5. Remove the casserole from the oven, carefully remove the lid or foil, and stir in the sweet peppers. Cover and bake until the peppers are tender, about another 20 minutes.
6. Top with the green onions, sesame seeds, and red chili flakes and cashews if desired. Serve with the rice.

Vegan: Use pure maple syrup instead of honey. Use 2 packages (12 ounces/350 g each) extra-firm tofu, cubed, instead of the chicken.

Vegetarian: Use 2 packages (12 ounces/350 g each) extra-firm tofu, cubed, instead of the chicken.

Gluten-Free: Use gluten-free soy sauce.

Nut-Free: Omit the cashews.

STORAGE

Store the cooled casserole in a resealable container in the fridge for up to 4 days or in the freezer for up to 3 months. If frozen, thaw in the fridge overnight. Reheat in the microwave or on the stovetop in a pot over low heat, stirring occasionally.

Re-Fraiche

Serve the Sweet and Sour Chicken in lettuce cups instead of over rice.

DUMP-AND-BAKE CHICKEN PAPRIKASH CASSEROLE

Dairy-Free Option · *Gluten-Free Option* · *Nut-Free*

Serves 6

TIME
Prep: 15 MINUTES
Cook: 35 MINUTES
Total: 50 MINUTES

- 4 cups (1 L) chicken stock
- ¼ cup (60 mL) tomato paste
- 2 pounds (900 g) boneless, skinless chicken thighs, cut into ½-inch (1 cm) pieces
- 1 package (13 ounces/375 g) broad egg noodles
- 1 cup (250 mL) finely diced sweet onion
- 1 sweet green pepper, finely diced
- 1 tablespoon (15 mL) sweet paprika, preferably Hungarian
- 1 teaspoon (5 mL) salt
- ½ teaspoon (2 mL) black pepper
- ½ cup (125 mL) sour cream, plus more for serving
- Roughly chopped fresh flat-leaf parsley, for garnish

When my husband Charles and I were dating, he won me over with his chicken paprikash. It was slow-cooked while we enjoyed a couple of glasses of wine and Frank Sinatra tunes and served complete with homemade noodles. I do, was all I thought. These days, between work schedules, soccer games, and homework, life doesn't allow us as many leisurely evenings cooking together. This simplified version is such an incredible shortcut to those same rich chicken paprikash flavours, and you will love the dump-and-bake method. If you can get your hands on Hungarian paprika, this is the time to use it.

Note that there will be extra sauce when it is done cooking, much like traditional Hungarian paprikash. Be sure to cut your chicken to the size stated to ensure it cooks evenly and in the same time as the noodles.

1. Preheat the oven to 425°F (220°C) and grease a 13 × 9-inch (3.5 L) baking dish.

2. In a large bowl, whisk together the chicken stock and tomato paste. Stir in the chicken, egg noodles, onion, green pepper, sweet paprika, salt, and black pepper. Transfer the mixture to the prepared baking dish, spreading in an even layer. Cover tightly with foil.

3. Bake until the pasta is tender and the chicken is cooked through, about 35 minutes, stirring halfway through. Stir in the sour cream. Serve garnished with the parsley and extra sour cream if desired.

Dairy-Free: Use vegan sour cream.

Gluten-Free: Use gluten-free rotini noodles or similar.

PREP AHEAD

Prepare the casserole without the noodles (step 2), cover, and store in the fridge up to 1 day in advance. Stir in the noodles just before baking.

STORAGE

This dish is best served hot out of the oven, but you can store the cooled casserole in a resealable container in the fridge for up to 4 days. Reheat in the microwave until warmed through.

BUTTERNUT SQUASH RAVIOLI LASAGNA

Vegan Option · Vegetarian Option · Dairy-Free Option · Gluten-Free Option · Nut-Free Option

Serves 6 to 8

TIME
Prep: 15 MINUTES
Cook: 55 MINUTES
Total: 70 MINUTES

Butternut Squash Sauce

2 tablespoons (30 mL) extra-virgin olive oil or butter

2 cups (500 mL) chopped yellow onion

2 cloves garlic, minced

2 cups (500 mL) chicken or vegetable stock

6 cups (1.5 L) peeled butternut squash cut into ½-inch (1 cm) pieces

½ cup (125 mL) table (18%) cream or Cashew Cream (page 332)

Salt and pepper

½ teaspoon (2 mL) pepper

Filling

18 ounces (500 g) refrigerated or frozen spinach and cheese ravioli

1 tub (475 g) ricotta cheese

2 cups (500 mL) roughly chopped spinach

2 cups (500 mL) grated mozzarella cheese, divided

½ cup (125 mL) grated Parmesan cheese, divided

Just wait until you taste this dish—it's pure comfort food. Butternut squash and sage are a match made in heaven, and I love this modified lasagna that uses tender ravioli in place of the noodles. Topped with a Sage Pine Nut Panko Crisp, this prep-ahead meal will have your family or guests swooning. Prepare to fall in love with this simple yet sophisticated twist on a classic pasta bake!

If you have individual-size ovenproof dishes, this is the time to pull them out. I won't judge if you add a little extra cheese; I went a bit skimpy in the spirit of nutrition, but you do you.

1. **Make the Butternut Squash Sauce:** Heat the olive oil in a large pot with a lid over medium heat. Add the onion and cook, stirring occasionally, until soft and translucent, 3 to 4 minutes. Add the garlic and cook, stirring, until fragrant, about 1 minute. Stir in the chicken stock and butternut squash. Bring to a boil, then reduce the heat to low, cover, and cook, stirring occasionally, until the squash is fork-tender, about 25 minutes. Stir in the cream. Using an immersion blender or high-speed blender, carefully blend until smooth. Season to taste with salt and pepper. Set aside.

2. **Meanwhile, cook the ravioli:** Bring a large pot of salted water to a boil. Add the ravioli and cook until they float to the surface, about 3 minutes. Drain. Transfer the ravioli to a medium bowl and toss with a drizzle of olive oil to prevent them from sticking together.

Recipe and ingredients continue . . .

Sage Pine Nut Panko Crisp

½ cup (125 mL) panko crumbs

¼ cup (60 mL) pine nuts

¼ cup (60 mL) grated Parmesan cheese

¼ cup (60 mL) finely chopped fresh sage leaves

1 tablespoon (15 mL) extra-virgin olive oil

¼ teaspoon (1 mL) salt

PREP AHEAD

Prepare and assemble the lasagna ahead through step 5, cover tightly with foil or plastic wrap, and refrigerate for up to 2 days or freeze for up to 3 months. If frozen, thaw in the fridge overnight. Uncover, sprinkle with the Sage Pine Nut Panko Crisp, and bake as directed.

STORAGE

Store cooled lasagna covered or in a resealable container in the fridge for up to 5 days or in the freezer for up to 3 months. If frozen, thaw in the fridge overnight, then reheat in the oven or in the microwave until warmed through.

Tip

Assemble mini lasagnas in 6 to 8 individual-size ovenproof dishes, layering according to the directions. Bake for 25 to 30 minutes on a large baking sheet to make the transfer to the oven easier and bake at 450°F (230°C) for 25 to 30 minutes.

3. **Make the Sage Pine Nut Panko Crisp:** In a small bowl, stir together the panko, pine nuts, Parmesan, sage, olive oil, and salt. Set aside.

4. Preheat the oven to 450°F (230°C) and grease a 13 × 9-inch (3.5 L) baking dish or individual-size ovenproof dishes.

5. **Assemble the Lasagna:** Pour a third of the butternut squash sauce into the prepared baking dish and spread in an even layer. Cover with a single layer of half the ravioli. Spread the ricotta evenly over the ravioli. Sprinkle the spinach on top. Scatter half of the mozzarella on top, followed by half of the Parmesan. Pour another third of the butternut squash sauce on top and spread evenly. Lay the remaining ravioli in a single layer on top. Finish with the remaining sauce, followed by the remaining mozzarella and Parmesan.

6. Sprinkle the Sage Pine Nut Panko Crisp evenly on top of the lasagna. Bake until the top is just light golden brown and bubbling around the edges, about 20 minutes. Turn the oven to broil and broil until golden brown on top and the cheese bubbles, about 2 minutes. Set aside to rest for 5 minutes before cutting and serving.

Vegan: Use olive oil instead of butter. Use vegetable stock. Use Cashew Cream (page 332). Use vegan ravioli, vegan ricotta, vegan mozzarella cheese, and vegan parm.

Vegetarian: Use vegetable stock.

Dairy-Free: Use Cashew Cream (page 332). Use dairy-free ravioli. Use vegan ricotta, vegan mozzarella cheese, and vegan parm.

Gluten-Free: Use gluten-free ravioli.

Nut-Free: Use cream instead of Cashew Cream. Omit the pine nuts.

COTTAGE PIE

Vegan Option • Vegetarian Option • Dairy-Free Option • Gluten-Free Option • Nut-Free

Serves 4 to 6

TIME	
Prep:	20 MINUTES
Cook:	45 MINUTES
Total:	65 MINUTES

- 2 tablespoons (30 mL) extra-virgin olive oil
- 1 cup (250 mL) diced yellow onion
- 1 cup (250 mL) diced celery
- 1 cup (250 mL) diced peeled carrots
- 2 cloves garlic, minced
- 1 tablespoon (15 mL) all-purpose flour
- 4 cups (1 L) chopped cooked roast beef, plus pan drippings (from Pot Roast, page 231)
- 1 cup (250 mL) beef stock
- 1 cup (250 mL) frozen corn kernels
- 1 cup (250 mL) frozen peas
- Salt and pepper
- 1 batch Buttery Mashed Potatoes (page 326)

This cottage pie is reminiscent of the type of dishes I was raised on—wholesome ingredients that make use of leftovers in creative ways and that are also hearty enough to satisfy a hungry crowd. I can still picture my childhood dining room, a steaming casserole dish on the table, my mom inviting me to pull up a chair, grab a plate, and connect over a warm meal after hours of playing outside. I now get those same magical moments with my own family over meals like this, and I hope you do too.

This dish is designed to use leftover roast from my Pot Roast (page 231). It's okay if you don't have the exact amount of roast beef that's called for, but be sure to add all the extra veggies and pan drippings from the roast to the filling mixture; it will add an incredible amount of flavour. If you have leftover mashed potatoes, this is a perfect place to use them up instead of making them from scratch. You will need about 4 cups (1 L) of mashed potatoes for this dish, but don't worry if it's not exact.

1. Preheat the oven to 400°F (200°C).

2. Heat the olive oil in a large frying pan over medium heat. Add the onion, celery, and carrots and cook, stirring occasionally, until the carrots are soft, about 8 minutes. Add the garlic, sprinkle with the flour, and cook, stirring, for 2 minutes.

3. Stir in the cooked roast beef and drippings, beef stock, corn, and peas. Cook, stirring occasionally, until heated through and slightly thickened, about 5 minutes. Season to taste with salt and pepper.

4. Transfer the mixture to a 13 × 9-inch (3.5 L) baking dish. Top with the mashed potatoes, spreading to evenly cover.

5. Bake, uncovered, until golden brown on top and the mixture is bubbling, about 30 minutes. Let the cottage pie rest for 5 minutes before serving.

Recipe continues . . .

PREP AHEAD
The pie can be assembled through step 4 up to 2 days ahead. Cover and store in the fridge until ready to bake.

STORAGE
Store the cooled cooked pie in a resealable container in the fridge for up to 3 days or in the freezer for up to 3 months. If frozen, thaw in the fridge overnight, then reheat in the microwave until warmed through.

FREEZER-FRIENDLY
Prepare the pie through step 4. Store the unbaked pie, covered tightly, in the freezer for up to 3 months. Thaw in the fridge overnight, then uncover and bake as directed.

Vegan: Use 2 cans (19 ounces/540 mL each) lentils (drained and rinsed) instead of beef. Use beef-flavoured vegetarian stock. Make the dairy-free option of the Buttery Mashed Potatoes (page 326).

Vegetarian: Use 2 cans (19 ounces/540 mL each) lentils (drained and rinsed) instead of the beef. Use beef-flavoured vegetarian stock.

Dairy-Free: Make the dairy-free option of the Buttery Mashed Potatoes (page 326).

Gluten-Free: Use 1 teaspoon (5 mL) cornstarch instead of all-purpose flour.

Tip

For a beautiful presentation, bake in 4 to 6 individual-size ovenproof baking dishes. For easy transfer into the oven, place the individual dishes on a baking sheet before baking.

SHRIMP AND FETA SPINACH RICE

Vegan Option • *Vegetarian Option* • *Dairy-Free Option* • *Gluten-Free* • *Nut-Free*

Serves 4

TIME
Prep: 10 MINUTES
Cook: 15 MINUTES
Total: 25 MINUTES

Garlic Shrimp

2 tablespoons (30 mL) butter or extra-virgin olive oil

1 clove garlic, minced

1 pound (450 g) large fresh or thawed frozen shrimp, peeled and deveined

¼ teaspoon (1 mL) salt

¼ teaspoon (1 mL) pepper

Spinach Rice

2 tablespoons (30 mL) extra-virgin olive oil

1 cup (250 mL) diced yellow onion

2 cloves garlic, minced

4 cups (1 L) chopped spinach

¼ cup (60 mL) chopped fresh dill, plus more for garnish

¼ cup (60 mL) roughly chopped fresh flat-leaf parsley, plus more for garnish

2 green onions (white and light green parts only), sliced

4 cups (1 L) cooked rice

½ cup (125 mL) chicken or vegetable stock

½ cup (125 mL) crumbled feta cheese, plus more for serving

1 tablespoon (15 mL) fresh lemon juice

Salt and pepper

Lemon wedges, for serving (optional)

Tip

You will need about 2 cups (500 mL) of uncooked rice to yield 4 cups (1 L) of cooked rice.

I love everything about Mediterranean-style eating, from the flavours to the good nutrition. This dish is inspired by a traditional Greek spanakorizo, or spinach and rice in English, an elevated, nutritious rice dish. I love it as a main course, but it also makes an incredible side dish with Roast Chicken Dinner (page 235), with or without the shrimp. A medium-grain rice such as arborio is traditionally used in this dish, but you may use a long-grain rice such as jasmine or similar. This is a great place to use leftover or precooked rice if you're planning ahead.

1. **Cook the Garlic Shrimp:** Heat a large frying pan over medium-high heat. Add the butter and garlic and cook for 30 seconds. Add the shrimp, salt, and pepper and cook, tossing occasionally, until they start to brown around the edges on both sides and are opaque, about 5 minutes. Transfer the shrimp to a small dish and cover to keep warm.

2. **Make the Spinach Rice:** To the same pan (no need to wipe it) over medium heat, add the olive oil. Add the onion and cook, stirring occasionally, until soft and translucent, 3 to 4 minutes. Add the garlic and cook, stirring, until fragrant, about 1 minute. Stir in the spinach, dill, parsley, and green onions and cook, stirring occasionally, until the spinach has wilted, about 3 minutes. Stir in the rice, chicken stock, feta, and lemon juice and cook until heated through. Season to taste with salt and pepper.

3. To serve, arrange the shrimp along with any accumulated juices on top of the spinach rice. Garnish with dill and parsley, and lemon wedges if desired. Serve hot.

Vegan: Use vegan butter, if using. Use 1 package (12 ounces/350 g) extra-firm tofu, cubed, or 1 can (19 ounces/540 mL) white beans (drained and rinsed) instead of shrimp (or omit shrimp). Use vegetable stock. Use vegan feta.

Vegetarian: Use 1 package (12 ounces/350 g) extra-firm tofu, cubed, or 1 can (19 ounces/540 mL) white beans (drained and rinsed) instead of shrimp (or omit shrimp). Use vegetable stock.

Dairy-Free: Use vegan butter or olive oil for the shrimp. Use vegan feta.

STORAGE

Store cooled casserole in a resealable container in the fridge for up to 4 days. Reheat in a frying pan on the stovetop or in the microwave until warmed through.

MOM'S SNEAKY MEATLOAF MUFFINS

Dairy-Free Option · *Gluten-Free Option* · *Nut-Free*

Serves 6 to 8

TIME
Prep: 15 MINUTES
Cook: 20 MINUTES
Total: 35 MINUTES

2 pounds (900 g) ground beef, chicken, or turkey

1 egg, whisked

1 cup (250 mL) finely diced yellow onion

½ cup (125 mL) finely grated peeled carrot

½ cup (125 mL) finely grated zucchini

10 soda crackers, finely crushed

¼ cup (60 mL) table (18%) cream

1 teaspoon (5 mL) salt

½ teaspoon (2 mL) pepper

Tomato Sauce

1 can (10 ounces/284 mL) condensed tomato soup

¼ cup (60 mL) ketchup

¼ cup (60 mL) lightly packed brown sugar

For serving

2 batches Buttery Mashed Potatoes (page 326)

Steamed vegetables (corn, green beans, peas, broccoli, or carrots)

Tip

For the best texture, use the small holes of a box grater to finely grate the carrot and zucchini.

Re-Fraiche

Transform leftovers into meatloaf sandwiches or subs.

The '80s called and want their dinner back. My mom's meatloaf—always served with mounds of buttery mashed potatoes—was a core part of my childhood. I now live a stone's throw from my parents, and Sunday dinners are usually spent together. Every time my mom makes her meatloaf, my kids rave about it for days. This is a slightly modified version that is baked in muffin tins to speed up the cooking, and it also sneaks in extra veggies. I've experimented with replacements for the canned tomato soup, but none compares. Since these are already portioned, leftovers are a cinch for lunches! Serve with Buttery Mashed Potatoes (page 326) and a side of steamed veggies.

1. Preheat the oven to 375°F (190°C). If using ground chicken or turkey, spray a muffin tin with nonstick cooking spray.

2. In a large bowl, combine the ground meat, egg, onion, carrot, zucchini, crushed soda crackers, cream, salt, and pepper. Mix until well combined. Evenly divide the mixture among the muffin cups. Using your fingers, press evenly into the tins.

3. **Make the Tomato Sauce:** In a small bowl, whisk together the tomato soup, ketchup, and brown sugar.

4. Spread the sauce evenly on top of the meatloaf muffins. Bake until the meat is cooked through and the internal temperature reaches at least 160°F (70°C) on an instant-read thermometer, about 20 minutes. Serve hot with Buttery Mashed Potatoes and steamed vegetables.

Dairy-Free: Omit the cream. Use vegan butter and Cashew Cream (page 332) in the Buttery Mashed Potatoes (page 326).

Gluten-Free: Use gluten-free soda crackers and tomato soup.

PREP AHEAD
The tomato sauce (step 3) can be made up to 2 days ahead, covered, and refrigerated. The Buttery Mashed Potatoes can be cooked up to 2 days ahead, covered, and refrigerated. The meatloaf ingredients (step 2) can be mixed up to 1 day ahead, covered, and refrigerated.

STORAGE
Store cooled meatloaf muffins in a resealable container in the fridge for up to 4 days or in the freezer for up to 2 months. If frozen, thaw in the fridge overnight, then reheat in the oven on a baking sheet lined with parchment paper or in the microwave until warmed through

NO-LAYER GNOCCHI LASAGNA

Vegan Option · *Vegetarian Option* · *Dairy-Free Option* · *Gluten-Free Option* · *Nut-Free*

Serves 4

TIME
Prep: 15 MINUTES
Cook: 15 MINUTES
Total: 30 MINUTES

1 pound (450 g) ground beef, chicken, or turkey

1 cup (250 mL) diced yellow onion

1 cup (250 mL) finely grated peeled carrots

1 cup (250 mL) finely grated zucchini

3 cloves garlic, minced

2 teaspoons (10 mL) dried oregano

1 teaspoon (5 mL) Italian seasoning

2 tablespoons (30 mL) tomato paste

1 can (28 ounces/796 mL) diced tomatoes

1 cup (250 mL) chicken, beef, or vegetable stock

½ teaspoon (2 mL) red wine vinegar

1 teaspoon (5 mL) lightly packed brown sugar

Salt and pepper

18 ounces (500 g) shelf-stable or frozen gnocchi

¼ cup (60 mL) roughly chopped fresh basil, plus more for serving

¼ cup (60 mL) grated Parmesan cheese, divided

½ cup (125 mL) ricotta cheese

1 cup (250 mL) grated mozzarella cheese

This no-layer lasagna is the type of no-fuss meal we all need on busy days. Get all the comforting flavours you know and love from a traditional lasagna in only 30 minutes, with no added pressure of getting perfect layers. Serve with thick slices of Garlic Bread (page 321) and a simple salad, and you and your loved ones are in for a great meal!

If you don't have an ovenproof frying pan, simply transfer the gnocchi mixture to a 13 × 9-inch (3.5 L) baking dish before broiling.

1. Preheat the broiler.

2. Heat a large ovenproof frying pan with a lid over medium heat. Add the ground meat and cook, stirring occasionally, until lightly browned, 5 to 6 minutes. Add the onion, carrots, and zucchini and cook, stirring occasionally, until the vegetables are soft, about 5 minutes.

3. Add the garlic, oregano, Italian seasoning, and tomato paste and cook, stirring, until fragrant, about 1 minute.

4. Stir in the diced tomatoes, chicken stock, red wine vinegar, and brown sugar. Season to taste with salt and pepper. Bring to a boil, then reduce the heat to medium-low, stir in the gnocchi, cover, and cook until the gnocchi are tender, about 4 minutes.

5. Stir in the basil and half of the Parmesan. Season to taste with salt and pepper. Dollop large spoonfuls of the ricotta on top of the gnocchi. Sprinkle with the remaining Parmesan and the mozzarella.

6. Broil until the cheese is melted, bubbling, and golden on top, about 2 minutes. Garnish with basil and serve hot.

Vegan: Use veggie ground. Use vegetable stock. Use vegan parm, ricotta, and mozzarella cheese.

Vegetarian: Use veggie ground. Use vegetable stock.

Dairy-Free: Use vegan parm, ricotta, and mozzarella cheese.

Gluten-Free: Use gluten-free gnocchi.

STORAGE

Store cooled lasagna in a resealable container in the fridge for up to 4 days or in the freezer for up to 2 months. If frozen, thaw in the fridge overnight, then reheat in the microwave until warmed through.

PREP AHEAD

The lasagna can be prepped ahead through step 5. Cover tightly with foil and store in the fridge for up to 2 days or in the freezer for up to 2 months. If frozen, thaw in the fridge overnight. Bake, covered, in a 350°F (180°C) oven until heated through. Turn the oven to broil and broil until the cheese is melted, bubbling, and golden on top, about 2 minutes.

One-Pan MEALS

PREP AHEAD

FLANK STEAK WITH FETA SALSA

Dairy-Free Option • Gluten-Free Option • Nut-Free

Serves 4

TIME

Prep: 15 MINUTES, PLUS 2 HOURS MARINATING

Cook: 15 MINUTES

Total: 30 MINUTES, PLUS RESTING TIME

Flank Steak

2 pounds (900 g) flank steak

1 cup (250 mL) water

½ cup (125 mL) soy sauce

2 teaspoons (10 mL) lightly packed brown sugar

2 cloves garlic, minced

1 teaspoon (5 mL) pepper

Feta Salsa

1 cup (250 mL) crumbled feta cheese

¾ cup (175 mL) finely chopped fresh flat-leaf parsley

¼ cup (60 mL) finely diced red onion

2 cloves garlic, minced

1 tablespoon (15 mL) extra-virgin olive oil

½ teaspoon (2 mL) pepper

Grilled Peppers and Onions

2 red, orange, or yellow sweet peppers, sliced

1 sweet onion, sliced

1 tablespoon (15 mL) extra-virgin olive oil

1 clove garlic, minced

Salt and pepper

Garlic Bread (page 321), for serving

Marinated to perfection, this flank steak is juicy, tender, and full of bold flavours. And the Feta Salsa? You will want to add it to everything—and you can! From grilled chicken or fish to scrambled eggs, this incredibly flavourful salsa will elevate so many dishes. This is a very special recipe straight from my husband Charles—everyone raves about how delicious it is! Buy flank steak in bulk and marinate extra to freeze for quick future meals.

1. **Marinate the Flank Steak:** Place the steak in a shallow baking pan or in a large resealable bag. In a medium bowl, mix together the water, soy sauce, brown sugar, garlic, and pepper. Pour the marinade over the meat. Cover the dish or seal the bag and refrigerate for at least 2 hours or overnight, turning once.

2. **Make the Feta Salsa:** In a medium bowl, mix together the feta, parsley, red onion, garlic, olive oil, and pepper. Cover and store in the fridge until ready to use.

3. Remove the flank steak from the marinade. Place the steak on a plate and bring to room temperature, about 30 minutes. Discard the marinade.

4. If cooking on an outdoor grill, preheat the grill to medium-high (400 to 450°F/200 to 230°C). (Alternatively, you can cook the steak indoors on the stovetop.)

5. Cook the steak on the hot grill (or in a preheated cast-iron pan with a drizzle of avocado oil on medium-high heat) for about 5 minutes per side for medium doneness or until cooked to your preference (see Steak Doneness Guide, page 182). Transfer the steak to a cutting board, cover loosely with foil, and let rest for 5 to 10 minutes.

6. **Meanwhile, make the Grilled Peppers and Onions:** In a large bowl, toss together the peppers, onion, olive oil, and garlic. Season to taste with salt and pepper. On the grill over medium-high heat, grill the peppers and onion until they start to brown around the edges and are slightly softened, about 4 minutes. (Alternatively, cook the vegetables in the same pan you used for the steak over medium-high heat, stirring frequently, until browned around the edges and slightly softened.)

7. Using a sharp chef's knife, thinly slice the meat diagonally against the grain. Serve immediately with the Feta Salsa, Grilled Peppers and Onions, and Garlic Bread.

Recipe continues . . .

PREP AHEAD

The Feta Salsa and the pepper and onion mixture can be prepped up to 2 days ahead and stored in separate resealable containers in the refrigerator. The steak can be marinated up to 1 day in advance. The Garlic Bread can be prepped up to 1 day in advance and stored in a resealable bag at room temperature until ready to bake.

STORAGE

Store cooled flank steak and grilled vegetables in separate resealable containers in the fridge for up to 3 days.

Re-Fraiche

Transform the grilled flank into the ultimate steak sandwich. Use Garlic Bread (page 321) as the base. Top with leftover Grilled Peppers and Onions, sliced flank steak, and Feta Salsa. Broil until golden and serve immediately.

Dairy-Free: Use vegan feta. Make the dairy-free option of the Garlic Bread (page 321).

Gluten-Free: Use gluten-free soy sauce. Make the gluten-free option of the Garlic Bread (page 321).

Steak Doneness Guide

MEDIUM-RARE:

3 to 4 minutes per side
(internal temperature 130°F/55°C)

MEDIUM:

5 minutes per side
(internal temperature 140°F/60°C)

MEDIUM-WELL:

6 minutes per side
(internal temperature 150°F/65°C)

PREP AHEAD | MAKE AHEAD

JALAPEÑO POPPER CHICKEN PASTA

Dairy-Free Option • Gluten-Free Option • Nut-Free

Serves 4 to 6

TIME	
Prep:	10 MINUTES
Cook:	40 MINUTES
Total:	50 MINUTES

Spice Mixture

1 teaspoon (5 mL) ground cumin

1 teaspoon (5 mL) smoked paprika

1 teaspoon (5 mL) garlic powder

1 teaspoon (5 mL) onion powder

1 teaspoon (5 mL) dried oregano

1 teaspoon (5 mL) salt

½ teaspoon (2 mL) pepper

Jalapeño Popper Chicken Pasta

8 boneless, skinless chicken thighs (about 2 pounds/900 g total)

6 slices thick-cut bacon, diced

2 cups (500 mL) finely chopped yellow onion

2 cloves garlic, minced

2 jalapeño peppers, seeded and finely diced

2 cups (500 mL) frozen corn kernels

4 cups (1 L) medium shell pasta, bow ties, or similar shape

3½ cups (875 mL) chicken stock

1 cup (250 mL) whole milk or half-and-half (10%) cream, plus more for thinning

½ cup (125 mL) panko crumbs (optional)

1 tablespoon (15 mL) extra-virgin olive oil

½ cup (125 mL) cream cheese, room temperature

1½ cups (375 mL) grated extra-old white cheddar

Sliced jalapeño peppers (optional)

A good cheesy pasta is a timeless staple in any home. Let this be your new go-to. The iconic flavours of a jalapeño popper meet the ooey-gooey goodness of mac and cheese in this one-pan jalapeño popper pasta. Smoky bacon, jalapeños, and cream cheese, along with perfectly seasoned chicken and a crispy panko topping, is always a huge hit in my house. I'm talking no-leftovers, *plate-licking* kind of hit!

1. **Make the Spice Mixture:** In a small bowl, stir together the cumin, smoked paprika, garlic powder, onion powder, oregano, salt, and pepper. Scoop out 2 teaspoons (10 mL) of the spice mixture into a separate small bowl and set aside.

2. **Make the Chicken Pasta:** In a medium bowl, toss the chicken with the remaining spice mixture to coat.

3. Heat a large ovenproof frying pan with a lid over medium heat. Add the bacon and cook until slightly crispy, about 5 minutes, stirring occasionally. Using a slotted spoon, transfer the bacon to a small dish. Drain off all but 2 tablespoons (30 mL) of fat from the pan.

4. Return the pan to medium heat. Add the chicken and cook until golden brown on both sides and the internal temperature reaches 165°F (74°C) on an instant-read thermometer, about 12 minutes total. Transfer the chicken to a plate and cover to keep warm.

5. To the same pan (no need to wipe it—I like the added flavour from the bacon) over medium heat, add the onion (add a drizzle of oil if needed) and cook, stirring occasionally, until soft and translucent, 3 to 4 minutes.

6. Add the garlic, jalapeños, and reserved spice mixture and cook, stirring, until fragrant, about 2 minutes. Stir in the corn, pasta, chicken stock, and milk, cover, and cook, stirring occasionally, until the pasta is tender, about 15 minutes.

Recipe continues . . .

PREP AHEAD
The chicken can be prepared through step 2 up to 2 days ahead, then stored in a resealable container before cooking. Alternatively, you can prepare the recipe through step 10, let cool, then cover and refrigerate for up to 3 days. Preheat the broiler, loosen the pasta mixture with some hot water or extra milk, and proceed with step 11.

STORAGE
Store cooled pasta in a resealable container in the fridge for up to 3 days. Reheat in the microwave until warmed through.

7. While the pasta cooks, preheat the broiler.

8. Roughly chop the cooked chicken, reserving any juices.

9. In small bowl, stir together the panko and olive oil.

10. Stir the cream cheese into the pasta mixture to combine. Add the cooked chicken with any juices and the cooked bacon and stir until incorporated. Add more milk to thin into a creamy consistency if needed.

11. Sprinkle the cheddar over the pasta mixture, followed by the panko, if using. Top with jalapeño slices if desired and broil until golden, about 2 minutes.

Dairy-Free: Use Cashew Cream (page 332) or non-dairy milk instead of milk or cream. Use vegan cream cheese and vegan cheddar cheese.

Gluten-Free: Use gluten-free bacon, pasta, and panko.

SKILLET ENCHILADAS

Vegan Option · *Vegetarian Option* · *Dairy-Free Option* · *Gluten-Free Option* · *Nut-Free*

Serves 6 to 8

TIME
Prep: 15 MINUTES
Cook: 15 MINUTES
Total: 30 MINUTES

- 2 tablespoons (30 mL) extra-virgin olive oil
- 1 cup (250 mL) finely diced yellow onion
- 1 red, orange, or yellow sweet pepper, finely diced
- 2 cloves garlic, minced
- 2 teaspoons (10 mL) ground cumin
- 1 teaspoon (5 mL) dried oregano
- 1 teaspoon (5 mL) chili powder
- 1 teaspoon (5 mL) garlic powder
- 1 teaspoon (5 mL) sweet paprika
- 4 cups (1 L) shredded rotisserie chicken
- 2 cups (500 mL) enchilada sauce (or make your own, page 316)
- 1 can (19 ounces/540 mL) black beans or pinto beans, drained and rinsed
- 1 cup (250 mL) frozen or drained canned corn kernels
- ½ cup (125 mL) chicken or vegetable stock
- Juice of 1 lime
- Salt and pepper
- 1½ cups (375 mL) grated Monterey Jack or Tex-Mex cheese
- 4 medium (7-inch/18 cm) flour tortillas, cut into triangles

For serving

- 1 cup (250 mL) roughly chopped fresh cilantro
- 1 avocado, pitted, peeled, and diced
- Sliced jalapeño peppers
- 1 cup (250 mL) cherry tomatoes, cut into quarters
- Sour cream or plain full-fat Greek yogurt
- Lime wedges

Everyone loves enchiladas, and when you're short on time, this skillet version delivers all those big flavours in a quick and easy way that helps you get dinner on the table fast. Light on steps but packed with flavour, these skillet enchiladas use rotisserie chicken for a low-lift dinner. It's also a great way to use up leftover chicken from my Roast Chicken Dinner (page 235). Make your own Enchilada Sauce (page 316) if you have the time—it's simple, I promise!

If you don't have an ovenproof frying pan, simply transfer the filling to a 13 × 9-inch (3.5 L) baking dish before topping with the cheese and tortillas and broiling.

1. Heat the olive oil in a large ovenproof frying pan over medium heat. Add the onion, sweet pepper, garlic, cumin, oregano, chili powder, garlic powder, and sweet paprika and cook, stirring frequently, until the veggies are soft, about 4 minutes.

2. Add the chicken, enchilada sauce, black beans, corn, and chicken stock and bring to a boil. Reduce the heat to low and simmer until slightly thickened, about 5 minutes. Add the lime juice and season to taste with salt and pepper.

3. Meanwhile, preheat the broiler.

4. Evenly top the enchilada mixture with half the cheese. Cover with the tortilla triangles, followed by the remaining cheese. Broil until the cheese is golden brown and bubbling, about 4 minutes.

5. Serve with the cilantro, avocado, jalapeños, cherry tomatoes, sour cream, and lime wedges.

Vegan: Omit the chicken and double the beans. Use vegetable stock. Use vegan cheese and vegan sour cream.

Vegetarian: Omit the chicken and double the beans. Use vegetable stock.

Dairy-Free: Use vegan cheese and vegan sour cream.

Gluten-Free: Use gluten-free tortillas.

PREP AHEAD
The enchiladas can be prepared up to 1 day ahead; prepare through step 2 and assemble (step 4), but don't broil. Cover with foil and refrigerate. Bake, covered, in a 350°F (180°C) oven until heated through, around 30 minutes. Turn the oven to broil and broil until the cheese is golden brown and bubbling, about 4 minutes.

STORAGE

Store cooled skillet enchiladas in a resealable container in the fridge for up to 3 days. Reheat in the microwave until warmed through.

FREEZER-FRIENDLY

Prepare the enchiladas through step 2, then assemble the enchiladas in step 4 but don't broil. Cover tightly with foil and store in the freezer for up to 2 months. Bake from frozen, covered with foil, in a 350°F (180°C) oven until heated through, about 45 minutes. Turn the oven to broil, remove the foil, and broil until the cheese is golden brown and bubbling, about 4 minutes.

TUSCAN ORZO

Vegan Option • Vegetarian Option • Dairy-Free Option • Gluten-Free Option • Nut-Free

Serves 4

TIME	
Prep:	10 MINUTES
Cook:	20 MINUTES
Total:	30 MINUTES

- 2 Italian sausages (6 ounces/170 g each), casings removed
- ½ cup (125 mL) diced yellow onion
- 2 cloves garlic, minced
- ¼ cup (60 mL) drained oil-packed sun-dried tomatoes, roughly chopped
- ¼ teaspoon (1 mL) dried oregano
- ½ cup (125 mL) white wine or chicken stock
- 3 cups (750 mL) chicken stock
- 1½ cups (375 mL) orzo
- ¼ cup (60 mL) heavy (35%) cream or Cashew Cream (page 332)
- 4 cups (1 L) spinach, roughly chopped
- ½ cup (125 mL) crumbled feta cheese, plus more for garnish
- Salt and pepper
- 2 tablespoons (30 mL) finely chopped fresh basil

STORAGE

Store cooled orzo in a resealable container in the fridge for up to 4 days or in the freezer for up to 2 months. If frozen, thaw in the fridge overnight, then reheat in the microwave on medium or in a saucepan over low heat on the stovetop with about ½ cup (125 mL) of chicken stock to loosen it, stirring occasionally.

I see you, busy moms—this creamy, comforting, one-pan wonder has got your back. This creamy Tuscan Orzo is everything you want in a weeknight dinner—quick, simple, comforting, and packed with bold, sun-drenched flavours. Orzo is a lovely quick-cooking pasta that I highly recommend you keep stocked at home—it is one of my favourite pantry staples for fast, no-fuss meals.

1. Heat a medium frying pan with a lid over medium-high heat. Add the sausage and cook, breaking the meat into small pieces with a wooden spoon, until browned, 4 to 5 minutes. Add the onion and cook, stirring occasionally, until soft and translucent, 3 to 4 minutes.

2. Add the garlic, sun-dried tomatoes, and oregano and cook, stirring, until fragrant, about 30 seconds. Add the white wine and cook until reduced by half, about 2 minutes.

3. Stir in the stock and orzo. Bring to a simmer, cover, and cook, stirring occasionally, until the orzo is tender, about 8 minutes.

4. Stir in the cream, spinach, and feta and cook until the spinach is wilted, about 1 minute. Season to taste with salt and pepper. Garnish with the basil and extra feta if desired.

Vegan: Use plant-based Italian sausage; add a drizzle of oil to the pan if needed. Use vegetable stock. Use Cashew Cream (page 332) instead of heavy cream. Use vegan feta.

Vegetarian: Use plant-based Italian sausage; add a drizzle of oil to the pan if needed. Use vegetable stock.

Dairy-Free: Use Cashew Cream (page 332). Use vegan feta.

Gluten-Free: Use gluten-free chickpea orzo.

BROCCOLI AND CHEESE ORZO

Vegan Option · Vegetarian Option · Dairy-Free Option · Gluten-Free Option · Nut-Free

Serves 4

TIME	
Prep:	5 MINUTES
Cook:	15 MINUTES
Total:	20 MINUTES

2 tablespoons (30 mL) butter

1 cup (250 mL) finely diced yellow onion

2 cloves garlic, minced

3 cups (750 mL) chicken or vegetable stock

1½ cups (375 mL) orzo

½ cup (125 mL) table (18%) cream

4 cups (1 L) small broccoli florets

1 cup (250 mL) grated cheddar cheese

Salt and pepper

STORAGE
Store cooled orzo in a resealable container in the fridge for up to 5 days. Reheat in the microwave until warmed through.

For as long as I can remember, my kids have loved the classic combo of broccoli and cheese, and this orzo version is a fun, creamy twist on their favourite. It comes together in 20 minutes and uses only eight ingredients. This is a reliable recipe to lean on when you need a last-minute meal. Serve it as a vegetarian meal or add grilled chicken breast, grilled fillet of salmon, or pan-fried shrimp.

1. In a medium frying pan with a lid over medium heat, melt the butter. Add the onion and cook, stirring occasionally, until soft and translucent, 3 to 4 minutes. Add the garlic and cook, stirring, until fragrant, about 1 minute.

2. Stir in the chicken stock and orzo, bring to a simmer, then reduce the heat to medium-low, cover, and cook, stirring occasionally, until the orzo is tender, about 8 minutes.

3. Stir in the cream and broccoli and cook, stirring occasionally, until the broccoli is fork-tender but still bright green, 3 to 5 minutes. Stir in the cheese and season to taste with salt and pepper.

Vegan: Use vegan butter or olive oil. Use vegetable stock. Use Cashew Cream (page 332) instead of table cream. Use vegan cheddar cheese.

Vegetarian: Use vegetable stock.

Dairy-Free: Use Cashew Cream (page 332) and vegan cheese.

Gluten-Free: Use gluten-free chickpea orzo.

Re-Fraiche

To turn leftovers into a soup, add 1 cup (250 mL) of chicken or vegetable stock to every 1 cup (250 mL) of leftover orzo. Finish with extra grated cheese if desired.

STORAGE

Store the cooked chicken and potatoes in a resealable container in the fridge for up to 4 days. Enjoy cold or to reheat, place the chicken and potatoes in a skillet over medium heat with a splash of water or broth, cover, and cook for 5 to 7 minutes until heated through, stirring occasionally. Or, microwave in a covered dish on medium for 1 to 2 minutes, stirring halfway.

FREEZER-FRIENDLY

Place the uncooked chicken and marinade (step 1) in a resealable plastic bag and store in the freezer for up to 3 months. If frozen, thaw in the fridge overnight before cooking.

PREP AHEAD | FREEZER-FRIENDLY

LEMON DILL CHICKEN AND POTATOES

Dairy-Free Option • *Gluten-Free* • *Nut-Free*

Serves 4

TIME

Prep: 10 MINUTES, PLUS 20 MINUTES MARINATING

Cook: 35 MINUTES

Total: 40 MINUTES

- ¼ cup (60 mL) + 1 tablespoon (15 mL) extra-virgin olive oil, divided
- 4 cloves garlic, minced
- 2 tablespoons (30 mL) finely chopped fresh dill, plus more for serving
- 2 tablespoons (30 mL) finely chopped fresh flat-leaf parsley, plus more for serving
- 1 teaspoon (5 mL) lemon zest
- 2 tablespoons (30 mL) fresh lemon juice
- 1 teaspoon (5 mL) salt
- ½ teaspoon (2 mL) pepper
- 4 boneless, skinless chicken breasts (about 3 pounds/1.35 kg total)
- 1 pound (450 g) baby potatoes, halved

For serving

- 2 cups (500 mL) diced English cucumber
- 1 cup (250 mL) halved cherry tomatoes
- ½ cup (125 mL) tzatziki
- ¼ cup (60 mL) crumbled feta cheese
- Lemon wedges

PREP AHEAD

The chicken can be marinated ahead and stored in a resealable container in the fridge for up to 2 days or in a resealable plastic bag in the freezer for up to 3 months. If frozen, thaw in the fridge overnight before cooking.

This lemon dill chicken with potatoes is a one-pan wonder you'll want on repeat. Inspired by the fresh, wholesome flavours of the Mediterranean diet, it brings together tender, herb-marinated chicken, vibrant Greek-style veggies, and golden roasted potatoes—all in one dish. The bright pop of lemon and fragrant dill makes it feel fresh and flavourful, without any fuss.

Pro tip: Double the chicken and marinade—cook half now and freeze the rest for a ready-to-go dinner on a busy night. If you don't have a large ovenproof frying pan, in step 4 simply transfer the chicken and potatoes to a 13 × 9-inch (3.5 L) baking dish before baking.

1. In a large bowl, whisk together ¼ cup (60 mL) of the olive oil, garlic, dill, parsley, lemon zest, lemon juice, salt, and pepper. Place half of the dressing in a small resealable container and store in the fridge until ready to serve. Add the chicken to the remaining dressing and turn to evenly coat. Cover and marinate in the fridge for at least 20 minutes or up to 2 days.

2. When ready to cook, preheat the oven to 425°F (220°C).

3. Heat a large cast-iron or ovenproof frying pan over medium-high heat. Add the remaining 1 tablespoon (15 mL) olive oil. Using tongs, remove the chicken from the marinade (reserve the marinade for the potatoes) and sear until golden brown, about 2 minutes per side. Remove from the heat. Transfer the chicken to a plate and cover to keep warm.

4. To the same pan (no need to wipe it), add the potatoes along with the reserved marinade. Transfer to the oven and bake for 15 minutes. Toss the potatoes, return the chicken to the pan, and bake until the internal temperature of the chicken reaches 165°F (74°C) on an instant-read thermometer, about 15 minutes.

5. Assemble bowls with a base of chicken and potatoes. Top with the cucumber, tomatoes, tzatziki, feta, dill, parsley, and lemon wedges for squeezing. Serve with a drizzle of the reserved dressing.

Dairy-Free: Use vegan tzatziki and vegan feta.

Re-Fraiche

Transform leftover chicken into Santorini Bowls (see page 22).

LUMPIA LETTUCE WRAPS

Vegan Option • Vegetarian Option • Dairy-Free • Gluten-Free Option • Nut-Free

Serves 4

TIME
Prep: 15 MINUTES
Cook: 15 MINUTES
Total: 30 MINUTES

1 cup (250 mL) jasmine rice

Spring Roll Crisps

8 spring roll wrappers, thawed if frozen

Salt

Lumpia Filling

1 pound (450 g) ground chicken or pork

1 can (8 ounces/227 mL) water chestnuts, drained and rinsed, finely diced

1 cup (250 mL) finely diced yellow onion

½ cup (125 mL) finely diced cremini mushrooms

½ cup (125 mL) finely diced peeled carrot

½ cup (125 mL) finely diced celery

4 cloves garlic, minced

2 tablespoons (30 mL) sesame oil, divided

1 tablespoon (15 mL) soy sauce, plus more to taste

1 tablespoon (15 mL) oyster sauce

Salt and pepper

Lumpia Shanghai are similar to crispy spring rolls but longer and thinner. Common in Filipino cuisine, lumpia are usually filled with seasoned ground pork and vegetables and served with a sweet, tangy chili dipping sauce. On a trip to Maui with my family I got the chance to dive into the kitchen and cook with my dear friends at the Fairmont Kea Lani. Chef Jonathan Pasion taught me how to make lumpia, a delicious highlight of my vacation! This is my "unwrapped" version complete with crispy spring roll chips for that signature crunch. It is delicious served as a bowl over rice or simply wrapped in butter or iceberg lettuce leaves.

1. Cook the rice. Set aside and keep warm.

2. Meanwhile, make the Spring Roll Crisps. Preheat the oven to 400°F (200°C) and line a baking sheet with parchment paper.

3. Use a sharp knife to cut the spring roll wrappers in half corner to corner to form triangles. Lightly spray both sides of the wrapper triangles with cooking spray and sprinkle with salt. Arrange them in a single layer on the prepared baking sheet. Bake until golden, about 5 minutes. Set aside.

4. **Make the Lumpia Filling:** In a medium bowl, combine the ground chicken, water chestnuts, onion, mushrooms, carrot, celery, garlic, 1 tablespoon (15 mL) of the sesame oil, soy sauce, and oyster sauce. Mix together well.

5. Heat a large frying pan over medium-high heat. Add the remaining 1 tablespoon (15 mL) sesame oil. Add the chicken mixture and cook, stirring occasionally, until golden brown and cooked through, about 10 minutes. Season to taste with salt and pepper.

Recipe and ingredients continue . . .

Sweet Chili Sauce

½ cup (125 mL) sweet chili sauce

½ cup (125 mL) unseasoned rice vinegar

For serving

1 head of iceberg or butter lettuce, leaves separated

Chopped fresh cilantro

Sliced green onions

PREP AHEAD
The Sweet Chili Sauce can be made up to 1 week ahead and stored in a resealable container in the fridge. The Spring Roll Crisps (steps 2 and 3) can be made up to 2 days ahead and stored in a loosely covered container at room temperature. The Lumpia Filling (steps 4 through 5) can be made up to 1 day ahead; cool and store in a resealable container in the fridge.

STORAGE
Store the cooled rice and filling in separate resealable containers in the fridge for up to 3 days. Store the Sweet Chili Sauce in a resealable container in the fridge for up to 1 week.

FREEZER-FRIENDLY
Make the Lumpia Filling (steps 4 and 5), let cool completely, and freeze in a resealable container for up to 2 months. Thaw in the fridge overnight. Reheat in a lightly oiled frying pan on the stovetop or in the microwave until warmed through.

6. Make the Sweet Chili Sauce: In a small bowl, stir together the chili sauce and rice vinegar.

7. To serve family-style so everyone can assemble their own, stack the lettuce leaves on a plate in the centre of the table, along with small dishes with cilantro, green onions, and the Sweet Chili Sauce. Transfer the cooked rice and hot filling to separate serving dishes and place on the table.

Vegan and Vegetarian: Use veggie ground. Omit the oyster sauce.

Gluten-Free: Use gluten-free spring roll wrappers or omit the Spring Roll Crisps. Use gluten-free soy sauce.

Re-Fraiche

For an easy bowl meal, reheat leftover filling and serve over cooked rice or transform into Lumpia Rice Bowls (see page 22).

SMASHED CHICKEN CAESAR TACOS

Vegan Option • Vegetarian • Dairy-Free Option • Gluten-Free Option • Nut-Free

Makes 8 tacos, serves 4

TIME
Prep: 15 MINUTES
Cook: 20 MINUTES
Total: 35 MINUTES

Simple Caesar Dressing

½ cup (125 mL) extra-virgin olive oil

¼ cup (60 mL) grated Parmesan cheese

¼ cup (60 mL) mayonnaise

2 tablespoons (30 mL) white wine vinegar

1 tablespoon (15 mL) drained capers, chopped

4 teaspoons (20 mL) Dijon mustard

1 teaspoon (5 mL) Worcestershire sauce

1 teaspoon (5 mL) anchovy paste

4 cloves garlic, minced

Juice of 1 lemon

Salt and pepper

Caesar Salad

1 heart of romaine lettuce, roughly chopped

½ cup (125 mL) grated Parmesan cheese

½ cup (125 mL) crumbled cooked bacon

½ cup (125 mL) Simple Caesar Dressing (page 197) or store-bought

I still remember making these tacos for my family for the first time. We all enjoyed it so much that I knew it was destined for this cookbook. If you like Caesar salad *and* tacos, then you will love these. Seasoned ground chicken gets smashed onto a tortilla and pan-fried until golden, topped with vibrant crunchy Caesar salad, and drizzled with an umami bomb of homemade Caesar dressing. Add Cajun spice to really level them up! The Caesar dressing is zesty, garlicky, and perfectly creamy. Made with simple ingredients, it's lighter than traditional versions but just as delicious.

1. **Make the Simple Caesar Dressing:** In a medium bowl with tall sides, combine the olive oil, Parmesan, mayonnaise, white wine vinegar, capers, mustard, Worcestershire sauce, anchovy paste, garlic, and lemon juice. Blend with an immersion blender. (If you don't have an immersion blender, add the ingredients to a tall jar with a lid and shake well to combine.) Season to taste with salt and pepper.

2. **Make the Caesar Salad:** In a medium bowl, combine the romaine, Parmesan, and bacon, if using. Set aside.

3. **Make the Taco Filling:** In a medium bowl, combine the ground chicken, Cajun seasoning (if using), garlic powder, salt, and pepper. Mix well.

4. Divide the ground chicken into 8 equal portions. Place a portion of chicken on top of each tortilla and, using a rubber spatula, your fingers, a fork, or a butter knife, spread the chicken evenly across the tortilla.

5. Heat 1 teaspoon (5 mL) of olive oil in a large frying pan over medium-high heat. Working in batches to avoid crowding the pan, place the tortillas, chicken mixture side down, in the hot pan and cook until golden brown, 2 to 3 minutes. Flip and continue cooking until the chicken is cooked through and the tortillas are golden brown, about 3 minutes. Remove from the pan and cover to keep warm. Repeat with the remaining tortillas.

Recipe and ingredients continue . . .

Taco Filling

1 pound (450 g) ground chicken

2 teaspoons (10 mL) Cajun seasoning (optional)

½ teaspoon (2 mL) garlic powder

½ teaspoon (2 mL) salt

¼ teaspoon (1 mL) pepper

For assembly

8 medium (7-inch/18 cm) flour tortillas

Extra-virgin olive oil, for cooking

½ cup (125 mL) Crispy Panko (page 325), for serving

PREP AHEAD

The Simple Caesar Dressing can be made up to 5 days ahead and stored in a resealable container in the fridge. The Caesar Salad can be mixed (without the dressing) up to 2 days in advance; cover and refrigerate. The Taco Filling can be mixed up to 2 days ahead; refrigerate in a resealable container.

STORAGE

Stored cooled tacos, without the salad, in a resealable container in the fridge for up to 3 days or in the freezer for up to 2 months. Heat in a 300°F (150°C) oven or an air fryer until hot.

6. Just before serving, toss the salad with Simple Caesar Dressing to taste.

7. Top the tortillas with the Caesar Salad and a sprinkle of Crispy Panko. Fold in half like a taco.

Vegan: Use vegan parm. Use vegan mayonnaise. Omit the anchovy paste.

Dairy-Free: Use vegan parm.

Gluten-Free: Use gluten-free Worcestershire sauce or gluten-free soy sauce. Use gluten-free tortillas.

SMASHED GREEK CHICKEN TACOS

Dairy-Free Option • Gluten-Free Option • Nut-Free

Makes 8 tacos, serves 4

TIME	
Prep:	10 MINUTES
Cook:	20 MINUTES
Total:	30 MINUTES

Greek Salad

1 cup (250 mL) halved cherry tomatoes

1 cup (250 mL) diced English cucumber

2 tablespoons (30 mL) finely diced red onion

½ teaspoon (2 mL) dried oregano

1 clove garlic, minced

1 tablespoon (15 mL) extra-virgin olive oil

1 teaspoon (5 mL) red wine vinegar

1 teaspoon (5 mL) fresh lemon juice

Salt

Taco Filling

1 pound (450 g) ground chicken

½ teaspoon (2 mL) lemon zest

1 teaspoon (5 mL) fresh lemon juice

1 teaspoon (5 mL) garlic powder

½ teaspoon (2 mL) dried oregano

½ teaspoon (2 mL) salt

¼ teaspoon (1 mL) pepper

For assembly

8 medium (7-inch/18 cm) flour tortillas

Extra-virgin olive oil, for cooking

For serving

Tzatziki

Hummus

Feta, crumbled

These Smashed Greek Chicken Tacos are a light and flavourful twist on classic Mediterranean flavours. Seasoned ground chicken is smashed into a flour tortilla and seared until golden, served with creamy tzatziki, a simple crisp Greek salad, and finished with a sprinkle of feta. Quick, fresh, and packed with flavour, these tacos make the perfect easy weeknight meal.

1. **Make the Greek Salad:** In a medium bowl, toss together the cherry tomatoes, cucumber, red onion, oregano, garlic, olive oil, red wine vinegar, and lemon juice. Season to taste with salt. Store in the fridge until ready to serve.

2. **Make the Taco Filling:** In a medium bowl, combine the ground chicken, lemon zest, lemon juice, garlic powder, oregano, salt, and pepper. Mix well.

3. Divide the ground chicken into 8 equal portions. Place a portion of chicken on top of each tortilla and, using a rubber spatula, your fingers, a fork, or a butter knife, spread the chicken evenly across the tortilla.

4. Heat 1 teaspoon (5 mL) of olive in a large frying pan over medium-high heat. Working in batches to avoid crowding the pan, place the tortillas, chicken mixture side down, in the hot pan and cook until golden brown, 2 to 3 minutes. Flip and continue cooking until the chicken is cooked through and the tortillas are golden brown, about 3 minutes. Remove from the pan and cover to keep warm. Repeat with the remaining tortillas.

5. Top the tortillas with the Greek Salad, tzatziki, hummus, and feta as desired. Fold in half like a taco.

Dairy-Free: Use vegan tzatziki and vegan feta.

Gluten-Free: Use gluten-free tortillas.

PREP AHEAD

The Greek Salad (without the dressing) can be mixed up to 2 days in advance; cover and refrigerate. The Taco Filling can be mixed up to 2 days in advance; refrigerate in a resealable container.

STORAGE

Stored cooled tacos, without the salad, in a resealable container in the fridge for up to 3 days or in the freezer for up to 2 months. Reheat in a 350°F (180°C) oven or an air fryer until hot.

Makes 12 tacos, serves 6

TIME
Prep: 15 MINUTES
Cook: 15 MINUTES
Total: 30 MINUTES

SMASHED DUMPLING TACOS

Dairy-Free • *Gluten-Free Option*

Like a deconstructed dumpling, these super-speedy, super-easy Smashed Dumpling Tacos are such fun to make. The Cucumber Coleslaw is a refreshing addition to these mouthwatering tacos, and it makes enough to enjoy on the side for an extra helping of veggies!

Dumpling Dip

½ cup (125 mL) low-sodium soy sauce

1 tablespoon (15 mL) pure maple syrup

2 teaspoons (10 mL) sesame oil

1 teaspoon (5 mL) sesame seeds

Pinch of red chili flakes (optional)

Cucumber Coleslaw

¼ cup (60 mL) unseasoned rice vinegar

2 teaspoons (10 mL) sesame oil

1 teaspoon (5 mL) sugar

½ teaspoon (2 mL) red chili flakes (optional)

Salt

5 cups (1.25 L) coleslaw mix (397 g package)

1 English cucumber, diced

2 green onions (white and light green parts only), sliced

½ cup (125 mL) fresh cilantro, roughly chopped

Taco Filling

1 pound (450 g) large fresh or thawed frozen shrimp, peeled, deveined, and minced

1 pound (450 g) ground chicken or pork

4 green onions (white and light green parts only), sliced

4 cloves garlic, minced

1 tablespoon (15 mL) grated peeled fresh ginger

2 teaspoons (10 mL) soy sauce

1 teaspoon (10 mL) sesame oil, plus more for cooking

For assembly

12 medium (7-inch/18 cm) flour tortillas

Fresh cilantro, for garnish

Sesame seeds, for garnish

1. **Make the Dumpling Dip:** In a small bowl, whisk together the soy sauce, maple syrup, sesame oil, sesame seeds, and red chili flakes, if using. Set aside.

2. **Make the Cucumber Coleslaw:** In a small bowl, whisk together the rice vinegar, sesame oil, sugar, red chili flakes (if using), and salt to taste. Set aside.

3. In a medium bowl, toss together the coleslaw mix, cucumber, green onions, and cilantro. Set aside.

4. **Make the Taco Filling:** In a large bowl, combine the shrimp, ground chicken, green onions, garlic, ginger, soy sauce, and sesame oil. Mix well.

5. Divide the shrimp and chicken mixture into 12 equal portions. Place a portion of shrimp and chicken mixture on top of each tortilla and, using a rubber spatula, your fingers, a fork, or a butter knife, spread the mixture evenly across the tortilla.

6. Heat 1 teaspoon (5 mL) of sesame oil in a large frying pan over medium-high heat. Working in batches to avoid crowding the pan, place the tortillas, shrimp and chicken mixture side down, and cook until golden brown on the bottom, 2 to 3 minutes. Flip and continue cooking until the mixture is cooked through and the tortillas are golden brown, about 3 minutes. Repeat with the remaining tortillas.

7. Top the tortillas with the Cucumber Coleslaw, cilantro, and a sprinkle of sesame seeds. Fold like a taco. Serve with the Dumpling Dip on the side.

Gluten-Free: Use gluten-free tortillas and gluten-free soy sauce.

PREP AHEAD

The Dumpling Dip can be made up to 4 days in advance; cover and refrigerate. The Taco Filling can be mixed up to 2 days in advance; refrigerate in a resealable container.

STORAGE

Store cooled tacos, without the coleslaw and dip, in a resealable container in the fridge for up to 3 days or in the freezer for up to 2 months. Reheat in a 350°F (180°C) oven or an air fryer until hot.

MAKE AHEAD | FREEZER-FRIENDLY | SOS

CREAMY PESTO TOMATO TORTELLINI

Vegan Option · *Vegetarian Option* · *Dairy-Free Option* · *Gluten-Free Option* · *Nut-Free Option*

Serves 4

TIME
Prep: 5 MINUTES
Cook: 20 MINUTES
Total: 25 MINUTES

¼ cup (60 mL) pine nuts

1 tablespoon (15 mL) extra-virgin olive oil

4 cups (1 L) cherry tomatoes

2 cloves garlic, minced

3 cups (750 mL) chicken or vegetable stock

1 package (500 g) refrigerated or frozen cheese tortellini

¼ cup (60 mL) pesto

¼ cup (60 mL) cream cheese, room temperature

6 cups (1.5 L) roughly chopped spinach

Salt and pepper

¼ cup (60 mL) grated Parmesan cheese, plus more for garnish

Roughly chopped fresh basil, for serving

STORAGE

Store cooled tortellini in a resealable container in the fridge for up to 5 days or in the freezer for up to 2 months. If frozen, thaw in the fridge overnight. Reheat in the microwave or in a saucepan over low heat on the stovetop; add about ½ cup (125 mL) of stock or cream to loosen the pasta if needed.

This Creamy Pesto Tomato Tortellini is both effortless and impressive. It will surprise you with how the rich tomato pesto flavour develops in such a short time. This is the type of dish you can throw together with less than 30 minutes to spare, using minimal ingredients, and feel great about serving. For added protein, coat chicken thighs with pesto and grill to add on top, or stir in cooked Italian sausage.

1. Toast the pine nuts in a large nonstick frying pan with a lid over medium-low heat, stirring frequently, until they are golden brown and have a nutty aroma, 1 to 2 minutes. Transfer to a small bowl.

2. In the same pan, heat the olive oil over medium-high heat. Add the tomatoes and cook, gently stirring occasionally, until blistered and starting to soften, about 8 minutes. Add the garlic and cook, stirring, until fragrant, about 1 minute.

3. Pour in the chicken stock and bring to a boil. Reduce the heat to low, stir in the tortellini, cover, and cook for 5 minutes. Stir in the pesto, cream cheese, and spinach and cook for another 1 to 2 minutes, until the spinach is wilted. Season to taste with salt and pepper and top with the toasted pine nuts and Parmesan. Serve with the basil and extra Parmesan if desired.

Vegan: Use vegetable stock, dairy-free tortellini, vegan cream cheese, and vegan parm.

Vegetarian: Use vegetable stock.

Dairy-Free: Use dairy-free tortellini, vegan cream cheese, and vegan parm.

Gluten-Free: Use gluten-free tortellini.

Nut-Free: Omit the pine nuts. Use nut-free pesto.

COCONUT CURRY LENTILS

Vegan · Vegetarian · Dairy-Free · Gluten-Free · Nut-Free

Serves 4

TIME	
Prep:	10 MINUTES
Cook:	15 MINUTES
Total:	25 MINUTES

2 tablespoons (30 mL) coconut oil

2 cups (500 mL) diced yellow onion

4 cloves garlic, minced

1 tablespoon (15 mL) grated peeled fresh ginger

2 tablespoons (30 mL) curry powder

1 teaspoon (5 mL) ground cumin

1 teaspoon (5 mL) ground coriander

¼ cup (60 mL) tomato paste

2 cans (19 ounces/540 mL each) lentils, drained and rinsed

1 can (14 ounces/400 mL) full-fat coconut milk

4 cups (1 L) loosely packed chopped spinach

1 tablespoon (15 mL) fresh lime juice

1 tablespoon (15 mL) pure maple syrup

Salt

For serving

Cooked rice and/or warmed naan bread

Chopped fresh cilantro

Lime wedges

This cozy one-pan-wonder is creamy, filled with warm aromatic spices, and incredibly satisfying. The best part? It tastes better the next day, making it the perfect make-ahead meal. Lentils must be one of the most underrated ingredients; they are filled with fibre, plant-based protein, and essential vitamins and minerals. Serve this curry over rice or with naan to scoop up every bite. To add a bit of spice and zing, serve with cilantro chutney. To boost the nutrition, stir in 4 cups (1 L) of 1-inch (2.5 cm) cubed peeled butternut squash plus 2 cups (500 mL) chicken or vegetable stock with the ingredients in step 2 and cook until the squash is fork-tender, about 15 minutes.

1. Melt the coconut oil in a large frying pan over medium heat. Add the onion and cook, stirring occasionally, until soft and translucent, 3 to 4 minutes. Add the garlic, ginger, curry powder, cumin, and coriander and cook, stirring, until fragrant, about 2 minutes.

2. Stir in the tomato paste, lentils, and coconut milk and cook, stirring occasionally, until slightly thickened, about 8 minutes. Stir in the spinach until just wilted.

3. Stir in the lime juice and maple syrup. Season to taste with salt.

4. Serve the coconut curry lentils hot over rice and/or with warmed naan bread, with cilantro and lime wedges if desired.

STORAGE

Store cooled coconut curry lentils, without rice or naan, in a resealable container in the fridge for up to 5 days or in the freezer for up to 3 months. If frozen, thaw in the fridge overnight, then reheat in the microwave until warmed through.

MAKE AHEAD | FREEZER-FRIENDLY | SOS

CHICKEN RICOTTA MEATBALLS

Dairy-Free Option • *Gluten-Free Option* • *Nut-Free*

Makes 16 meatballs, serves 4

TIME
Prep: 15 MINUTES
Cook: 15 MINUTES
Total: 30 MINUTES

1 pound (450 g) ground chicken
½ cup (125 mL) finely grated zucchini
1 egg, whisked
½ cup (125 mL) panko crumbs
⅓ cup (75 mL) ricotta cheese
¼ cup (60 mL) grated Parmesan cheese, plus more for serving
¼ cup (60 mL) roughly chopped fresh flat-leaf parsley
¼ cup (60 mL) roughly chopped fresh basil, plus more for serving
2 cloves garlic, minced
1 teaspoon (5 mL) salt
¼ teaspoon (1 mL) pepper
1 tablespoon (15 mL) extra-virgin olive oil
1 jar (700 mL) marinara sauce (or 1 batch of SOS Spaghetti Sauce, page 312)
Toasted sourdough bread or Garlic Bread (page 321), for serving

These chicken and ricotta meatballs fit the bill when you are craving comfort food but still want something wholesome and packed with protein. Chicken and ricotta are both good sources of protein, so you are getting a solid satisfying combo. My favourite way to eat these meatballs is in a simmering tomato sauce with a generous slice of garlic bread, but you can also enjoy them on pasta or transform into a grade-A meatball sub. The meatballs are also freezer-friendly, so do yourself a favour and freeze extras for a future last-minute meal.

1. In a large bowl, combine the ground chicken, zucchini, egg, panko, ricotta, Parmesan, parsley, basil, garlic, salt, and pepper. Mix until well combined. Shape into 16 meatballs, slightly smaller than a golf ball.

2. Heat the olive oil in a large frying pan with a lid over medium-high heat. Add the meatballs and cook, turning occasionally, until golden brown on all sides, about 5 minutes total.

3. Add the marinara sauce, reduce the heat to low, cover, and simmer until the meatballs are cooked through, about 10 minutes.

4. Garnish with Parmesan and basil and serve with toasted sourdough or Garlic Bread.

Dairy-Free: Use vegan parm and vegan ricotta.

Gluten-Free: Use gluten-free panko crumbs. Serve with gluten-free bread or gluten-free pasta.

STORAGE

Store cooled cooked meatballs and sauce in a resealable container in the fridge for up to 4 days or in the freezer for up to 2 months. If frozen, thaw in the fridge overnight, then reheat on the stovetop or in the microwave until warmed through.

Re-Fraiche

- Make into meatball subs.
- Make into burgers. Double the recipe and form the ground chicken mixture into 4 burger patties. Store in a resealable container (with parchment paper between patties) in the freezer for up to 3 months.

PREP AHEAD | FREEZER-FRIENDLY

SKILLET CURRY CHICKEN POT PIE

Vegan Option • Vegetarian Option • Dairy-Free Option • Nut-Free

Serves 4

TIME
Prep: 20 MINUTES
Cook: 40 MINUTES
Total: 1 HOUR

- 1 tablespoon (15 mL) extra-virgin olive oil
- 2 tablespoons (30 mL) butter
- 1 cup (250 mL) diced yellow onion
- 2 cloves garlic, minced
- 2 boneless, skinless chicken breasts (about 1½ pounds/675 g total), cubed
- 2 cups (500 mL) diced peeled carrots
- 1 cup (250 mL) diced celery
- 2 tablespoons (30 mL) all-purpose flour
- 1 tablespoon (15 mL) curry powder
- 1 cup (250 mL) chicken stock
- 2 cups (500 mL) frozen peas
- ½ cup (125 mL) table (18%) cream or full-fat coconut milk, plus more for brushing
- 1 tablespoon (15 mL) fresh lime juice
- 2 tablespoons (30 mL) finely chopped fresh flat-leaf parsley or cilantro
- Salt and pepper
- 1 package (1 pound/400 g) puff pastry, thawed

Elevate the everyday and add a little spice to your life with this easy curry chicken pot pie. This remix on a classic chicken pot pie will fill your home with the aromatic scents of curry as the pie bakes to golden perfection with a flaky puff pastry top. Perfect for a winter meal to warm your belly.

If you don't have an ovenproof frying pan, transfer the filling to a 13 × 9-inch (3.5 L) baking dish before topping with the puff pastry and baking.

1. Preheat the oven to 400°F (200°C).

2. Heat the olive oil and butter in a medium ovenproof frying pan over medium heat. Add the onion and cook, stirring occasionally, until soft and translucent, 3 to 4 minutes. Add the garlic and cook, stirring, until fragrant, 1 to 2 minutes. Add the chicken and cook, stirring occasionally, for 2 minutes. Add the carrots and celery and cook, stirring occasionally, until softened, another 3 to 4 minutes. Sprinkle with the flour and curry powder and stir to combine. Add the chicken stock and simmer until the mixture thickens, about 2 minutes. Remove from the heat and stir in the peas, cream, lime juice, and parsley. Season to taste with salt and pepper.

3. On a lightly floured work surface with a lightly floured rolling pin, roll out the puff pastry into a 16-inch (40 cm) square (it doesn't have to be perfect). Using a sharp knife, cut the pastry into 2-inch (5 cm) squares. Gently place the squares, slightly overlapping, on top of the filling to cover. Brush the pastry lightly with more cream.

4. Bake until the mixture is bubbling and the pastry is golden brown, about 30 minutes. Serve hot.

Vegan: Use vegan butter. Use 1 can (19 ounces/540 mL) chickpeas (drained and rinsed) instead of the chicken. Use vegetable stock instead of chicken stock and coconut milk instead of table cream.

Vegetarian: Use 1 can (19 ounces/540 mL) chickpeas (drained and rinsed) instead of the chicken. Use vegetable stock instead of chicken stock.

Dairy-Free: Use vegan butter and coconut milk.

PREP AHEAD

The filling (step 2) can be prepared up to 2 days in advance; cover and refrigerate.

STORAGE

Store the cooled pot pie, covered, in the fridge for up to 4 days or in the freezer for up to 1 month. To reheat, place the pot pie on baking sheet lined with parchment paper and bake in a 350°F (180°C) oven until heated through and the filling is bubbling, 20 minutes if refrigerated or 45 to 60 minutes if frozen.

FREEZER-FRIENDLY

Prepare the pot pie through step 2. Let cool, cover tightly, and store in the freezer for up to 3 months. Thaw before topping with the puff pastry and baking according to directions.

EVERYDAY

CREAMY DILL SALMON AND BABY POTATOES

Dairy-Free Option • *Gluten-Free* • *Nut-Free*

Serves 4

TIME
Prep: 10 MINUTES
Cook: 20 MINUTES
Total: 30 MINUTES

1 pound (450 g) baby potatoes, halved

4 skinless salmon fillets (about 6 ounces/170 g each)

Salt and pepper

2 tablespoons (30 mL) extra-virgin olive oil, divided

1 cup (250 mL) finely diced yellow onion

4 cloves garlic, minced

½ cup (125 mL) chicken or vegetable stock

½ cup (125 mL) heavy (35%) cream or full-fat coconut cream

4 cups (1 L) lightly packed baby spinach

For serving

¼ cup (60 mL) chopped fresh dill

1 lemon, cut into wedges

PREP AHEAD
The potatoes can be prepared up to 3 days ahead. Cook, drain, let cool, and store in a resealable container in the fridge.

STORAGE
Store cooled leftovers in a resealable container in the fridge for up to 3 days. Reheat in a frying pan on the stovetop or in the microwave until warmed through.

I love this restaurant-quality seafood dinner that combines the simple flavours of lemon, dill, and tender baby potatoes with a creamy sauce filled with spinach. This dish takes only 30 minutes from the time you walk in the door until the time dinner is served—less time than it takes to order in, making it the ultimate fast food. Don't miss a drop of the sauce; pair this with thick slices of Garlic Bread (page 321) or warm Sour Cream and Onion Biscuits (page 106).

1. Bring a large pot of salted water to a boil. Add the potatoes and cook until tender, about 10 minutes. Drain and set aside.

2. While the potatoes are cooking, season the salmon with salt and pepper. Heat a medium frying pan over medium heat. Add 1 tablespoon (15 mL) of the olive oil and cook the salmon until golden and just cooked through, 4 to 6 minutes per side. Remove the salmon from the pan and cover to keep warm.

3. To the same pan (no need to wipe it) over medium heat, add the remaining 1 tablespoon (15 mL) olive oil. Add the onion and cook, stirring occasionally, until soft and translucent, 3 to 4 minutes. Add the garlic and cook, stirring, until fragrant, about 1 minute. Stir in the chicken stock, cream, and spinach and cook, stirring occasionally, until the spinach has wilted. Season to taste with salt and pepper.

4. Stir in the potatoes. Gently nestle the salmon among the potatoes and cook for another 1 to 2 minutes to warm the salmon. Sprinkle with the dill and serve with lemon wedges.

Dairy-Free: Use full-fat coconut cream instead of heavy cream.

CAJUN SKILLET SHRIMP BOIL

Dairy-Free Option · *Gluten-Free Option* · *Nut-Free*

Serves 4

TIME

Prep: 5 MINUTES (NOT INCLUDING MAKING THE GARLIC BREAD)

Cook: 20 MINUTES

Total: 25 MINUTES

9 ounces (250 g) farmer's sausage, sliced ¼ inch (5 mm) thick

¼ cup (60 mL) butter

2 cloves garlic, minced

1 pound (450 g) baby potatoes, halved

3 cups (750 mL) chicken or vegetable stock

2 ears of sweet corn, husked and cut into 2-inch (5 cm) pieces

2 teaspoons (10 mL) Cajun seasoning

1 teaspoon (5 mL) Old Bay seasoning

1 pound (450 g) large fresh or thawed frozen shrimp, peeled and deveined

Juice of ½ lemon

Salt and pepper

Fresh flat-leaf parsley, for garnish

Lemon wedges, for squeezing

1 batch Garlic Bread (page 321), for serving

STORAGE

Store cooled shrimp boil in a resealable container in the fridge for up to 2 days. Reheat in a frying pan on the stovetop until warmed through.

A shrimp boil is the kind of meal that brings everyone to the table, sleeves rolled up and smiles wide. Inspired by classic coastal seafood boils, this Cajun one-pan wonder is made for families: no fussy prep, no fancy tools—just simple ingredients, big flavour, and a whole lot of fun. With juicy shrimp, tender potatoes, sweet corn, and savoury sausage all tossed in a buttery garlic spice blend, it's the kind of messy, hands-on dinner that becomes a memory. Because let's be honest: the messiest dinners are often the best ones. Place this skillet right on the table and serve it up family-style with thick slices of Garlic Bread (page 321).

1. Heat a large, deep frying pan with a lid over medium heat. Add the sausage and cook, stirring occasionally, until lightly browned, about 4 minutes. Transfer the sausage to a plate and cover to keep warm.

2. In the same pan (no need to wipe it) over medium heat, melt the butter. Add the garlic and cook, stirring, until fragrant, about 1 minute. Add the potatoes, chicken stock, corn, Cajun seasoning, and Old Bay seasoning. Bring to a boil, then reduce the heat to a simmer, cover, and cook until the potatoes are tender and the corn is cooked, about 10 minutes.

3. Add the shrimp, cover, and cook, stirring occasionally, until they are pink and cooked through, about 5 minutes. Stir in the sausage and lemon juice. Season to taste with salt and pepper. Garnish with parsley. Serve hot with lemon wedges for squeezing and Garlic Bread on the side.

Dairy-Free: Use vegan butter.

Gluten-Free: Use gluten-free sausage and gluten-free baguette if serving with Garlic Bread.

GARLIC BUTTER PORK CHOPS WITH CREAMY MUSHROOM SAUCE

Dairy-Free Option • *Gluten-Free*

Serves 4

TIME
Prep: 10 MINUTES
Cook: 20 MINUTES
Total: 35 MINUTES

Garlic Butter Pork Chops

4 boneless pork loin chops (about 1½ pounds/675 g total)

1 teaspoon (5 mL) salt

½ teaspoon (2 mL) pepper

½ teaspoon (2 mL) sweet paprika

1 tablespoon (15 mL) extra-virgin olive oil

2 tablespoons (30 mL) butter

4 cloves garlic, smashed

4 sprigs fresh thyme (or 1 teaspoon/5 mL dried thyme)

Creamy Mushroom Sauce

1 tablespoon (15 mL) butter

1 cup (250 mL) finely diced yellow onion

1 pound (450 g) cremini or button mushrooms, sliced

2 cloves garlic, minced

½ cup (125 mL) chicken stock

½ cup table (18%) cream

1 teaspoon (5 mL) Dijon mustard

1 teaspoon (5 mL) fresh thyme leaves (or ½ teaspoon/2 mL dried thyme)

¼ cup (60 mL) grated Parmesan cheese (optional)

Salt and pepper

Chopped fresh flat-leaf or curly parsley, for garnish (optional)

STORAGE
Store cooled pork chops with the mushroom sauce in a resealable container in the fridge for up to 3 days. Reheat in a frying pan on the stovetop or in the microwave until warmed through.

I grew up eating pork chops with mushroom sauce. It was one of those staple dinner recipes that my mom knew we would always love. Back then the sauce came from a can of condensed cream of mushroom soup. I've given this nostalgic dish an upgrade—rich, comforting, and packed with herbaceous earthy flavours. The pan-seared chops are juicy and golden brown and smothered in a luscious creamy mushroom thyme sauce. Perfect for a cozy dinner!

1. **Prepare the Garlic Butter Pork Chops:** Trim the pork chops of any excess fat and pat dry. Working with one chop at a time, place between 2 sheets of parchment paper on a cutting board. Using a meat mallet, pound until about ½ inch (1 cm) thick. Season both sides of the pork with the salt, pepper, and sweet paprika.

2. Heat the olive oil in a large frying pan over medium-high heat. Add the pork and sear until golden brown, about 4 minutes per side.

3. Reduce the heat to medium. Add the butter, smashed garlic, and thyme. Tilt the pan and spoon the melted butter over the pork chops as they cook, for another 1 to 2 minutes, until the chops have reached an internal temperature of 145°F (65°C). Transfer the pork to a plate and cover with foil to keep warm.

4. **Make the Creamy Mushroom Sauce:** In the same pan (no need to wipe it) over medium heat, melt the butter. Add the onion and cook, stirring occasionally, until soft and translucent, 3 to 4 minutes. Add a splash of water if it starts to scorch. Add the mushrooms and garlic and continue to cook, stirring occasionally, until the mushrooms soften, 4 to 5 minutes. Stir in the chicken stock, scraping up any browned bits from the bottom of the pan to add flavour.

5. Stir in the cream, mustard, and thyme. Bring to a boil, then reduce the heat to low and simmer until slightly thickened, about 2 minutes. Stir in the Parmesan for extra creaminess if desired. Season to taste with salt and pepper.

6. Return the pork to the frying pan, spoon the sauce over top, and simmer for 2 minutes. Garnish with the parsley if desired and serve warm with mashed potatoes, buttered pasta, or rice and steamed vegetables.

Dairy-Free: Use vegan butter. Use Cashew Cream (page 332) instead of cream. Use vegan parm, if using.

One-Pot MEALS

MAKE AHEAD | FREEZER-FRIENDLY

BUFFALO WHITE CHICKEN CHILI

Vegan Option · Vegetarian Option · Gluten-Free · Nut-Free

Serves 4 to 6

TIME
Prep: 10 MINUTES
Cook: 30 MINUTES
Total: 40 MINUTES

1 tablespoon (15 mL) extra-virgin olive oil

1 cup (250 mL) diced yellow onion

1 can (4 ounces/113 g) diced green chilies

2 cloves garlic, minced

1 tablespoon (15 mL) dried parsley

1 tablespoon (15 mL) dried chives

1½ teaspoons (7 mL) sweet paprika

1 teaspoon (5 mL) salt

½ teaspoon (2 mL) pepper

4 cups (1 L) chicken stock

2 boneless, skinless chicken breasts (about 1½ pounds/675 g total)

1 can (19 ounces/540 mL) white beans, drained and rinsed

1 cup (250 mL) frozen corn kernels

¼ cup (60 mL) Frank's hot sauce

⅓ cup (75 mL) cream cheese, room temperature

1 tablespoon (15 mL) cornstarch

1 tablespoon (15 mL) water

Toppings (optional)

Grated cheddar or Monterey Jack cheese

Sliced green onions

Sliced avocado

Sour cream

Corn chips

There's nothing like coming home to a pot of something warm and comforting after a busy, chilly day, especially when you've been juggling work, soccer practice, and just trying to keep up with life! Enter Buffalo White Chicken Chili. Anything but boring, this creamy make-ahead chili has the perfect kick of spice. Freezer-friendly, potluck-ready, and ideal for cozy family dinners. Whether it's simmering away on the stove or pulled out of the freezer, it's guaranteed to hit the spot and warm everyone up! Serve it up with warm Sour Cream and Onion Biscuits (page 106).

1. Heat the olive oil in a large pot over medium heat. Add the onion and chilies and cook, stirring occasionally, until the onion is soft and translucent, 3 to 4 minutes. Add the garlic, parsley, chives, sweet paprika, salt, and pepper and cook, stirring, until fragrant, about 1 minute.

2. Add the chicken stock and chicken, stir, cover, and cook until the chicken is cooked through and the internal temperature reaches 165°F (74°C) on an instant-reader thermometer, 15 to 20 minutes. Using tongs, transfer the chicken to a large bowl.

3. Use two forks or an electric mixer to shred the chicken. Return the chicken to the pot.

4. Stir in the beans, corn, and hot sauce. Reduce the heat to medium-low and simmer, uncovered and stirring occasionally, for 5 minutes.

5. Stir in the cream cheese to combine.

6. In a small bowl, stir together the cornstarch and water until the cornstarch is dissolved. Stir into the chili and cook until the chili has thickened slightly, 2 to 3 minutes. Season to taste with salt and pepper. Serve with the desired toppings.

Vegan: Omit the chicken and double the beans. Use vegan cream cheese and vegan cheese.

Vegetarian: Omit the chicken and double the beans.

STORAGE

Store cooled chili in a resealable container in the fridge for up to 4 days or in the freezer for up to 3 months. If frozen, thaw in the fridge overnight, then reheat on the stovetop or in the microwave until warmed through.

THAI GREEN CURRY POT

Vegan Option • Vegetarian Option • Dairy-Free • Gluten-Free • Nut-Free

Serves 4

TIME
Prep: 15 MINUTES
Cook: 15 MINUTES
Total: 30 MINUTES

2 tablespoons (30 mL) canola oil or avocado oil

2 cloves garlic, minced

1 tablespoon (15 mL) grated peeled fresh ginger

2 shallots, thinly sliced

2 tablespoons (30 mL) green curry paste

4 cups (1 L) chicken or vegetable stock

1 can (14 ounces/400 mL) full-fat coconut milk

2 cups (500 mL) sliced peeled carrots

4-inch (10 cm) stalk lemongrass, trimmed and sliced crosswise into 1-inch (2.5 cm) pieces

4 makrut lime leaves

2 teaspoons (10 mL) lightly packed brown sugar

2 teaspoons (10 mL) fish sauce

2 teaspoons (10 mL) soy sauce

3½ ounces (100 g) thick rice noodles

1 package (12 ounces/350 g) extra-firm tofu, drained and cut into ½-inch (1 cm) cubes

2 cups (500 mL) snow peas, trimmed and cut in half

Juice of 1 lime

For serving

¼ cup (60 mL) roughly chopped fresh Thai basil

2 cups (500 mL) bean sprouts

2 green onions (white and light green parts only), sliced diagonally

Lime wedges

Make this one-pot, two-step flavour bomb of a meal on those cozy nights when you're craving Thai takeout but know you can whip it up faster than it can get to your door. The one dish I always order when I dine at a Thai restaurant is a coconut curry. The creamy coconut broth with a touch of lime is simply the best. With its vibrant flavours, I eat this soup year-round.

If you can't find Thai basil, substitute another variety. Red curry paste will work if you can't find green curry paste. Boost the protein by stirring in cooked shrimp or shredded cooked chicken with the tofu.

1. Heat the canola oil in a large pot with a lid over medium heat. Add the garlic, ginger, and shallots and cook, stirring occasionally, for 2 minutes. Add the curry paste and cook, stirring occasionally, until fragrant, about 2 minutes. Stir in the chicken stock, coconut milk, carrots, lemongrass, lime leaves, brown sugar, fish sauce, and soy sauce. Cover and simmer until the carrots are tender, about 5 minutes.

2. Add the rice noodles and cook, uncovered, until tender, about 3 minutes. Remove the lime leaves and lemongrass. Stir in the tofu, snow peas, and lime juice. Serve garnished with the Thai basil, bean sprouts, green onions, and lime wedges.

Vegan and Vegetarian: Omit the fish sauce and use vegetable stock.

PREP AHEAD
The rice noodles can be cooked up to 1 day ahead and added just before serving. Gently loosen the noodles by running them under hot water.

STORAGE
Store cooled curry in a resealable container in the fridge for up to 4 days. Reheat in a pot on the stovetop until warmed through.

PIZZA PASTA

Vegan Option · *Vegetarian Option* · *Dairy-Free Option* · *Gluten-Free Option*

Serves 4

TIME	
Prep:	10 MINUTES
Cook:	15 MINUTES
Total:	25 MINUTES

3½ ounces (100 g) sliced pepperoni
1 clove garlic, minced
5 cups (1.25 L) chicken or vegetable stock
1 can (14 ounces/398 mL) pizza sauce
4 cups (1 L) fusilli pasta (or similar shape)
½ cup (125 mL) roughly chopped fresh basil, divided
1 teaspoon (5 mL) dried oregano
Salt and pepper
1 cup (250 mL) grated mozzarella cheese

STORAGE
Store cooled pasta in a resealable container in the fridge for up to 4 days. Reheat in the microwave until warmed through.

Pizza and pasta are two ultimate kid-friendly meals—they're always winners at the dinner table. But combine the two? Now *that's* next-level brilliance. This one-pot Pizza Pasta brings together all the cheesy, saucy, comforting flavours kids (and let's be honest, grown-ups too) can't get enough of. It's quick to make, fun to eat, and destined to become a weeknight favourite. Think of it as the best of both worlds, baked into one cozy, family-pleasing dish.

1. Position an oven rack about 6 inches (15 cm) below the broiler and preheat the broiler.

2. Heat a large ovenproof pot with a lid over medium-high heat. When the pot is hot, add the pepperoni slices and cook until crisp. Transfer the pepperoni to a plate lined with paper towel. Set aside.

3. To the same pot (no need to wipe it) over medium-high heat, add the garlic and cook, stirring, until fragrant, about 1 minute. Stir in the chicken stock and pizza sauce, cover, and bring to a boil. Add the pasta to the pot, stir, cover, and cook, stirring occasionally, until the pasta is tender, about 12 minutes. Remove from the heat.

4. Stir in ¼ cup (60 mL) of the basil, half of the pepperoni slices, and the oregano. Season to taste with salt and pepper. Top with the mozzarella and remaining pepperoni slices. Broil until the cheese is melted and golden brown. Garnish with the remaining ¼ cup (60 mL) basil and serve hot.

Vegan: Use vegan pepperoni and dairy-free cheese.

Vegetarian: Use vegan pepperoni.

Dairy-Free: Use dairy-free cheese.

Gluten-Free: Use gluten-free pasta.

MAKE AHEAD | FREEZER-FRIENDLY | SOS

PIZZA BEANS

Vegan Option · *Vegetarian* · *Dairy-Free* · *Gluten-Free Option* · *Nut-Free*

Serves 4

TIME
Prep: 10 MINUTES
Cook: 20 MINUTES
Total: 30 MINUTES

- 2 tablespoons (30 mL) extra-virgin olive oil
- 1 cup (250 mL) finely diced yellow onion
- 1 cup (250 mL) finely diced celery
- 1 cup (250 mL) finely diced yellow, orange, or red sweet pepper
- 2 carrots, peeled and finely diced
- 3 cloves garlic, minced
- 2 teaspoons (10 mL) dried oregano
- 1 can (14 ounces/398 mL) pizza sauce
- 2 tablespoons (30 mL) tomato paste
- 2 cups (500 mL) chicken or vegetable stock
- 2 cans (19 ounces/540 mL each) navy beans, drained and rinsed
- ½ cup (125 mL) chopped fresh basil, plus more for serving
- Salt and pepper
- 1 cup (250 mL) grated mozzarella cheese
- 1 batch Garlic Bread (page 321)

STORAGE
Store cooled pizza beans in a resealable container in the fridge for up to 5 days or in the freezer for up to 2 months. If frozen, thaw in the fridge overnight, then reheat on the stovetop or in the microwave until warmed through.

Imagine all the saucy, cheesy flavours of your favourite pizza—only cozier, heartier, and eaten with a spoon. These Pizza Beans are baked to bubbly perfection with a golden, melty topping and packed with wholesome ingredients like fibre-rich beans and fresh veggies. Scoop them up with Garlic Bread (page 321) or enjoy straight from the bowl for a nourishing, feel-good meal. This versatile vegetarian dish is perfect for busy weeknights or laid-back get-togethers. It's endlessly customizable too—add your favourite pizza toppings like pepperoni, sautéed veggies, feta, pesto, or banana peppers just before broiling to make it your own.

If you don't have an ovenproof frying pan, simply transfer the mixture to a 9-inch (2.5 L) square baking dish before broiling.

1. Position an oven rack about 6 inches (15 cm) under the broiler and preheat the broiler.

2. Heat the olive oil in a large ovenproof frying pan over medium heat. Add the onion and cook, stirring occasionally, until soft and translucent, 3 to 4 minutes. Add the celery, sweet pepper, carrots, and garlic and cook, stirring occasionally, until the vegetables are tender, about 8 minutes.

3. Add the oregano, pizza sauce, tomato paste, chicken stock, and beans and stir to combine. Bring to a boil, then reduce the heat to low and cook, stirring occasionally, for about 5 minutes. Stir in the basil and season to taste with salt and pepper.

4. Evenly scatter the grated cheese over the top and broil until the cheese bubbles and is golden brown, about 3 minutes. Garnish with basil if desired. Serve hot with garlic bread.

Vegan: Use vegetable stock. Use vegan cheese.

Gluten-Free: Serve with gluten-free garlic bread.

MAKE AHEAD | FREEZER-FRIENDLY

CHEESEBURGER CHILI

Vegan Option · Vegetarian Option · Gluten-Free Option · Nut-Free

Serves 8

TIME
Prep: 10 MINUTES
Cook: 30 MINUTES (FOR STOVETOP METHOD)
Total: 40 MINUTES

6 slices thick-cut bacon, diced
1 cup (250 mL) diced yellow onion
2 cloves garlic, minced
1 pound (450 g) ground turkey, chicken, or beef
1 tablespoon (15 mL) chili powder
1 tablespoon (15 mL) sweet paprika
1 teaspoon (5 mL) onion powder
1 cup (250 mL) chicken, beef, or vegetable stock
1 can (28 ounces/796 mL) diced tomatoes
1 can (14 ounces/398 mL) kidney beans, drained and rinsed
1 can (14 ounces/398 mL) black beans, drained and rinsed
1 cup (250 mL) finely grated zucchini
1 cup (250 mL) finely grated peeled carrots
1 tablespoon (15 mL) Worcestershire sauce
1 tablespoon (15 mL) ketchup
1 tablespoon (15 mL) yellow mustard
2 tablespoons (30 mL) sweet relish
Salt and pepper

For serving (optional)
Grated cheddar cheese
Shredded iceberg lettuce
Diced yellow onion
Sliced dill pickles

Cheeseburger Chili is the ultimate family-friendly comfort food—with a wholesome twist. It's loaded with classic burger flavours thanks to the clever combo of ketchup, mustard, and relish, then finished with all your favourite toppings: grated cheese, crisp lettuce, fresh onion, and pickles. A hearty mix of black beans, kidney beans, and finely grated zucchini and carrots are added for a boost of fibre, protein, and hidden veggies even picky eaters won't notice. Serve it with Focaccia Cheese Buns (page 101) for the full burger experience.

Stovetop Instructions

1. In a large, heavy pot over medium heat, cook the bacon, stirring occasionally, until slightly crisp, about 4 minutes.

2. Add the onion and cook, stirring occasionally, until soft and translucent, 3 to 4 minutes. Add the garlic and cook until the garlic is fragrant, about 1 minute.

3. Stir in the ground turkey, chili powder, sweet paprika, and onion powder and cook, stirring occasionally, until slightly browned. Add the chicken stock, scraping up any browned bits from the bottom of the pot to add flavour. Add the tomatoes, kidney beans, black beans, zucchini, carrots, Worcestershire sauce, ketchup, mustard, and sweet relish. Stir. Reduce the heat to a low simmer, cover, and cook, stirring occasionally, for 20 minutes. Season to taste with salt and pepper.

4. Ladle the chili into bowls and top with cheese, lettuce, onions, and pickles as desired.

Recipe and ingredients continue . . .

STORAGE
Store cooled chili in a resealable container in the fridge for up to 4 days or in the freezer for up to 3 months. If frozen, thaw in the fridge overnight, then reheat on the stovetop or in the microwave until warmed through.

Slow Cooker Instructions

1. Heat a large frying pan over medium heat. Add the bacon and cook, stirring occasionally, until slightly crisp, about 4 minutes.

2. Add the onion and cook, stirring occasionally, until soft and translucent, 3 to 4 minutes. Add the garlic and cook, stirring, until the garlic is fragrant, about 1 minute.

3. Add the ground turkey and cook, stirring, until almost cooked through, 5 to 6 minutes.

4. Scrape the contents of the pan into the slow cooker. Add the chili powder, sweet paprika, onion powder, chicken stock, tomatoes, kidney beans, black beans, zucchini, carrots, Worcestershire sauce, ketchup, mustard, and sweet relish. Season to taste with salt and pepper. Stir. Cover and cook on low for 6 to 7 hours or on high for 3 to 4 hours.

5. Ladle the chili into bowls and top with cheese, lettuce, onions, and pickles as desired.

Vegan: Omit the bacon and use a drizzle of olive oil instead. Use vegetable stock and veggie ground. Use vegan cheese.

Vegetarian: Omit the bacon and use a drizzle of olive oil instead. Use vegetable stock and veggie ground.

Gluten-Free: Use gluten-free bacon and Worcestershire sauce.

MAKE AHEAD

POT ROAST

Dairy-Free • Gluten-Free Option • Nut-Free

Serves 6 to 8

TIME	
Prep:	20 MINUTES
Cook:	4 HOURS
Total:	4 HOURS 20 MINUTES

- 4 pounds (1.8 kg) boneless beef chuck roast
- Salt and pepper
- 4 sprigs fresh rosemary
- 4 sprigs fresh thyme
- 2 tablespoons (30 mL) extra-virgin olive oil
- 6 cups (1.5 L) beef stock
- 2 tablespoons (30 mL) tomato paste
- 2 tablespoons (30 mL) Worcestershire sauce
- 1 large yellow onion, peeled and cut into wedges
- 4 cloves garlic, smashed
- 2 bay leaves
- 4 to 6 carrots, peeled and cut crosswise into 2-inch (5 cm) pieces

STORAGE
Store cooled pot roast in a resealable container in the fridge for up to 4 days or in the freezer for up to 2 months. If frozen, thaw in the fridge overnight, then reheat in a pot on the stovetop over low heat, stirring occasionally and adding a splash of beef stock if needed, until warmed through.

There are some things in life that can't be rushed, and this pot roast is one of them. This slow-cooked dish is perfectly tender with an incredible sauce that is best enjoyed with those you love on a quiet Sunday evening. Serve with Buttery Mashed Potatoes (page 326), warm Popovers (page 105), and your favourite steamed veggies for a simple down-home dinner. I included slow cooker instructions for the ultimate low-touch dinner: what a lovely thing to come home to after a long day out of the house.

Oven Instructions

1. Preheat the oven to 350°F (180°C). Season the roast on all sides with salt and pepper. Tie the rosemary and thyme together with cooking twine and set aside.

2. Heat the olive oil in a large Dutch oven with a lid over medium-high heat. Add the beef and sear until browned on all sides, about 8 minutes total. Transfer the roast to a plate. Add the stock to the pan and stir to loosen the browned bits on the bottom. Stir in the tomato paste and Worcestershire sauce.

3. Return the roast to the pot. Arrange the onion, garlic, bay leaves, and the tied herbs around the roast. Cover and roast for 2 hours.

4. After 2 hours, add the carrots to the pot and continue to cook, covered, until the beef is tender and shreds easily, about another 2 hours.

5. Remove the bay leaves and herb sprigs before serving. Serve hot.

Slow Cooker Instructions

Reduce the beef stock to 4 cups (1 L). Prepare through step 2. In step 3, place the seared roast, pan liquid, onion, garlic, bay leaves, tied herbs, and carrots in the slow cooker. Cover and cook on low for 8 hours. Remove the bay leaves and herb sprigs before serving.

Gluten-Free: Use gluten-free Worcestershire sauce.

Re-Fraiche

Turn leftover pot roast into French Dip Sandwiches (page 239) or Cottage Pie (page 169).

PREP AHEAD

ROAST CHICKEN DINNER

Dairy-Free Option • Gluten-Free Option • Nut-Free

Serves 4

TIME	
Prep:	15 MINUTES
Cook:	1 HOUR 15 MINUTES
Total:	1 HOUR 30 MINUTES

Roast Chicken

1 whole chicken (4 pounds/1.8 kg), giblets discarded, room temperature

1 yellow onion, peeled and quartered

Bunch of mixed fresh herbs (rosemary, thyme, oregano, parsley), tied with cooking twine

4 cloves garlic, minced

Extra-virgin olive oil

1 teaspoon (5 mL) salt

1 teaspoon (5 mL) coarsely ground pepper

1 cup (250 mL) chicken stock

Buttery Mashed Potatoes

2 pounds (900 g) Yukon gold potatoes, peeled and cut into 1- to 2-inch (2.5 to 5 cm) pieces

¼ cup (60 mL) butter

½ cup (125 mL) half-and-half (10%) cream or whole milk

Salt and pepper

Gravy

2 tablespoons (30 mL) all-purpose flour

Pan juices from the chicken

¼ to ½ cup (60 to 125 mL) potato cooking water, for thinning

Salt and pepper

Steamed vegetables, for serving

Nothing brings back memories of family meals for me quite like a roast chicken. My mom would usually cook a roast chicken on a Sunday, and not a bit would go to waste. Since then, my husband Charles has proudly taken over the roast chicken dinner, which is requested regularly by our two sons. Served with a generous scoop of Buttery Mashed Potatoes (page 326) and pools of gravy, this is how down-home cooking was meant to taste.

Cooking the chicken with a splash of stock adds flavour and helps keep the chicken moist. If desired, you can add carrots and baby potatoes to the roaster along with the chicken and skip the steamed vegetables and mashed potatoes. I highly recommend making a batch of Chicken Stock (page 318) with the carcass (and any of the drippings if you don't make gravy). If you're feeling ambitious, make a batch of Milk and Honey Bread (page 89) or Greek Yogurt Biscuits (page 109) to serve alongside the chicken.

1. **Make the Roast Chicken:** Preheat the oven to 450°F (230°C).

2. Rinse the chicken, then pat dry with paper towel. (It's important to get the chicken as dry as possible so it browns nicely.) Stuff the cavity with half of the onion and herbs, then tie the legs together with cooking twine. Place the chicken breast side up in a 13 × 9-inch (3.5 L) baking dish or a roasting pan. Arrange the remaining onion and herbs in the pan around the chicken and scatter with the garlic. Drizzle olive oil over the chicken, onion, and herbs, and rub the oil into the chicken to cover. Season the chicken generously with salt and pepper. Pour the chicken stock around the base of the chicken.

3. Roast for 15 minutes. Reduce the oven temperature to 375°F (190°C) and continue to roast until the chicken is golden brown, the juices run clear, and the internal temperature reaches 165°F (74°C) on an instant-read thermometer, about 45 minutes.

4. Meanwhile, make the Buttery Mashed Potatoes: Place the potatoes in a large pot and add cold water to cover by 1 inch (2.5 cm). Salt the water. Bring to a boil, then reduce the heat to medium and cook until the potatoes are fork-tender, 10 to 15 minutes.

Recipe continues . . .

PREP AHEAD
The chicken can be prepped (step 2) up to 2 days ahead; cover tightly with plastic wrap and foil and refrigerate. Uncover and bring to room temperature while the oven preheats. Veggies such as peeled carrots or quartered potatoes may be nestled around the chicken before roasting if desired. Buttery Mashed Potatoes can be made up to 2 days ahead and refrigerated. Reheat in the microwave or stovetop.

STORAGE
Store cooled cut-up roast chicken in a resealable container in the fridge for up to 4 days or in the freezer for up to 2 months. If frozen, thaw in the fridge overnight, then reheat in the microwave until warmed through.

Tip

You can scale up this recipe to roast 2 or 3 chickens at a time using a larger pan. The herbs can be omitted if desired.

5. Meanwhile, in a small microwave-safe bowl, microwave the butter and cream until warmed and the butter has melted (watch that it doesn't boil over).

6. Once the potatoes are cooked, reserve 1 cup (250 mL) of the cooking water. Drain the potatoes and return them to the pot. Using a potato masher, or a potato ricer over a large bowl, mash or press the potatoes until smooth. Stir in the warmed butter and cream mixture to combine. Season to taste with salt and pepper. Cover and keep warm until ready to serve.

7. Transfer the roasted chicken to a platter and tent with foil to keep warm.

8. Make the Gravy: Pour the pan juices through a fine-mesh sieve into a medium bowl. Discard the solids. In a medium saucepan over medium heat, cook the flour, stirring constantly, until it turns light brown and smells nutty, about 1 minute. Gradually add the strained pan juices, whisking constantly. Add in ¼ cup (60 mL) of reserved potato cooking water while whisking and cook until slightly thickened, adding up to ¼ cup (60 mL) more to thin if needed, 2 to 3 minutes. Season to taste with salt and pepper.

9. Cut the roast chicken into manageable pieces and serve hot with the Buttery Mashed Potatoes, gravy, and a side of steamed veggies.

Dairy-Free: Use vegan butter. Use Cashew Cream (page 332) instead of half-and-half cream.

Gluten-Free: Use a 1:1 gluten-free flour blend.

FRENCH DIP SANDWICHES

Gluten-Free Option • *Nut-Free*

Serves 4

TIME	
	Prep: 5 MINUTES (NOT INCLUDING COOKING THE POT ROAST)
	Cook: 10 MINUTES
	Total: 15 MINUTES

2 cups (500 mL) roughly chopped cooked Pot Roast (page 231), plus pan drippings

2 cups (500 mL) beef stock

1 teaspoon (5 mL) Worcestershire sauce

4 hoagie buns or Italian rolls

4 slices Swiss cheese

Prepared horseradish (optional)

STORAGE

Store cooled pot roast mixture (step 2) in a resealable container in the fridge for up to 4 days from when the pot roast was cooked. Reheat in the microwave until warmed through.

My parents owned an Arby's restaurant when we were young, and I'll never forget the French dip sandwiches. Turns out that the homemade version is a million times better (no surprise!). I love to turn leftover Pot Roast (page 231) into these cheesy sandwiches that my family loves. Serve with veggies and dip or a green salad.

1. Position an oven rack about 6 inches (15 cm) under the broiler and preheat the broiler. Line a baking sheet with parchment paper.

2. In a large pot with a lid, combine the beef and drippings, beef stock, and Worcestershire sauce. Bring to a boil over medium heat, stirring occasionally. Remove from the heat. Using tongs, transfer the beef to a medium bowl and cover to keep warm. Cover the pot to keep the broth hot.

3. Split the rolls in half and place cut side up on the prepared baking sheet; butter if desired. Broil until light golden brown, about 1 minute. Top each bun with about ½ cup (125 mL) of the roast beef and a slice of Swiss cheese. Broil until the cheese has melted and is bubbly, 1 to 2 minutes. Serve with horseradish if desired and a small bowl of the hot beef broth on the side for dipping.

Gluten-Free: Make the gluten-free option of the Pot Roast (page 231). Use gluten-free Worcestershire sauce and buns.

MANGO
Sauce

Sheet-Pan MEALS

BOLOGNAISE FLATBREAD

Vegan Option · *Vegetarian Option* · *Gluten-Free Option* · *Nut-Free*

Makes 2 flatbreads, serves 8

TIME
Prep: 10 MINUTES (NOT INCLUDING MAKING THE BETTER-FOR-YOU BOLOGNAISE)
Cook: 15 MINUTES
Total: 25 MINUTES

2 (12-inch/30 cm) store-bought pizza crusts or flatbreads

4 cups (1 L) Better-for-You Bolognaise (page 315)

1½ cups (375 mL) grated mozzarella cheese

1 cup (250 mL) thinly sliced cremini mushrooms

1 green sweet pepper, thinly sliced

½ cup (125 mL) thinly sliced red onion

For serving (optional)

Red chili flakes

Dried oregano

STORAGE

Store cooled flatbread, covered, in the fridge for up to 4 days. Reheat in a 425°F (220°C) oven or an air fryer until the cheese just starts to bubble, about 4 minutes.

This recipe should come with a warning! Our friends took us to a restaurant in Maui called Flatbread Pizza Company, and bolognaise flatbread was the feature pizza. My son Charlie and his buddy Asher ordered it for dinner and turned feral at first bite, fighting over each slice like it was their last meal. I promised Charlie that I would make it for him at home so long as the boys could keep it together while they ate. All to say, it's that good! As with any flatbread, the world is your oyster when it comes to toppings. If you want to make the zucchini extra sneaky, peel it before shredding. Add greens by simply tossing arugula with a pinch of salt and a drizzle of extra-virgin olive oil and serve alongside the flatbread for topping.

1. Preheat the oven to 425°F (220°C) and line 2 baking sheets with parchment paper.

2. Place 1 pizza crust on each prepared baking sheet. Evenly spread a thin layer of the Better-for-You Bolognaise over each crust, stopping about 1 inch (2.5 cm) from the edge.

3. Evenly scatter the cheese, mushrooms, green peppers, and red onion over the flatbreads.

4. Bake, one at a time, until the edges are golden and the cheese is melted and bubbly, about 10 minutes. Turn the oven to broil and broil until the cheese is golden on top, about 1 minute. Serve sprinkled with red chili flakes and oregano if desired.

Vegan: Make the vegan option of the Better-for-You Bolognaise (page 315). Use vegan mozzarella cheese and vegan parm.

Vegetarian: Make the vegan option of the Better-for-You Bolognaise (page 315).

Gluten-Free: Use gluten-free pizza crust or flatbread.

CHEESEBURGER NACHOS

Vegan Option · *Vegetarian Option* · *Gluten-Free* · *Nut-Free*

Serves 4

TIME
Prep: 5 MINUTES
Cook: 10 MINUTES
Total: 15 MINUTES

Burger Sauce

½ cup (125 mL) mayonnaise
¼ cup (60 mL) ketchup
2 tablespoons (30 mL) sweet relish
2 tablespoons (30 mL) yellow mustard

Meat Mixture

1 pound (450 g) ground beef, chicken, or turkey
2 teaspoons (10 mL) garlic powder
2 teaspoons (10 mL) sweet paprika
2 teaspoons (10 mL) onion powder
½ teaspoon (2 mL) salt
¼ teaspoon (1 mL) pepper

For assembly

4 cups (1 L) tortilla chips
2 cups (500 mL) grated cheddar cheese
1 head of iceberg lettuce, shredded
2 tomatoes, diced
4 large dill pickles, diced
½ white onion, diced

These Cheeseburger Nachos are piled high with all the good stuff—melted cheese, savoury beef, and all your favourite burger fixings. I'm a sucker for a fully loaded nacho situation, and serving them family-style right on the table makes it feel like a party (even if it's just Tuesday). The shredded lettuce adds that fresh crunch that makes every bite ridiculously good. To boost the veggies, add 1 cup (250 mL) of finely grated zucchini or carrots with the spices in step 2. Cook until the vegetables are soft.

1. Position an oven rack about 6 inches (15 cm) under the broiler and preheat the broiler. Line a baking sheet with parchment paper.

2. **Make the Burger Sauce:** In a small bowl, stir together the mayonnaise, ketchup, relish, and mustard. Set aside.

3. **Make the Meat Mixture:** Heat a medium frying pan over medium-high heat. Add the ground meat and cook, stirring occasionally, until browned and cooked through, about 4 minutes. Stir in the garlic powder, sweet paprika, onion powder, salt, and pepper. Remove from the heat.

4. **Assemble and Broil:** Spread half the tortilla chips in an even layer on the prepared baking sheet. Top with half the meat mixture. Scatter half the cheese over the meat. Repeat with the remaining tortilla chips, meat mixture, and cheese. Broil until the cheese is golden, melted, and bubbly, 3 to 4 minutes.

5. Top the nachos with shredded lettuce, tomatoes, pickles, and onion. Serve hot with the Burger Sauce on the side or drizzled over top.

Vegan: Use vegan cheese and vegan mayonnaise. Use veggie ground instead of ground meat.

Vegetarian: Use veggie ground instead of ground meat.

PREP AHEAD
The Burger Sauce can be made up to 3 days ahead and stored in a resealable container in the fridge. Cook the meat mixture, cool, and store in a resealable container in the fridge for up to 2 days or in the freezer for up to 3 months. If frozen, thaw in the fridge overnight, then reheat in the microwave until warmed through.

STORAGE
The nachos are best eaten hot out of the oven, but you can store leftovers, covered, in the fridge for up to 3 days. Reheat in a 275°F (140°C) oven for 5 to 10 minutes or until the chips have crisped up.

PREP AHEAD | FREEZER-FRIENDLY

CRISPY HOT HONEY CHICKEN SLIDERS

Vegetarian Option • Gluten-Free Option • Nut-Free

Makes 8 sliders, serves 4

TIME	
Prep:	15 MINUTES
Cook:	20 MINUTES
Total:	35 MINUTES

This is a dinner my family always agrees on. An easy sheet-pan version of fried chicken that delivers all the sweet, spicy, and sticky goodness without the mess or extra effort. Piled onto a bun with crispy Dill Pickle Slaw, it's next level, and better than takeout. I get rave reviews every time I make them. Now it's your turn to get the credit!

Crispy Chicken

½ cup (125 mL) all-purpose flour

2 teaspoons (10 mL) sweet paprika

1 teaspoon (5 mL) garlic powder

1 teaspoon (5 mL) onion powder

¼ teaspoon (1 mL) salt

¼ teaspoon (1 mL) pepper

2 eggs

2 tablespoons (30 mL) canola oil or avocado oil

2 cups (500 mL) panko crumbs

8 boneless, skinless chicken thighs (about 2 pounds/900 g total)

Hot Honey Sauce

¼ cup (60 mL) pure liquid honey

2 tablespoons (30 mL) butter, melted

2 tablespoons (30 mL) Frank's hot sauce

1. **Make the Crispy Chicken:** Preheat the oven to 425°F (220°C) and line a baking sheet with parchment paper.

2. In a shallow bowl, stir together the flour, sweet paprika, garlic powder, onion powder, salt, and pepper. Whisk the eggs in another shallow bowl.

3. Heat the canola oil in a medium frying pan over medium-high heat. When the pan is hot, add the panko and toast, stirring constantly, until golden brown, 1 to 2 minutes. Transfer the crumbs to a third shallow bowl.

4. Working with one chicken thigh at a time, coat in the flour mixture (shaking off the excess), then dip in the egg, followed by coating in the panko. As they are coated, transfer to the prepared baking sheet. Repeat until all the chicken thighs are coated.

5. Bake until the chicken is golden brown, cooked through, and the internal temperature reaches 165°F (74°C) on an instant-read thermometer, about 15 minutes. For extra crispiness, flip halfway through baking.

6. **Meanwhile, make the Hot Honey Sauce:** In a small bowl, stir together the honey, melted butter, and hot sauce.

7. **Make the Dill Pickle Slaw:** In a medium bowl, whisk together the mayonnaise, yogurt, pickles, pickle brine, dill, rice vinegar, and sugar. Add the coleslaw mix and green onion and toss to coat. Season to taste with salt and pepper.

8. When the chicken is done, drizzle about half of the Hot Honey Sauce on top, reserving the remaining sauce for dipping.

Recipe and ingredients continue . . .

Dill Pickle Slaw

2 tablespoons (30 mL) mayonnaise

2 tablespoons (30 mL) plain full-fat Greek yogurt

2 dill pickles, finely chopped

2 tablespoons (30 mL) dill pickle brine

2 tablespoons (30 mL) roughly chopped fresh dill

1 teaspoon (5 mL) unseasoned rice vinegar

¼ teaspoon (1 mL) sugar

5 cups (1.25 L) coleslaw mix (397 g package)

1 green onion, sliced

Salt and pepper

For serving

8 slider buns

Mayonnaise or Herb Ranch Dressing (page 133)

Sliced dill pickles

9. **Assemble the Sliders:** Slice the buns horizontally in half. Toast until lightly browned. Thinly spread mayonnaise on the bottom halves, then top with Crispy Hot Honey Chicken. Arrange some Dill Pickle Slaw and sliced pickles on top, then close with the tops.

Vegetarian: Use extra-firm tofu or cauliflower steaks instead of chicken.

Gluten-Free: Use gluten-free flour, panko crumbs, and buns.

PREP AHEAD

The Hot Honey Sauce can be made up to 5 days in advance and stored in a resealable container in the fridge (warm before using). The dressing for the slaw can be made up to 5 days ahead; refrigerate in a resealable container. Prepare the chicken with the coating (steps 2 through 4) up to 1 day in advance; place the chicken on a baking sheet, cover with plastic wrap or foil, and refrigerate.

STORAGE

Store the cooled cooked chicken and Hot Honey Sauce in separate resealable containers in the fridge for up to 4 days. Reheat the chicken in a 400°F (200°C) oven for about 8 minutes or an air fryer until warmed through and crisp.

FREEZER-FRIENDLY

Coat the chicken (steps 2, 3, and 4) and place on the prepared baking sheet. Freeze until firm, 1 to 2 hours. Transfer the frozen chicken to a resealable container or freezer bag, separating the layers with parchment paper, and freeze for up to 3 months. Preheat the oven or air fryer to 400°F (200°C). Place the frozen breaded chicken on a lined baking sheet and lightly spray or brush with oil. Bake for 25 to 30 minutes, or until golden, cooked through, and the internal temperature reaches 165°F (74°C). For extra crispiness, flip halfway through baking.

Re-Fraiche

Transform the Crispy Chicken and Hot Honey Sauce into Hot Honey Chicken Bowls (see page 22).

MANGO COCONUT SHRIMP TACOS

Vegan Option • Vegetarian Option • Dairy-Free • Gluten-Free Option • Nut-Free

Makes 8 tacos, serves 4

TIME
Prep: 10 MINUTES
Cook: 20 MINUTES
Total: 30 MINUTES

Coconut Rice

1 cup (250 mL) rice (I use jasmine)

1 cup (250 mL) water

¾ cup (175 mL) canned full-fat coconut milk

½ teaspoon (2 mL) sugar

Pinch of salt

Spicy Mango Sauce

2 cups (500 mL) fresh or thawed frozen mango chunks

¼ cup (60 mL) mayonnaise

1 tablespoon (15 mL) sriracha, or to taste

2 teaspoons (10 mL) unseasoned rice vinegar

1 teaspoon (5 mL) pure liquid honey or sugar, or to taste

Zest and juice of 1 lime

Salt

Coconut Shrimp

2 tablespoons (30 mL) coconut oil or avocado oil, divided

½ cup (125 mL) panko crumbs

½ cup (125 mL) sweetened shredded coconut

½ cup (125 mL) all-purpose flour

2 eggs

Salt and pepper

1 pound (450 g) large fresh or thawed frozen shrimp, peeled and deveined

These Mango Coconut Shrimp Tacos are sunshine in every bite—sweet, savoury, crunchy, and creamy all at once. Coconut-crusted shrimp are cooked to golden perfection, then tucked into warm tortillas and topped with fresh mango salsa, crisp slaw, and a drizzle of creamy lime sauce. It's a flavour-packed, tropical twist on taco night that feels like a mini vacation. Perfect for warm-weather casual entertaining or a regular weeknight dinner.

1. Preheat the oven to 400°F (200°C) and line a baking sheet with parchment paper.

2. **Make the Coconut Rice:** Combine the rice, water, coconut milk, sugar, and salt in a medium saucepan with a lid. Bring to a boil, then reduce the heat to low, cover, and simmer until the rice is tender, 18 to 20 minutes. Remove from the heat and keep warm.

3. **Meanwhile, make the Spicy Mango Sauce:** In a small blender or food processor, combine the mango, mayonnaise, sriracha, rice vinegar, honey, lime zest, and lime juice. Blend until smooth. Season with salt and more sriracha as needed. Transfer to a squeeze bottle or small bowl, cover, and refrigerate.

4. **Make the Coconut Shrimp:** Heat 1 tablespoon (15 mL) of the coconut oil in a medium frying pan over medium heat. Add the panko and cook, stirring occasionally, until golden, about 3 minutes. Transfer the toasted panko to a shallow bowl.

5. In the same pan (no need to wipe it) over medium heat, heat the remaining 1 tablespoon (15 mL) coconut oil. Add the shredded coconut and cook, stirring constantly, until golden brown, about 3 minutes. Transfer the toasted coconut to the bowl with the panko and stir to combine.

6. Place the flour in a shallow bowl. In a second shallow bowl, whisk the eggs. Season each bowl with salt and pepper; stir.

7. Working with one shrimp at a time, coat in the flour (shaking off the excess), then dip in the egg, followed by coating in the coconut panko mixture. As they are coated, transfer to the prepared baking sheet. Repeat until all the shrimp are coated.

8. Bake until the shrimp are golden brown and cooked through, 8 to 10 minutes.

Recipe and ingredients continue . . .

For assembly

8 medium (7-inch/18 cm) flour tortillas

2 cups (500 mL) finely shredded purple cabbage

2 mangoes, peeled and diced

1 avocado, pitted, peeled, and sliced

Quick Pickled Red Onions (page 331)

PREP AHEAD

The Coconut Rice and Spicy Mango Sauce can be made up to 2 days in advance and stored in separate resealable containers in the fridge. Reheat the rice in the microwave until warm just before serving.

STORAGE

Store cooled cooked Coconut Rice and Coconut Shrimp in separate resealable containers in the fridge for up to 3 days. Reheat the rice in the microwave and the shrimp in a 350°F (180°C) oven or air fryer until warmed through.

9. **Assemble the Tacos:** In the centre of the tortilla, layer some Coconut Rice and Coconut Shrimp. Top with cabbage, mango, avocado, and Quick Pickled Red Onions, as desired. Drizzle the Spicy Mango Sauce over top and fold like a taco. Serve immediately.

Vegan: Use vegan mayonnaise. Use cubed extra-firm tofu or cauliflower florets instead of shrimp. Use sugar instead of honey.

Vegetarian: Use cubed extra-firm tofu or cauliflower florets instead of shrimp.

Gluten-Free: Use a 1:1 gluten-free flour blend and gluten-free panko crumbs.

Re-Fraiche

Make into Mango Coconut Shrimp Bowls (see page 22) or Mango Coconut Shrimp Lettuce Wraps.

PREP AHEAD

The taquitos can be prepared through step 4 up to 1 day in advance. Cover tightly with plastic wrap and refrigerate. Uncover, lightly brush with avocado oil, and bake as directed.

STORAGE

Store cooled taquitos in a resealable container in the fridge for up to 4 days or in the freezer for up to 1 month. Reheat frozen taquitos in an air fryer or on a baking sheet lined with parchment paper in a 375°F (190°C) oven for 10 to 15 minutes, until golden and crispy, turning halfway through.

PREP AHEAD | MAKE AHEAD | FREEZER-FRIENDLY

SNEAKY SHEET-PAN TAQUITOS

Vegan Option • Vegetarian Option • Dairy-Free Option • Gluten-Free Option • Nut-Free

Makes 12 taquitos, serves 4

TIME
Prep: 20 MINUTES
Cook: 25 MINUTES
Total: 45 MINUTES

Filling

1 pound (450 g) ground beef, chicken, or turkey

½ cup (125 mL) grated yellow onion

2 teaspoons (10 mL) ground cumin

2 teaspoons (10 mL) garlic powder

2 teaspoons (10 mL) dried oregano

2 teaspoons (10 mL) sweet paprika

½ teaspoon (2 mL) chipotle chili powder, or to taste

3 tablespoons (45 mL) tomato paste

½ cup (125 mL) finely grated zucchini

½ cup (125 mL) finely grated carrot

½ cup (125 mL) beef or chicken stock or water

Juice of 1 lime

Salt and pepper

For assembly

12 medium (7-inch/18 cm) flour tortillas

1½ cups (375 mL) grated cheddar or Monterey Jack cheese

Avocado oil or canola oil, for brushing

For serving

Sour cream

Guacamole

Hot sauce

Who says comfort food can't come with a side of healthy? These taquitos are everything you love about crispy, cheesy taquitos—with a hidden twist. Packed with veggies so stealthy even the pickiest eaters won't notice, they're the ultimate win for both flavour and nutrition. Perfect for busy weeknights, meal prep, or snack attacks, these fun-to-eat taquitos come together quickly and freeze well. Whether you serve them up for dinner, pack them for lunch, or enjoy them as a crowd-pleasing appetizer, you'll love this feel-good spin on a classic favourite. Serve with a green salad.

The chipotle chili powder makes these a bit spicier: you may omit it or add more, depending on the taste of your crowd.

1. Preheat the oven to 425°F (220°C) and line a baking sheet with parchment paper.

2. **Make the Filling:** Heat a large frying pan over medium-high heat; add a drizzle of olive oil to the pan if your meat is extra lean. Add the ground beef and cook, stirring occasionally, until lightly browned, 5 to 6 minutes. Add the onion and cook, stirring occasionally, until the onion is soft and translucent, 3 to 4 minutes. Add the cumin, garlic powder, oregano, sweet paprika, chili powder, and tomato paste and cook, stirring, until fragrant, about 2 minutes.

3. Add the zucchini, carrots, and beef stock. Cook, stirring occasionally, until the vegetables are very soft, about 8 minutes. Stir in the lime juice to taste and season to taste with salt and pepper.

4. **Assemble and Bake:** Spoon about 2 tablespoons (30 mL) of cheese down the centre of a tortilla and top with about ¼ cup (60 mL) of the filling. Roll tightly and place seam side down on the prepared baking sheet. Repeat with the remaining tortillas. Brush the taquitos lightly with avocado oil.

5. Bake until golden and crispy, 10 to 15 minutes, turning halfway through. Serve hot with sour cream, guacamole, and hot sauce.

Vegan: Use veggie ground. Use vegan cheese. Use water or vegetable stock. Serve with vegan sour cream.

Vegetarian: Use veggie ground and vegetable stock.

Dairy-Free: Use vegan cheese. Serve with vegan sour cream.

Gluten-Free: Use gluten-free tortillas.

PREP AHEAD | MAKE AHEAD | FREEZER-FRIENDLY

SHAWARMA CHICKEN PITA WRAPS

Vegan Option · Vegetarian Option · Dairy-Free Option · Gluten-Free Option · Nut-Free

Serves 4

TIME
Prep: 15 MINUTES, PLUS 30 MINUTES MARINATING
Cook: 20 MINUTES
Total: 35 MINUTES

Marinated Chicken

8 boneless, skinless chicken thighs (about 2 pounds/900 g total)

2 tablespoons (30 mL) extra-virgin olive oil

1 teaspoon (5 mL) fresh lemon juice

1 tablespoon (15 mL) cornstarch

2 teaspoons (10 mL) ground cumin

2 teaspoons (10 mL) smoked paprika

1 teaspoon (5 mL) ground coriander

1 teaspoon (5 mL) salt

½ teaspoon (2 mL) ground turmeric

¼ teaspoon (1 mL) cinnamon

2 cloves garlic, minced

Garlic Yogurt Sauce

1 cup (250 mL) plain full-fat Greek yogurt

2 tablespoons (30 mL) mayonnaise

2 to 4 tablespoons (30 to 60 mL) fresh lemon juice

4 cloves garlic, minced

Salt

For serving

4 pitas, warmed

Quick Pickled Red Onions (page 331)

1 cup (250 mL) diced English cucumber

1 cup (250 mL) diced tomato

1 cup (250 mL) shredded green lettuce

¼ cup (60 mL) roughly chopped fresh flat-leaf parsley

This flavour-packed dish brings all the bold, crave-worthy vibes of your favourite takeout right from your own oven. Chicken is marinated to spice perfection and roasted until golden and tender, filling your kitchen with the most irresistible aroma. It's all tucked into warm pitas with a cool, creamy Garlic Yogurt Sauce that adds just the right zing. Layer in crisp cucumbers, juicy tomatoes, and whatever veggies your heart desires for the perfect balance of textures. Serve it family-style and let everyone build their own shawarma masterpiece.

Double or triple the marinated chicken and freeze meal-size portions for future quick meals.

1. **Marinate the Chicken:** Place the chicken thighs in a medium bowl. Add the olive oil, lemon juice, cornstarch, cumin, smoked paprika, coriander, salt, turmeric, cinnamon, and garlic. Toss to coat well. Cover and marinate in the fridge for at least 30 minutes or overnight.

2. When ready to bake the chicken, preheat the oven to 450°F (230°C) and line a baking sheet with parchment paper.

3. Arrange the chicken thighs on the prepared baking sheet and bake until golden brown, cooked through, and the internal temperature reaches 165°F (74°C) on an instant-read thermometer, about 20 minutes. Remove from the oven, cover with foil, and let rest for 5 minutes.

4. **Meanwhile, make the Garlic Yogurt Sauce:** In a small bowl, whisk together the yogurt, mayonnaise, lemon juice to taste, and garlic. Season to taste with salt.

5. Thinly slice the chicken. Top the warmed pita with chicken and desired toppings. Drizzle with the Garlic Yogurt Sauce.

Vegan: Use rehydrated soy curls (follow package instructions) instead of chicken. Use non-dairy Greek yogurt and vegan mayonnaise.

Vegetarian: Use rehydrated soy curls (follow package instructions) instead of chicken.

Dairy-Free: Use non-dairy Greek yogurt.

Gluten-Free: Use gluten-free pitas.

Re-Fraiche

Transform leftover chicken and Garlic Yogurt Sauce into Shawarma Bowls (see page 22).

PREP AHEAD

The Garlic Yogurt Sauce can be made up to 5 days ahead; store in a resealable container in the fridge. The chicken can be prepared through step 3 up to 4 days in advance; let cool and store in a resealable container in the fridge.

STORAGE

Tightly wrap individual pita wraps, without the sauce, in foil or parchment paper. Store in a resealable container in the fridge for up to 2 days.

FREEZER-FRIENDLY

Place the chicken with marinade in a resealable plastic bag and store in the freezer for up to 3 months. Thaw in the fridge overnight, then bake as directed.

PREP AHEAD

EVERYTHING BAGEL SALMON

Gluten-Free • Nut-Free

Serves 4

TIME	
Prep:	15 MINUTES
Cook:	35 MINUTES
Total:	50 MINUTES

Crispy Smashed Potatoes

1 pound (450 g) baby potatoes

1 tablespoon (15 mL) extra-virgin olive oil

½ teaspoon (2 mL) garlic powder

½ teaspoon (2 mL) onion powder

1 tablespoon (15 mL) everything bagel seasoning (or make your own, page 334)

Salmon

4 skinless salmon fillets (about 6 ounces/170 g each)

2 tablespoons (30 mL) mayonnaise

1 teaspoon (5 mL) Dijon mustard

2 tablespoons (30 mL) everything bagel seasoning (or make your own, page 334)

Cream Cheese Sauce

¼ cup (60 mL) soft cream cheese

1 tablespoon (15 mL) everything bagel seasoning (or make your own, page 334)

½ teaspoon (2 mL) Dijon mustard

Juice of ½ lemon

1 green onion (white and light green parts only), thinly sliced

Salt and pepper

Ever get caught in a rut of cooking salmon the same way every time? This Everything Bagel Salmon is such a creative yet simple way to change up your cooking routine. The salmon gets topped with a crunchy, flavourful coating of everything bagel seasoning, then baked to golden perfection. Serve with Crispy Smashed Potatoes, the fresh and crunchy Cucumber Salad to contrast, and a drizzle of Cream Cheese Sauce for good measure. Use store-bought everything bagel seasoning to save time.

1. Position the racks in the upper and lower thirds of the oven and preheat to 425°F (220°C). Line 2 baking sheets with parchment paper.

2. **Make the Crispy Smashed Potatoes:** Bring a pot of salted water to a boil. Add the potatoes and boil until just fork-tender, 10 to 15 minutes. Drain and transfer the potatoes to a medium bowl.

3. Toss the potatoes with the olive oil, garlic powder, and onion powder. Evenly spread the potatoes on a prepared baking sheet. Using the bottom of a glass, press each potato until ½ inch (1 cm) thick. Sprinkle with the everything bagel seasoning. Bake on the bottom rack until golden and crispy, 25 to 30 minutes, flipping halfway through.

4. **Meanwhile, bake the Salmon:** Place the salmon fillets on the second prepared baking sheet and pat dry. In a small bowl, stir together the mayonnaise and mustard. Evenly spread the mixture on top of the fillets. Evenly sprinkle the top of the fish with the everything bagel seasoning. Bake on the top rack until cooked through, 12 to 15 minutes (bake time will depend on thickness of the fish).

5. **Make the Cream Cheese Sauce:** In a small bowl, stir together the cream cheese, everything bagel seasoning, mustard, lemon juice, and green onion. Season to taste with salt and pepper.

Recipe and ingredients continue . . .

Cucumber Salad

2 tablespoons (30 mL) unseasoned rice vinegar

1 teaspoon (5 mL) sesame oil

1 teaspoon (5 mL) sugar

1 English cucumber, thinly sliced

¼ red onion, thinly sliced

Salt

PREP AHEAD
The potatoes can be boiled, drained, and refrigerated in a resealable container up to 3 days ahead. The Cream Cheese Sauce can be made up to 3 days ahead; refrigerate in a resealable container.

STORAGE
Store cooled cooked salmon and potatoes in a resealable container in the fridge for up to 2 days. Reheat in the microwave until warmed through. Store the Cucumber Salad in a resealable container in the fridge for up to 1 day.

6. **Make the Cucumber Salad:** In a small bowl, whisk together the rice vinegar, sesame oil, and sugar until the sugar has dissolved. Add the cucumber and red onion; stir to combine. Season to taste with salt.

7. Serve the baked salmon, potatoes, and Cucumber Salad on a platter. Drizzle with the Cream Cheese Sauce just before serving.

Re-Fraiche

Transform leftover salmon into Everything Bagel Salmon Salad (page 120).

Tips

- When buying salmon, look for firm, moist flesh and a fresh, ocean-like smell—never fishy. If you're shopping at a fish counter, you can often ask to inspect it. But if you're buying pre-packaged salmon from the supermarket, check that the flesh looks vibrant (not dull or grey), and avoid any packages with excess liquid or broken fibres, which can be signs of aging.

- Don't shy away from frozen salmon either! It's usually flash-frozen at peak freshness, often making it just as nutritious—if not fresher—than "fresh" fish that's been sitting on ice for days. Look for wild-caught and sustainably sourced options when you can.

PREP AHEAD | MAKE AHEAD

CORN CHOWDER SEAFOOD CAKES

Vegetarian Option • Dairy-Free • Gluten-Free Option • Nut-Free

Serves 4

TIME
Prep: 10 MINUTES
Cook: 30 MINUTES
Total: 40 MINUTES

Seafood Cakes

- 2 slices thick-cut bacon
- 1 pound (450 g) large fresh or thawed frozen shrimp, peeled, deveined, and finely chopped
- 2 skinless white fish fillets (10 ounces/280 g each), cut into ¼-inch (5 mm) pieces
- ½ cup (125 mL) frozen corn kernels
- ¼ cup (60 mL) mayonnaise
- 1 egg, whisked
- 2 green onions (white and light green parts only), thinly sliced
- ½ teaspoon (2 mL) salt
- ¼ teaspoon (1 mL) pepper
- 2 cups (500 mL) panko crumbs, divided
- 2 tablespoons (30 mL) extra-virgin olive oil

My husband Charles and I are kind of known for these seafood cakes in our friend circle. Make-ahead, easy to cook, and always impressive—what's not to love! This is one of those dishes you see at a fine-dining restaurant but can make so easily right at home. These seafood cakes have a touch of sweetness from the corn and smokiness from the bacon, and the most perfectly balanced Lemon Dill Sauce rounds out the entire dish. Serve them as an appetizer or as a meal with a salad alongside such as my Herby Green Salad (page 119) or Caesar Salad with Simple Caesar Dressing (page 197).

1. Preheat the oven to 400°F (200°C) and line a baking sheet with parchment paper.

2. Arrange the bacon on the prepared baking sheet and bake until slightly crispy, about 12 minutes. Transfer the cooked bacon to a plate lined with paper towel to absorb excess oil, pat with paper towel if needed, and let cool. Chop into ¼-inch (5 mm) pieces.

3. **Meanwhile, make the Seafood Cakes:** In a medium bowl, combine the shrimp, fish, corn, mayonnaise, egg, green onions, salt, pepper, and ⅔ cup (150 mL) of the panko. Mix thoroughly. Stir in the cooked bacon until well combined. Set aside for about 10 minutes to allow the mixture to bind.

4. Heat the olive oil in a medium frying pan over medium heat. Add the remaining 1¼ cups (300 mL) panko (there's a bit extra—add it too) and cook, stirring occasionally, until golden, about 3 minutes. Transfer the toasted panko to a shallow bowl.

5. Using an ice-cream scoop or your hands, form about ⅓ cup (75 mL) of the seafood mixture into a 3-inch (8 cm) round cake. Gently place it on the panko and lightly press crumbs onto all sides of the cake. Transfer the seafood cake to the prepared baking sheet. Repeat with the remaining seafood mixture.

6. Bake until golden and the internal temperature reaches 155°F (68°C) on an instant-read thermometer, about 15 minutes.

Recipe and ingredients continue . . .

Lemon Dill Sauce

½ cup (125 mL) mayonnaise

2 tablespoons (30 mL) fresh lemon juice

1 green onion (white and light green parts only), thinly sliced

1 tablespoon (15 mL) finely chopped fresh dill, plus more for garnish

1 teaspoon (5 mL) Dijon mustard

Salt

Lemon wedges, for serving

PREP AHEAD

The Seafood Cakes can be made through step 6 up to 2 days ahead. Place cooled cakes in a resealable container, separating the layers with parchment, and refrigerate. The Lemon Dill Sauce can be made up to 5 days ahead and stored in a resealable container in the fridge.

STORAGE

Store cooled seafood cakes in a resealable container in the fridge for up to 2 days or in the freezer for up to 1 month. If frozen, thaw in the fridge overnight, then reheat in a 350°F (180°C) oven or in an air fryer until warmed through.

7. **Meanwhile, make the Lemon Dill Sauce:** In a small bowl, whisk together the mayonnaise, lemon juice, green onion, dill, and mustard. Season to taste with salt.

8. Serve the Seafood Cakes hot with Lemon Dill Sauce, garnished with fresh dill, if desired, and lemon wedges alongside.

Vegetarian: Omit the bacon. Use drained chopped jackfruit instead of the shrimp and fish.

Gluten-Free: Use gluten-free bacon and gluten-free panko crumbs.

PREP AHEAD
The Lime Crema can be made up to 5 days ahead; refrigerate in a resealable container. The Shrimp Mixture (step 2) can be prepared up to 2 days ahead; refrigerate in a resealable container.

Re-Fraiche

Transform into Chipotle Shrimp Pineapple Fajita Bowls (see page 22).

CHIPOTLE SHRIMP PINEAPPLE FAJITAS

Vegan Option • Vegetarian Option • Dairy-Free Option • Gluten-Free Option • Nut-Free

Serves 4

TIME	
Prep:	15 MINUTES
Cook:	15 MINUTES
Total:	30 MINUTES

Shrimp Mixture

1 teaspoon (5 mL) onion powder

1 teaspoon (5 mL) garlic powder

½ teaspoon (2 mL) chipotle chili powder, or to taste

½ teaspoon (2 mL) sweet paprika

½ teaspoon (2 mL) smoked paprika

½ teaspoon (2 mL) ground cumin

¼ teaspoon (1 mL) salt

2 red, orange, or yellow sweet peppers, sliced

1 green sweet pepper, sliced

½ large yellow onion, sliced

½ fresh pineapple, peeled and cut into 1- to 2-inch (2.5 to 5 cm) pieces

2 tablespoons (30 mL) avocado oil, divided

2 tablespoons (30 mL) fresh lime juice, divided

1 pound (450 g) large fresh or thawed frozen shrimp, peeled and deveined

Lime Crema

½ cup (125 mL) plain full-fat Greek yogurt

Zest and juice of 1 lime

2 cloves garlic, minced

½ teaspoon (2 mL) pure liquid honey

Salt

For serving

8 medium (7-inch/18 cm) flour tortillas

1 avocado, pitted, peeled, and diced

Cilantro

Lime wedges

These quick and flavour-packed fajitas are the perfect balance of spicy and sweet—a combo that makes them one of my all-time favourite weeknight meals. They come together in a flash and make delicious leftovers for lunch the next day. Want to tone down the heat? Simply reduce or skip the chipotle chili powder. And for a smoky twist, try swapping in poblano peppers for the green peppers, especially if you're craving a bit more depth of flavour. If you don't have a fresh pineapple or want to save time, you can use one 14-ounce (398 mL) can of drained pineapple chunks.

1. Preheat the oven to 450°F (230°C) and line a baking sheet with parchment paper.

2. **Make the Shrimp Mixture:** In a small bowl, stir together the onion powder, garlic powder, chipotle chili powder, sweet paprika, smoked paprika, cumin, and salt.

3. Place the sweet peppers, onion, and pineapple on the prepared baking sheet. Sprinkle with half the spice mix, 1 tablespoon (15 mL) of the avocado oil, and 1 tablespoon (15 mL) of the lime juice. Toss to evenly coat and spread in an even layer. Bake for 8 minutes.

4. Meanwhile, wrap the tortillas tightly in foil.

5. In a small bowl, toss the shrimp with the remaining spice mix, remaining 1 tablespoon (15 mL) of the olive oil, and remaining 1 tablespoon (15 mL) of the lime juice. Spread the shrimp on the baking sheet in a single layer with the peppers, along with the packet of wrapped tortillas to warm, and bake until the shrimp are opaque and cooked through, about 7 minutes.

6. **Meanwhile, make the Lime Crema:** In a small bowl, stir together the yogurt, lime zest and juice, garlic, and honey. Season to taste with salt.

7. Serve the shrimp mixture with warm tortillas, avocado, cilantro, lime wedges, and Lime Crema for building fajitas.

Vegan: Omit the shrimp and use 1 package (12 ounces/350 g) extra-firm tofu, cubed or drained canned jackfruit instead. Use non-dairy yogurt. Omit the honey and use sugar instead.

Vegetarian: Use extra-firm tofu or drained canned jackfruit instead.

Dairy-Free: Use non-dairy yogurt.

Gluten-Free: Use gluten-free tortillas.

BAKED CHICKEN PARMESAN

Dairy-Free Option • Gluten-Free Option • Nut-Free

Serves 4

TIME
Prep: 15 MINUTES
Cook: 20 MINUTES
Total: 35 MINUTES

- 4 boneless, skinless chicken breasts (about 3 pounds/1.35 kg total)
- 1 cup (250 mL) all-purpose flour
- 2 teaspoons (10 mL) garlic powder
- 2 teaspoons (10 mL) onion powder
- 2 teaspoons (10 mL) sweet paprika
- Salt and pepper
- 4 eggs
- 2 cups (500 mL) panko crumbs
- ¼ cup (60 mL) extra-virgin olive oil
- ½ cup (125 mL) grated Parmesan cheese, divided
- 1 cup (250 mL) marinara sauce or SOS Spaghetti Sauce (page 312)
- 2 balls (340 g each) fresh mozzarella cheese, thinly sliced
- 2 tablespoons (30 mL) finely chopped fresh basil or flat-leaf parsley

PREP AHEAD

The chicken can be prepared ahead through step 4; cover and refrigerate for up to 1 day or store in a resealable container in the freezer for up to 3 months. If frozen, thaw in the fridge overnight before cooking.

STORAGE

Store cooled chicken Parmesan in a resealable container in the fridge for up to 4 days.

The first week that I met Charles (my hubby), he suggested that he come over to my parents' house and cook them dinner. I thought, This guy is gutsy. It truly was the best night ever! My dad jokes that he traded his daughter for a chicken cutlet. While this may be true, I can't totally fault him, as this is a spectacularly good dish. Charles always fries his chicken, but for simplicity and to make it a bit healthier, this is my baked version, which is equally good. Serve with a green salad and buttered pasta with Parmesan if desired.

1. Preheat the oven to 425°F (220°C) and line a baking sheet with parchment paper.

2. Working with one chicken breast at a time, place between 2 sheets of parchment paper on a cutting board. Using a meat mallet, pound until ¼ to ½ inch (5 mm to 1 cm) thick. Season both sides of the chicken with salt and pepper. Set aside on a plate.

3. Set out 3 shallow medium bowls. In one bowl, stir together the flour, garlic powder, onion powder, paprika, salt, and pepper. In the second bowl, whisk the eggs. In the third bowl, stir together the panko, olive oil, and ¼ cup (60 mL) of the Parmesan and season with salt and pepper.

4. Working with one piece of chicken at a time, lightly dredge in the flour mixture, coating both sides, then place in the egg, turning to coat and letting the excess drip off. Finish with the panko mixture, lightly coating both sides. Transfer to the prepared baking sheet. Repeat to coat the remaining chicken.

5. Bake until the chicken is golden and the internal temperature reaches 165°F (74°C) on an instant-read thermometer, about 15 minutes.

6. Turn the oven to broil. Top the chicken with the remaining ¼ cup (60 mL) Parmesan, marinara sauce, and mozzarella slices and broil until the cheese has melted, 1 to 2 minutes. Garnish with the basil.

Dairy-Free: Use vegan parm and vegan mozzarella.

Gluten-Free: Use a 1:1 gluten-free flour blend. Use gluten-free panko.

Re-Fraiche

Transform into Chicken Parmesan Bowls (see page 22) or a sandwich.

CAJUN CHICKEN SHEET-PAN BURGERS

Vegan Option · *Vegetarian Option* · *Dairy-Free Option* · *Gluten-Free Option* · *Nut-Free*

Serves 4

TIME
Prep: 10 MINUTES
Cook: 15 MINUTES
Total: 25 MINUTES

4 boneless, skinless chicken breasts (about 3 pounds/1.35 kg total)

2 tablespoons (30 mL) Cajun spice

¼ teaspoon (1 mL) salt

2 tablespoons (30 mL) extra-virgin olive oil

For serving

4 ciabatta buns or your favourite burger buns

Mayonnaise

Sliced tomatoes

1 avocado, pitted, peeled, and sliced

½ red onion, thinly sliced

4 slices cheddar cheese

Iceberg lettuce

When that craving to hit the drive-thru strikes, make these smoky, spicy chicken burgers instead. It's a restaurant-quality meal from the comfort of your own kitchen. I often prep this ahead, including chopping up all the toppings we love, so it's ready for my hungry kids right at 5 p.m. when they inevitably start asking, "What's for dinner?"

These burgers are great served on any bun, but my go-to is ciabatta or Focaccia Cheese Buns (page 101). Serve with a light salad or Oven Fries (page 269). This chicken is delicious, so consider making a double batch to go on salads, bowls, and in sandwiches throughout the week.

1. Preheat the oven to 425°F (220°C) and line a baking sheet with parchment paper.

2. Working with one chicken breast at a time, place between 2 sheets of parchment paper on a cutting board. Using a meat mallet, pound until about ½ inch (1 cm) thick. Season both sides of the chicken with the Cajun spice and salt.

3. Heat the olive oil in a large frying pan over medium-high heat. Add the chicken and cook until golden brown, about 2 minutes per side. Transfer the chicken to the prepared baking sheet and bake until cooked through and the internal temperature reaches 165°F (74°C) on an instant-read thermometer, about 10 minutes.

4. Slice the buns horizontally in half. Toast until lightly browned. Thinly spread mayonnaise on the bottom halves, then top with Cajun chicken, sliced tomatoes, avocado, red onion, a slice of cheddar cheese, and lettuce. Close with the tops.

Vegan: Use 2 packages (12 ounces /350 g each) extra-firm tofu instead of chicken. Press the tofu to remove excess moisture, then slice it lengthwise into ½- to ¾-inch-thick (1 to 2 cm) slabs. Pat dry again, then season before frying; skip the baking. Use vegan mayonnaise and vegan cheese.

Vegetarian: Use extra-firm tofu instead of chicken (see Vegan instructions).

Dairy-Free: Use vegan cheese.

Gluten-Free: Use gluten-free buns.

PREP AHEAD
The chicken (step 2) can be prepared ahead and stored in a resealable container in the fridge for up to 2 days or in the freezer for up to 3 months. If frozen, thaw in the fridge overnight before cooking. The chicken can also be cooked up to 2 days ahead, stored in the fridge in a resealable container, then reheated in an air fryer or microwave until warmed through.

Re-Fraiche

Turn leftover burgers into Cajun Chicken Lettuce Wraps. Chop the cooked chicken burgers and serve in iceberg lettuce cups. Serve with the same toppings as desired.

PREP AHEAD

The panko can be toasted (step 4) up to 5 days ahead and stored in a resealable container at room temperature. The Tartar Sauce can be made up to 1 week ahead and refrigerated in a resealable container. The potatoes can be prepped up to 1 day ahead: cut the potatoes, place in a large bowl, cover with water, then cover with plastic wrap and refrigerate.

STORAGE

Store the cooled cooked fish burgers in a resealable container in the fridge for up to 2 days. Store the Tartar Sauce in a separate resealable container in the fridge for up to 1 week.

Re-Fraiche

Make into Fish Taco Bowls (see page 22).

PREP AHEAD

CRISPY FISH BURGERS WITH OVEN FRIES

Dairy-Free Option · *Gluten-Free Option* · *Nut-Free*

Serves 4

TIME
Prep: 15 MINUTES
Cook: 30 MINUTES
Total: 45 MINUTES

Oven Fries

2 skin-on russet potatoes, scrubbed and cut into ½-inch (1 cm) wedges

1 tablespoon (15 mL) avocado oil

Salt and pepper

Crispy Fish Burgers

2 tablespoons (30 mL) extra-virgin olive oil or avocado oil

1 cup (250 mL) panko crumbs

½ cup (125 mL) all-purpose flour

1 teaspoon (5 mL) garlic powder

1 teaspoon (5 mL) onion powder

¼ teaspoon (1 mL) salt

¼ teaspoon (1 mL) pepper

2 eggs

4 skinless cod fillets (about 6 ounces/170 g each)

Tartar Sauce

½ cup (125 mL) mayonnaise

2 dill pickles, finely diced

2 tablespoons (30 mL) finely diced red onion

2 tablespoons (30 mL) fresh lemon juice

For serving

4 hamburger buns

4 slices cheddar cheese

Sliced dill pickles

2 cups (500 mL) shredded iceberg lettuce

Crispy, golden fillets are piled with crisp lettuce, sliced cheddar, and dill pickles and topped with homemade Tartar Sauce (the true key to these burgers). Serve with a side of crispy Oven Fries. I used cod for this recipe, but you can swap in any fish, such as salmon or halibut.

1. Preheat the oven to 450°F (230°C) and line 2 baking sheets with parchment paper.

2. **Make the Oven Fries:** Bring a large pot of salted water to a boil. Add the potatoes and boil until just fork-tender, about 10 minutes. Drain and spread on a rack to dry out, about 5 minutes.

3. Transfer the potato wedges to a prepared baking sheet. Drizzle with the avocado oil and toss to evenly coat. Season to taste with salt and pepper, toss again, and spread out in an even layer. Bake until golden brown, 20 to 25 minutes, turning halfway through.

4. **Meanwhile, make the Fish Burgers:** Heat the olive oil in a medium frying pan over medium heat. Add the panko and toast, stirring occasionally, until golden, about 3 minutes. Transfer to a shallow bowl.

5. Set out 2 shallow bowls. In one bowl, stir together the flour, garlic powder, onion powder, salt, and pepper. In the second bowl, whisk the eggs.

6. Working with one fillet at a time, coat in the flour mixture (shaking off the excess), then dip in the egg, followed by coating in the panko. As they are coated, transfer to the prepared baking sheet. Repeat.

7. Bake until the fish is cooked through, 10 to 15 minutes (the cook time will depend on the thickness of the fillets).

8. **Meanwhile, make the Tartar Sauce:** In a small bowl, stir together the mayonnaise, pickles, red onion, and lemon juice until combined. Cover and store in the fridge until ready to use.

9. Slice the buns horizontally in half. Toast until lightly browned. Spread the Tartar Sauce on the bottom halves of the buns. Top with a piece of crispy cod, cheese, pickles, and lettuce. Close with the tops. Serve with the Oven Fries.

Dairy-Free: Use vegan cheese.

Gluten-Free: Use a 1:1 gluten-free flour blend. Use gluten-free panko and gluten-free buns.

Simple SWEETS

PREP AHEAD | MAKE AHEAD | FREEZER-FRIENDLY

APPLE SLAB PIE

Vegan Option · Vegetarian · Dairy-Free Option · Nut-Free

Serves 16

TIME
Prep: 40 MINUTES PLUS 1 HOUR CHILLING
Bake: 30 MINUTES
Total: 1 HOUR 10 MINUTES

Pie Dough

5 cups (1.25 L) all-purpose flour

4 teaspoons (20 mL) sugar

2 teaspoons (10 mL) salt

1 cup (250 mL) vegetable shortening, cut into chunks

1 cup (250 mL) cold butter, cut into ½-inch (1 cm) cubes

4 teaspoons (20 mL) fresh lemon juice or white vinegar

½ cup (125 mL) + 2 to 4 tablespoons (30 to 60 mL) ice water, divided

Apple Filling

12 cups (3 L) thinly sliced peeled Granny Smith or Gala apples (about 10 apples)

1 to 1½ cups (250 to 375 mL) lightly packed brown sugar

¼ cup (60 mL) butter

2 tablespoons (30 mL) all-purpose flour

1 tablespoon (15 mL) cinnamon

Pinch of salt

2 tablespoons (30 mL) fresh lemon juice

Egg Wash

1 egg

1 tablespoon (15 mL) of water

Coarse sugar, for sprinkling

This is the ultimate party pie! Designed to feed a hungry crowd, it is so easy to slice and serve. With a buttery, flaky crust filled with sweet cinnamon-spiced apples, it's a crowd-pleasing dessert for any type of gathering. The apple pie filling freezes beautifully, so why not make a double batch and freeze half to use later? Same goes for the pie crust.

I give a range for brown sugar depending on how sweet you like your apple pie. I use a 14-cup (3.5 L) food processor for this recipe. If yours is smaller, process the dough in two batches.

1. **Make the Pie Dough:** In a large-capacity food processor, combine the flour, sugar, and salt. Pulse to mix. Add the shortening and pulse until just incorporated. Add the butter and pulse until the butter is the size of peas. Do not overmix.

2. Drizzle the lemon juice and ½ cup (125 mL) of the ice water over the flour mixture. Pulse until the dough just starts to stick together in clumps, adding the remaining 2 to 4 tablespoons (30 to 60 mL) water if needed.

3. Divide the dough in half. Shape each piece into a disc, wrap tightly in plastic wrap, and refrigerate for at least 1 hour before rolling it out.

4. **Meanwhile, make the Apple Filling:** In a large saucepan, combine the apples, brown sugar, butter, flour, cinnamon, salt, and lemon juice. Cook, stirring occasionally, over medium-low heat, until the apples have softened, 15 to 20 minutes. Set aside to cool.

5. Preheat the oven to 425°F (220°C) and line a 15 × 10-inch (38 × 25 cm) baking sheet with parchment paper, leaving extra overhang on the sides to make it easier to remove the pie.

6. **Make the Egg Wash:** In a small bowl, whisk together the egg and water; set aside.

Recipe continues . . .

PREP AHEAD
The pie dough can be prepared ahead through step 3; refrigerate for up to 3 days or freeze for up to 3 months. If frozen, thaw in the fridge overnight before rolling it out. The Apple Filling can be made ahead and stored in a resealable container in the fridge for up to 3 days or in the freezer for up to 3 months. If frozen, thaw in the fridge overnight before using.

STORAGE
Store the cooled pie, covered, at room temperature for up to 2 days, in the fridge for up to 5 days, or tightly wrapped in the freezer for up to 2 months. To reheat from frozen, preheat the oven to 350°F (180°C). Unwrap the pie and place it on a baking sheet, cover loosely with foil to prevent over-browning, and bake for 30 to 40 minutes, removing the foil for the last 10 to 15 minutes, until the pie is golden and the filling is bubbling.

FREEZER-FRIENDLY
Prepare the pie through step 10, then wrap tightly with plastic wrap and foil and store in the freezer for up to 2 months. Brush the frozen pie with the egg wash and sprinkle with coarse sugar. Bake from frozen in a 425°F (220°C) oven for 15 minutes, then reduce the oven temperature to 375°F (190°C) and continue baking for another 35 to 45 minutes until the pie is golden brown and the filling is bubbling. Let cool slightly in the pan before serving.

7. **Roll Out the Dough and Assemble the Slab Pie:** On a lightly -floured work surface, use a rolling pin to roll out 1 disc of dough into an 18 × 13-inch (46 × 33 cm) rectangle. Carefully roll the dough around the rolling pin, brushing off any excess flour. Unroll the dough over the prepared baking sheet, making sure the dough extends slightly over all sides of the pan. Gently tuck the dough into the edges of the pan.

8. Scrape the apple filling into the prepared pie crust, spreading in an even layer.

9. On a lightly floured surface, roll out the second disc of dough into an 18 × 13-inch (46 × 33 cm) rectangle. Using a pastry wheel or a pizza cutter, cut the dough lengthwise into long strips, about 1 inch (2.5 cm) wide. You can re-roll the scraps to make more strips of dough if you run short in step 10.

10. Lay half the strips diagonally across the entire pie, about 1 inch (2.5 cm) apart. Weave the remaining strips diagonally through the first strips to make a lattice pattern. Trim the lattice ends, leaving an overhang. Press together the ends and the edge of the bottom crust to seal, then fold and crimp the edge as desired.

11. Brush the lattice with the egg wash and finish with a sprinkle of coarse sugar.

12. Bake until the pastry is golden brown and the filling is bubbling, 30 to 40 minutes. Cool slightly in the pan before serving.

Vegan and Dairy-Free: Use vegan butter.

MAKE AHEAD | FREEZER-FRIENDLY

STRAWBERRY YOGURT LEMON LOAF

Vegetarian • Gluten-Free Option • Nut-Free

Serves 8 to 10

TIME
Prep: 15 MINUTES
Bake: 1 HOUR
Total: 1 HOUR 15 MINUTES

Strawberry Yogurt Loaf

- 2 cups (500 mL) + 1 tablespoon (15 mL) all-purpose flour, divided
- 1½ teaspoons (7 mL) baking powder
- 1 teaspoon (5 mL) baking soda
- ¼ teaspoon (1 mL) salt
- ½ cup (125 mL) full-fat vanilla Greek yogurt (I used 5%)
- 3 tablespoons (45 mL) lemon zest
- 1 tablespoon (15 mL) fresh lemon juice
- 2 teaspoons (10 mL) pure vanilla extract
- 1 cup (250 mL) finely diced fresh strawberries
- ¾ cup (175 mL) + 1 tablespoon (15 mL) sugar, divided
- ½ cup (125 mL) butter, room temperature
- 2 eggs

Lemon Glaze

- ½ cup (125 mL) icing sugar
- 1 tablespoon (15 mL) fresh lemon juice

STORAGE
Store the cooled loaf, with or without the glaze, in a resealable container in the fridge for up to 5 days or in the freezer for up to 3 months.

I have a soft spot for lemon loaf. If you do too, you'll want to make this moist and citrusy loaf. The combination of Greek yogurt, lemon zest, and juicy strawberries creates a soft, tender crumb with just the right amount of sweetness. Finished with a simple lemon glaze, it's perfect for an afternoon snack with a cup of tea or as a light dessert.

You will need 3 to 4 lemons for this recipe. Be sure to cut the strawberries small for best results.

1. Preheat the oven to 325°F (160°C) and line a 9 × 5-inch (2 L) loaf pan with parchment paper, leaving extra overhang on the sides to make it easier to remove the loaf.

2. In a medium bowl, stir together 2 cups (500 mL) of the flour, baking powder, baking soda, and salt.

3. In a small bowl, mix together the yogurt, lemon zest, lemon juice, and vanilla.

4. In a small bowl, combine the strawberries, remaining 1 tablespoon (15 mL) flour, and 1 tablespoon (15 mL) of the sugar and toss together.

5. In a large bowl using an electric mixer, or in the bowl of a stand mixer fitted with the paddle attachment, beat the butter with the remaining ¾ cup (175 mL) of the sugar on high speed until light and fluffy, about 2 minutes. Add the eggs, one at a time, beating well after each addition. While mixing on medium speed, add the flour mixture and yogurt mixture in two parts, alternating between them and mixing after each addition, until just combined, stopping to scrape down the sides of the bowl as needed. The batter will be thick. Fold in the strawberries.

6. Scrape the batter into the prepared loaf pan and spread evenly. Bake until the loaf is golden brown and a wooden skewer inserted into the centre comes out clean, about 60 minutes. Cool the loaf in the pan for 5 minutes, then carefully turn out onto a rack and cool completely before glazing.

7. **Make the Lemon Glaze:** In a small bowl, whisk together the icing sugar and lemon juice. Drizzle the glaze over the cooled loaf before serving.

Gluten-Free: Use a 1:1 gluten-free flour blend.

HONEY NUT CEREAL SQUARES

Vegan Option • Vegetarian Option • Dairy-Free Option • Gluten-Free Option

Makes 20 squares

TIME — *Prep:* 10 MINUTES, PLUS 30 MINUTES CHILLING

- ½ cup (125 mL) butter
- ½ cup (125 mL) pure liquid honey
- ¾ cup (175 mL) smooth natural peanut butter
- 2 cups (500 mL) mini marshmallows
- 1 teaspoon (5 mL) pure vanilla extract
- 4 cups (1 L) mixed unsweetened cereal
- 1 cup (250 mL) salted roasted peanuts
- Pinch of salt

STORAGE
Store the cut cooled squares in a resealable container in the fridge for up to 1 week or in the freezer for up to 3 months.

These crunchy, sweet peanut-buttery squares are pure snack-time gold. What I love most about this recipe is how it uses up all those leftover bits of cereal at the bottom of the boxes (you know the ones!). Easy to make and impossible to resist, they're the perfect no-bake treat for after-school snacks, something sweet and satisfying after dinner, or anytime cravings.

1. Grease a 9-inch (2.5 L) square cake pan and line it with parchment paper, leaving extra overhang on the sides to make it easier to remove the squares.

2. In a large pot over medium-low heat, melt the butter and honey and bring to a low boil, stirring occasionally. Cook for about 1 minute, until the butter starts to foam, then reduce the heat to low. Stir in the peanut butter and marshmallows and cook, stirring constantly, until the marshmallows have completely melted and the mixture is smooth. Remove from the heat and stir in the vanilla. Add the cereal, peanuts, and salt and stir to combine well.

3. Scrape the mixture into the prepared cake pan. Using wet hands or the bottom of a glass, firmly press the mixture evenly into the bottom of the pan. Transfer to the fridge and chill for at least 30 minutes. Cut into 20 squares.

Vegan: Use vegan butter and marshmallows. Use brown rice syrup instead of honey.

Vegetarian: Use vegan marshmallows.

Dairy-Free: Use vegan butter.

Gluten-Free: Use gluten-free cereal.

MAKE AHEAD | FREEZER-FRIENDLY

PEAR GINGERBREAD BUNDT CAKE

Vegan Option · Vegetarian · Dairy-Free Option · Gluten-Free Option · Nut-Free

Serves 10 to 12

TIME
Prep: 10 MINUTES
Bake: 50 MINUTES
Total: 1 HOUR

2½ cups (625 mL) all-purpose flour
¾ cup (175 mL) lightly packed brown sugar
4 teaspoons (20 mL) gingerbread spice
2 teaspoons (10 mL) baking powder
1½ teaspoons (7 mL) baking soda
¼ teaspoon (1 mL) salt
2 eggs
2 cups (500 mL) grated Bartlett pear
1 cup (250 mL) fancy molasses
½ cup (125 mL) canola oil or avocado oil
½ cup (125 mL) water
1 teaspoon (5 mL) pure vanilla extract

Spiced Chantilly Whipped Cream

2 cups (500 mL) heavy (35%) cream
¼ cup (60 mL) sugar
1 teaspoon (5 mL) pure vanilla extract
½ teaspoon (2 mL) gingerbread spice

STORAGE
Store the cooled cake, covered, at room temperature for up to 4 days or in a resealable container in the freezer for up to 3 months. Store the Spiced Chantilly Whipped Cream in a resealable container in the fridge for up to 2 days or up to 4 days if a stabilizer is used.

This moist and utterly mouthwatering and showy festive Bundt cake is packed with holiday gingerbread flavours and earned five-star reviews from all our recipe testers! If you don't own a Bundt pan, you can divide the batter between two 8-inch (1.2 L) round cake pans and reduce the bake time to about 35 minutes or until a wooden skewer inserted into the centre comes out clean. To show off the Bundt cake pattern, lightly dust the cooled cake with icing sugar.

1. Preheat the oven to 350°F (180°C) and spray a 10-cup (2.5 L) Bundt pan with cooking spray.

2. In a large bowl, whisk together the flour, brown sugar, gingerbread spice, baking powder, baking soda, and salt.

3. In a medium bowl, whisk the eggs. Add the grated pear, molasses, canola oil, water, and vanilla and stir to combine.

4. Add the wet ingredients to the dry ingredients and stir to combine.

5. Pour the batter into the prepared pan and smooth the top. Bake until a wooden skewer inserted into the centre comes out clean, and the cake pulls away slightly from the edge of the pan, about 50 minutes.

6. Cool the cake in the pan for 10 minutes before inverting onto a rack (tap the bottom of the pan to dislodge the cake) and cooling slightly.

7. **Make the Spiced Chantilly Whipped Cream:** In a medium bowl with tall sides, whip the cream on high speed until it starts to thicken. Add the sugar, vanilla, and gingerbread spice and continue to whip until stiff peaks form.

8. Serve the warm Bundt cake topped with the whipped cream.

Vegan: Use a store-bought egg replacer or Flax Eggs (page 317) to replace the eggs. Serve with coconut whipped cream instead of the Spiced Chantilly Whipped Cream.

Dairy-Free: Serve with coconut whipped cream instead of the Spiced Chantilly Whipped Cream.

Gluten-Free: Use a 1:1 gluten-free flour blend.

MAKE AHEAD | FREEZER-FRIENDLY

PUMPKIN CHEESECAKE BARS

Vegan Option • Vegetarian • Dairy-Free Option • Gluten-Free Option

Makes 24 bars

TIME
Prep: 20 MINUTES
Bake: 1 HOUR
Total: 1 HOUR 20 MINUTES

Base

2 cups (500 mL) graham cracker crumbs

½ cup (125 mL) butter, melted

½ teaspoon (2 mL) pumpkin pie spice

2 tablespoons (30 mL) sugar

Pinch of salt

Pumpkin Cheesecake Filling

1 cup (250 mL) raw cashews

1 cup (250 mL) canned pumpkin purée

1 container (8 ounces/225 g) cream cheese, room temperature

¾ cup (175 mL) pure maple syrup

1 package (300 g) soft tofu, drained

1 tablespoon (15 mL) pumpkin pie spice

2 teaspoons (10 mL) pure vanilla extract

For serving

Chantilly Cream (page 333) or coconut whipped cream

Cinnamon

STORAGE
Store cooled bars in a resealable container in the fridge for up to 5 days or in the freezer for up to 1 month.

These Pumpkin Cheesecake Bars are so dreamy, made with a blend of cashews, tofu, pumpkin purée, and cream cheese for the perfect balance of indulgence and feel-good ingredients. These creamy bars get better with time, if you can resist (no judgment if you can't!).

Be sure to buy unsweetened canned pumpkin purée, not pumpkin pie filling. Either regular cream cheese or vegan cream cheese works in this recipe.

1. In a small bowl, pour boiling water over the cashews to cover them completely. Let soak for at least 15 minutes. Drain the cashews.

2. Preheat the oven to 350°F (180°C). Grease a 13 × 9-inch (3.5 L) baking pan and line it with parchment paper, leaving extra overhang on the sides to make it easier to remove the bars.

3. **Make the Base:** In a large bowl, stir together the graham cracker crumbs, melted butter, pumpkin pie spice, sugar, and salt until combined. Transfer to the prepared pan. Using the bottom of a glass, firmly press the mixture evenly into the bottom of the pan. Bake for 10 minutes.

4. **Meanwhile, make the Pumpkin Cheesecake Filling:** In a high-speed blender, combine the drained cashews, pumpkin purée, cream cheese, maple syrup, tofu, pumpkin pie spice, and vanilla. Blend until smooth, about 1 minute, scraping down the sides once halfway through.

5. Pour the filling into the prepared crust and evenly spread with a rubber spatula. Firmly tap the pan on the counter a few times to remove any air bubbles.

6. Bake until the edges are light golden brown and slightly pull away from the pan and the filling is set in the centre, about 1 hour. (If you give the pan a gentle shake back and forth, the filling shouldn't jiggle.) Let the bars cool completely in the pan, then cover with plastic wrap and chill in the fridge for at least 4 hours. Cut into 24 bars.

7. When ready to serve, top the bars with a dollop of Chantilly Cream and a sprinkle of cinnamon.

Vegan: Use vegan graham crackers, vegan butter, and vegan cream cheese. Top with coconut whipped cream.

Dairy-Free: Use vegan butter and vegan cream cheese. Top with coconut whipped cream.

Gluten-Free: Use gluten-free graham crackers.

MAKE AHEAD | FREEZER-FRIENDLY

DEEP-DISH CHOCOLATE BANANA CAKE

Vegan Option • Vegetarian • Dairy-Free Option • Gluten-Free Option • Nut-Free

Serves 12

TIME
Prep: 15 MINUTES
Bake: 30 MINUTES
Total: 45 MINUTES

Growing up in the '80s, I used to enjoy store-bought Deep'n Delicious cakes straight from the freezer as a delightful dessert. Inspired by those cherished memories, I've crafted a healthier alternative that boasts moist, chocolaty goodness—dare I say, even better than the version from my childhood. I prefer using Dutch-process cocoa powder to give this cake a dark and rich flavour. Instead of icing the cake, you can top it with heaps of lightly sweetened whipped cream and slices of fresh banana—an irresistible combination that elevates it to dessert perfection.

2 eggs

2 cups (500 mL) mashed ripe banana (about 4 large; see Tip)

¾ cup (175 mL) avocado oil or canola oil

2 teaspoons (10 mL) pure vanilla extract

2 cups (500 mL) all-purpose flour

¾ cup (175 mL) lightly packed brown sugar

½ cup (125 mL) Dutch-process cocoa powder, sifted

2 teaspoons (10 mL) baking powder

¼ teaspoon (1 mL) salt

2 tablespoons (30 mL) 2% milk

1 teaspoon (5 mL) baking soda

½ cup (125 mL) semisweet chocolate chips

Chocolate Icing (optional)

½ cup (125 mL) butter, room temperature

2 cups (500 mL) icing sugar

1 tablespoon (15 mL) Dutch-process cocoa powder, sifted

1 teaspoon (5 mL) pure vanilla extract

½ to 1 tablespoon (7 to 15 mL) 2% milk

1. Preheat the oven to 350°F (180°C) and grease a 13 × 9-inch (3.5 L) baking dish (or pan).

2. In a large bowl, whisk the eggs. Add the mashed banana, avocado oil, and vanilla. Stir to combine well.

3. In a medium bowl, whisk together the flour, brown sugar, cocoa powder, baking powder, and salt until well combined.

4. In a small microwave-safe bowl, microwave the milk until hot, about 30 seconds. Stir in the baking soda; it will froth up. Add to the banana mixture along with the dry ingredients and fold until combined. Fold in the chocolate chips. Pour the batter into the prepared baking dish (or pan) and smooth the top.

5. Bake until the cake slightly pulls away from the edges and a wooden skewer inserted into the centre comes out clean, about 30 minutes. Cool completely in the baking dish (or pan) before icing.

6. **Make the Chocolate Icing (if using):** In a medium bowl, using an electric mixer, beat the butter on high speed until light and fluffy, about 2 minutes. Add the icing sugar, cocoa powder, and vanilla and beat until light and fluffy, about 2 minutes. Add a drizzle of milk, 1 teaspoon (5 mL) at a time, adding just enough to make the icing spreadable.

7. Ice the cooled cake using an offset spatula or transfer the icing into a piping bag fitted with a star tip and decorate the cake as desired.

Vegan: Use a store-bought egg replacer or Flax Eggs (page 317) instead of eggs. Use non-dairy milk, dairy-free chocolate chips, and vegan butter.

Dairy-Free: Use non-dairy milk, dairy-free chocolate chips, and vegan butter.

Gluten-Free: Use a 1:1 gluten-free flour blend.

STORAGE
Store the iced cake in a resealable container in the fridge for up to 5 days or in the freezer for up to 1 month.

Tips

- For the best consistency, use an immersion blender to blend the bananas instead of mashing them.
- To make cupcakes, reduce the baking times to about 18 minutes.

MAKE AHEAD | FREEZER-FRIENDLY

OLD-FASHIONED COCONUT OATMEAL COOKIE BARS

Vegetarian • *Dairy-Free Option* • *Gluten-Free Option* • *Nut-Free*

Makes 24 bars

TIME
Prep: 10 MINUTES
Bake: 15 MINUTES
Total: 25 MINUTES

1 cup (250 mL) butter, room temperature

½ cup (125 mL) white sugar

½ cup (125 mL) lightly packed brown sugar

2 eggs

1 egg yolk

1 tablespoon (15 mL) pure vanilla extract

1½ cups (375 mL) quick rolled oats

1¼ cups (300 mL) all-purpose flour

1 cup (250 mL) sweetened shredded coconut

¼ cup (60 mL) ground flaxseed

1 teaspoon (5 mL) cinnamon

1 teaspoon (5 mL) baking soda

½ teaspoon (2 mL) salt

1 cup (250 mL) semisweet chocolate chips or raisins (see Tip)

I took a simple coconut oatmeal cookie recipe from my mom's collection that was handed down through the generations and turned it into bars. Perfectly chewy but crisp on the edges, and with a touch of coconut, these bars are a crowd-pleaser!

1. Preheat the oven to 350°F (180°C) and line a 15 × 10-inch (38 × 25 cm) baking sheet with parchment paper, leaving extra overhang on the sides to make it easier to remove the bars.

2. In a large bowl, using an electric mixer, beat the butter with the white sugar and brown sugar on medium-high speed until light and fluffy, about 2 minutes. Beat in the eggs, one at a time, then the egg yolk, beating until well combined. Add the vanilla and beat until smooth.

3. Add the oats, flour, coconut, ground flaxseed, cinnamon, baking soda, and salt and beat until well combined, about 2 minutes. Stir in the chocolate chips or raisins until combined.

4. Using a large cookie scoop, scoop the dough into evenly spaced mounds on the prepared baking sheet. Using wet hands, press the dough to flatten into an even layer; the dough will be soft.

5. Bake until golden brown around the edges, about 15 minutes, rotating the pan halfway through. Cool in the pan for 10 minutes. Use the overhanging parchment paper to gently lift the bars out of the pan onto a rack to cool completely. Cut into 24 bars.

Dairy-Free: Use vegan butter and dairy-free chocolate, if using.

Gluten-Free: Use a 1:1 gluten-free flour blend. Use certified gluten-free oats.

Tips

• To plump up raisins that are too dry, place the raisins in a small bowl, pour boiling water over them, and let them soak for 10 minutes. Drain well and pat dry before stirring into the cookie dough.

• To make cupcakes, reduce the baking time to about 13 minutes.

STORAGE

Store cut cooled bars in a resealable container at room temperature for up to 1 week or in the freezer for up to 2 months.

FREEZER-FRIENDLY

The unbaked bar slab can be frozen, wrapped well, for up to 3 months. Alternatively, the dough can be frozen in individual cookie portions. Simply line a baking sheet with parchment paper and scoop cookie-size portions of dough onto the sheet. Transfer to the freezer until frozen. Transfer the dough portions to a resealable bag and store in the freezer for up to 3 months. To bake from frozen, place the dough portions on a baking sheet lined with parchment paper, spaced about 2 inches (5 cm) apart and bake in a 350°F (180°C) oven until golden brown around the edges, about 13 minutes.

MAKE AHEAD | FREEZER-FRIENDLY

PINEAPPLE BANANA COCONUT CAKE

Vegan Option • Vegetarian • Dairy-Free Option • Gluten-Free Option • Nut-Free

Serves 8 to 12

TIME

Prep: 10 MINUTES (NOT INCLUDING MAKING THE CHANTILLY CREAM)

Bake: 30 MINUTES

Total: 40 MINUTES

- ¾ cup (175 mL) butter, room temperature
- ¾ cup (175 mL) lightly packed brown sugar
- 3 eggs
- 1½ cups (375 mL) all-purpose flour
- ¾ cup (175 mL) whole wheat flour
- ¾ cup (175 mL) sweetened shredded coconut, toasted
- 2 teaspoons (10 mL) baking powder
- ¼ teaspoon (1 mL) salt
- 2 tablespoons (30 mL) 2% milk
- 1 teaspoon (5 mL) baking soda
- 1 cup (250 mL) canned crushed pineapple (do not drain)
- ¾ cup (175 mL) mashed ripe banana
- 2 teaspoons (10 mL) pure vanilla extract

For serving

- Chantilly Cream (page 333) or coconut whipped cream
- ½ cup (125 mL) sweetened shredded coconut, toasted

STORAGE

Store the cooled cake in a resealable container at room temperature for up to 5 days or in the freezer for up to 1 month. Store the Chantilly Cream in a resealable container in the fridge for up to 2 days.

This cake will make any moment feel special. Made with a wholesome mix of whole wheat and all-purpose flour, toasted coconut, crushed pineapple, and mashed banana, it's incredibly moist, freezes well, and is packed with tropical flavour. I top it with fluffy Chantilly cream and finish with a sprinkle of toasted coconut, but the cake tastes wonderful all on its own.

1. Preheat the oven to 350°F (180°C) and grease a 13 × 9-inch (3.5 L) baking dish (or pan).

2. In a large bowl, using an electric mixer, beat the butter with the brown sugar on medium-high speed until light and fluffy, about 2 minutes. Beat in the eggs, one at a time, and beat until well incorporated and smooth.

3. In a medium bowl, whisk together the all-purpose flour, whole wheat flour, coconut, baking powder, and salt.

4. In a small microwave-safe bowl, microwave the milk until hot, about 30 seconds. Stir in the baking soda; it will froth up. Add to the wet ingredients along with the dry ingredients, pineapple with its juice, banana, and vanilla. Using the electric mixer, mix on medium speed until combined, scraping down the sides of the bowl with a rubber spatula halfway through.

5. Scrape the batter into the prepared baking dish (or pan) and smooth the top. Bake until golden brown around the edges and a wooden skewer inserted into the centre comes out clean, 30 to 35 minutes. Set aside to cool completely in the dish or (pan).

6. When ready to serve, spread the Chantilly Cream evenly over the cake and sprinkle the toasted coconut on top.

Vegan: Use vegan butter. Use a store-bought egg replacer or Flax Eggs (page 317) instead of eggs. Use non-dairy milk. Top with coconut whipped cream.

Dairy-Free: Use vegan butter and non-dairy milk. Top with coconut whipped cream.

Gluten-Free: Use a 1:1 gluten-free flour blend instead of all-purpose flour and whole wheat flour.

Tip

To make cupcakes, reduce the baking time to about 20 minutes.

MAKE AHEAD | FREEZER-FRIENDLY

TRIPLE BERRY COCONUT CRISP

Vegan Option • Vegetarian • Dairy-Free Option • Gluten-Free Option • Nut-Free Option

Serves 8 to 10

TIME	
Prep:	10 MINUTES
Bake:	50 MINUTES
Total:	1 HOUR

Coconut Oat Layer

1 cup (250 mL) old-fashioned rolled oats

½ cup (125 mL) unsweetened shredded coconut

½ cup (125 mL) chopped raw pecans

¼ cup (60 mL) whole wheat flour

¼ cup (60 mL) hemp hearts

¼ cup (60 mL) butter, melted

¼ cup (60 mL) pure maple syrup

1 teaspoon (5 mL) cinnamon

1 teaspoon (5 mL) pure vanilla extract

¼ teaspoon (1 mL) salt

Berry Layer

8 cups (2 L) mixed frozen berries

½ cup (125 mL) pure maple syrup

6 tablespoons (90 mL) cornstarch

¼ cup (60 mL) fresh lemon juice

Vanilla ice cream or vanilla Greek yogurt, for serving (optional)

Is it breakfast or is it dessert? Flip a coin to decide if you must, but in my home it's a toss-up. Lightly sweetened with maple syrup and topped with a mixture that tastes like a coconut cookie, this tastes delicious on its own or with a scoop of vanilla yogurt or ice cream.

If making this for a breakfast or simply if you prefer a less sweet dessert, you may reduce the maple syrup in the berry layer by half.

1. Preheat the oven to 350°F (180°C) and grease a 13 × 9-inch (3.5 L) baking dish.

2. **Make the Coconut Oat Layer:** In a medium bowl, combine the oats, coconut, pecans, flour, hemp hearts, melted butter, maple syrup, cinnamon, vanilla, and salt. Stir to combine.

3. **Make the Berry Layer:** In a large bowl, combine the berries, maple syrup, cornstarch, and lemon juice. Stir to combine.

4. Scrape the berry mixture into the prepared baking dish. Sprinkle evenly with the coconut oat mixture. Bake until the topping is golden brown and the berry mixture bubbles, about 50 minutes. Serve warm with a scoop of ice cream or yogurt if desired.

Vegan and Dairy-Free: Use vegan butter. Serve with vegan vanilla ice cream or vegan vanilla yogurt.

Gluten-Free: Use certified gluten-free oats.

Nut-Free: Omit the pecans.

STORAGE

Store the cooled crisp, covered, in the fridge for up to 5 days.

FREEZER-FRIENDLY

Assemble the crisp in advance, tightly cover, and freeze until ready to bake. You may also divide the crisp into 2 smaller pans and freeze to have a ready-to-bake dessert for smaller crowds. To bake from frozen, uncover and bake as directed.

MAKE AHEAD | FREEZER-FRIENDLY

NO-BAKE CHOCOLATE CHEESECAKE JARS

Vegan Option • Vegetarian • Dairy-Free Option • Gluten-Free Option • Nut-Free

Makes 8 (1-cup/250 mL) jars

TIME *Prep:* 15 MINUTES, PLUS 3 HOURS CHILLING

Chocolate Crust

1½ cups (375 mL) chocolate cookie crumbs

½ cup (125 mL) butter, melted

1 tablespoon (30 mL) sugar

Chocolate Cheesecake Filling

1 cup (250 mL) heavy (35%) cream

2 packages (8 ounces/250 g each) cream cheese, room temperature

½ cup (125 mL) sugar

2 tablespoons (30 mL) cocoa powder, sifted

2 teaspoons (10 mL) pure vanilla extract

1 cup (250 mL) semisweet chocolate chips

For serving

Whipped cream

Cocoa powder or shaved chocolate

STORAGE

Store cheesecakes, without the toppings, covered, in the fridge for up to 1 week or in the freezer for up to 1 month.

These no-bake cheesecakes are the ultimate shortcut to a creamy, dreamy dessert without the hassle of baking. They're lighter, quicker, and just as delicious as traditional cheesecake, but without all the fuss. Plus, how about that storage? Making them in jars turns them into the perfect individual-size treat, making cleanup a breeze and keeping them fresh for later.

1. **Make the Chocolate Crust:** In a medium bowl, stir together the chocolate cookie crumbs, melted butter, and sugar. Divide the mixture evenly among eight 1-cup (250 mL) mason jars (about 3 tablespoons/45 mL per jar). Press lightly into the bottom of the jars with the back of a small spoon.

2. **Make the Chocolate Cheesecake Filling:** In a medium bowl, whip the cream until stiff peaks form. Set aside.

3. In a large bowl, with the electric mixer, beat the cream cheese until light and fluffy. Add the sugar, cocoa powder, and vanilla and beat on high speed until smooth.

4. Melt the chocolate chips in a microwave-safe bowl in 30-second increments, stirring between each increment, until melted. Add the melted chocolate to the cream cheese mixture and beat to combine. Fold in the whipped cream to combine.

5. Divide the cheesecake mixture evenly among the prepared jars (about ½ cup/125 mL per jar), cover with lids, and refrigerate for at least 3 hours or overnight.

6. Before serving, top each jar with a dollop of whipped cream and a dusting of cocoa powder if desired.

Vegan and Dairy-Free: Use vegan chocolate cookie crumbs, vegan butter, and vegan cream cheese. Use 2 cups (500 mL) of coconut whipped cream instead of the heavy cream (fold in, no need to whip). Use dairy-free chocolate chips. Serve with coconut whipped cream and cocoa powder instead of shaved chocolate.

Gluten-Free: Use gluten-free chocolate cookie crumbs.

MAKE AHEAD | FREEZER-FRIENDLY

NO-BAKE STRAWBERRY YOGURT CHEESECAKE JARS

Vegan Option • Vegetarian • Dairy-Free Option • Gluten-Free Option • Nut-Free

Makes 8 jars (1 cup/250 mL each)

TIME *Prep:* 15 MINUTES, PLUS 3 HOURS CHILLING

1½ cups (375 mL) graham cracker crumbs

½ cup (125 mL) butter, melted

2 tablespoons (30 mL) lightly packed brown sugar

1 cup (250 mL) heavy (35%) cream

1 package (8 ounces/250 g) cream cheese, room temperature

1 cup (250 mL) plain 2% Greek yogurt

½ cup (125 mL) white sugar

1 teaspoon (5 mL) pure vanilla extract

1 teaspoon (5 mL) lemon zest (optional)

Fresh berries, for serving

STORAGE
Store cheesecakes, without berries, covered, in the fridge for up to 1 week or in the freezer for up to 1 month.

I'm rather famous for my no-bake cheesecake, and this is a slightly lightened-up version that uses yogurt to create the cutest individual cheesecakes to put smiles on faces. These make-ahead light and fluffy jars of cheesecake are ideal for entertaining or simply for a sweet something when the craving hits. Topped with mounds of fresh berries, this is my kind of dessert.

1. In a medium bowl, stir together the graham cracker crumbs, melted butter, and brown sugar. Divide the mixture evenly among 8 small mason jars (about 3 tablespoons/45 mL per jar). Press lightly into the bottom of the jars using a small spoon.

2. In a medium bowl, with an electric mixer, whip the cream until stiff peaks form.

3. In a separate medium bowl, with the electric mixer, beat the cream cheese until light and fluffy. Add the yogurt, white sugar, vanilla, and lemon zest (if using) and mix until smooth. Fold in the whipped cream to combine.

4. Divide the cheesecake mixture evenly among the prepared jars (about ½ cup/125 mL per jar), cover with lids, and refrigerate for at least 3 hours or overnight

5. Before serving, top each jar with fresh berries.

Vegan and Dairy-Free: Use vegan graham crumbs, vegan butter, vegan cream cheese, and vegan yogurt. Use 2 cups (500 mL) of coconut whipped cream instead of the heavy cream (fold in; no need to whip).

Gluten-Free: Use gluten-free graham crumbs.

MAKE AHEAD | FREEZER-FRIENDLY

CHOCOLATE PEANUT BUTTER QUINOA BARS

Vegan Option · Vegetarian · Dairy-Free Option · Gluten-Free · Nut-Free Option

Makes 16 bars

TIME *Prep:* 15 MINUTES, PLUS 30 MINUTES CHILLING

1 cup (250 mL) white quinoa

1 cup (250 mL) smooth natural peanut butter

¾ cup (175 mL) dark chocolate chips

¼ cup (60 mL) hemp hearts

¼ cup (60 mL) pure maple syrup

¼ cup (60 mL) coconut oil

1 teaspoon (5 mL) pure vanilla extract

Pinch of salt

2½ cups (625 mL) puffed rice cereal

STORAGE
Store cut bars in a resealable container in the fridge for up to 1 week or in the freezer for up to 2 months.

Quinoa and peanut butter might seem an unlikely pairing, but they are a match made in snack heaven! These naturally gluten-free bars are the perfect combination of nutty, crispy, and chocolaty goodness. They store for a week in the fridge or even longer in the freezer, but I'm willing to bet they won't last that long.

1. Line a 9-inch (2.5 L) square baking pan with parchment paper, leaving extra overhang on the sides to make it easier to remove the bars.

2. In a heavy medium pot over medium heat, toast the quinoa, shaking the pan every few seconds, until the quinoa is light golden brown and pops, 3 to 4 minutes. Reduce the heat to low and stir in the peanut butter, chocolate chips, hemp hearts, maple syrup, coconut oil, vanilla, and salt. Cook, stirring constantly, until smooth. Remove from the heat and stir in the puffed rice. Immediately scrape the mixture into the prepared pan and smooth into an even layer. Transfer to the fridge and chill for at least 30 minutes before cutting into 16 bars.

Vegan and Dairy-Free: Use dairy-free chocolate chips.

Nut-Free: Use tahini instead of peanut butter.

MAKE AHEAD | FREEZER-FRIENDLY

CINNAMON ROLL BUNDT CAKE

Vegetarian • Gluten-Free Option • Nut-Free

Serves 12

TIME	
Prep:	10 MINUTES
Bake:	35 MINUTES
Total:	45 MINUTES

Cinnamon Sugar

¼ cup (60 mL) sugar

1 tablespoon (15 mL) cinnamon

Cake

2 cups (500 mL) all-purpose flour

1 teaspoon (5 mL) baking powder

1 teaspoon (5 mL) baking soda

⅛ teaspoon (0.5 mL) salt

½ cup (125 mL) butter, room temperature

¾ cup (175 mL) sugar

2 eggs

¾ cup (175 mL) buttermilk

½ cup (125 mL) vanilla Greek yogurt

2 teaspoons (10 mL) pure vanilla extract

STORAGE

Store cooled cake in a resealable container in the fridge for up to 4 days or in the freezer for up to 1 month.

This Bundt is as simple as it gets when it comes to baking while still delivering that warm, comforting cinnamon roll flavour you know and love. Made with buttermilk and Greek yogurt to keep it moist and tender, this cake is easy to whip up and perfect for any occasion, from enjoying with your favourite tea to sharing with loved ones. Top with extra cinnamon sugar for that sweet finish or lightly dust with icing sugar. No fancy techniques required!

1. **Make the Cinnamon Sugar:** Stir together the sugar and cinnamon in a small bowl. Set aside.

2. **Make the Cake:** Preheat the oven to 350°F (180°C) and grease a 10-cup (2.5 L) Bundt pan with cooking spray.

3. In a medium bowl, whisk together the flour, baking powder, baking soda, and salt.

4. In a large bowl, with an electric mixer, or in a stand mixer fitted with the paddle attachment, beat the butter and sugar on high speed until light and fluffy, about 2 minutes. Add the eggs, one at a time, and beat after each addition until incorporated. Add the buttermilk, Greek yogurt, vanilla, and the flour mixture, and beat on low speed until smooth, scraping down the sides of the bowl with a rubber spatula as needed. The batter will be thick.

5. Scrape about half of the batter into the prepared pan and spread in an even layer. Sprinkle about half of the cinnamon sugar evenly over the batter. Using a spoon, drop heaping spoonfuls of the remaining batter on top. Sprinkle with the remaining cinnamon sugar. Using a rubber spatula, press and swirl the batter to incorporate the cinnamon sugar through the top and middle layer. Smooth the top.

6. Bake until golden brown and a wooden skewer inserted into the centre comes out clean, about 35 minutes. Cool the cake in the pan for 5 minutes, then invert onto a rack (tap the bottom of the pan to dislodge the cake) and cool completely.

Gluten-Free: Use a 1:1 gluten-free flour blend.

MAKE AHEAD | FREEZER-FRIENDLY

ORANGE CREAMSICLE CAKE

Vegan Option • Vegetarian • Dairy-Free Option • Gluten-Free Option • Nut-Free

Serves 12

TIME
Prep: 15 MINUTES
Bake: 25 MINUTES
Total: 40 MINUTES

Orange Creamsicle Cake

2 cups (500 mL) all-purpose flour
½ cup (125 mL) sugar
1 teaspoon (5 mL) baking powder
1 teaspoon (5 mL) baking soda
¼ teaspoon (1 mL) salt
2 eggs
1 cup (250 mL) plain full-fat Greek yogurt (2% or higher)
½ cup (125 mL) butter, melted
2 tablespoons (30 mL) packed orange zest
⅓ cup (75 mL) fresh orange juice
¼ cup (60 mL) pure liquid honey
1 teaspoon (5 mL) pure vanilla extract

Yogurt Cream Cheese Icing

½ cup (125 mL) cream cheese, room temperature
¼ cup (60 mL) plain full-fat Greek yogurt (2% or higher)
1 cup (250 mL) icing sugar, sifted
1 teaspoon (5 mL) packed orange zest
1 teaspoon (5 mL) pure vanilla extract

STORAGE
Store the cooled iced cake in a resealable container in the fridge for up to 1 week or in the freezer for up to 1 month.

I can almost hear the ice cream truck rolling into my neighbourhood just thinking about this dreamy cake. This cake captures all the nostalgia of that classic frozen treat with the perfect blend of Greek yogurt and orange; every bite tastes like summer. Topped with a creamy Yogurt Cream Cheese Icing, it's refreshing, light, and just the right amount of sweet. This is a recipe destined to bring smiles to any celebration, big or small, and it's impressively simple to make.

1. Preheat the oven to 350°F (180°C) and grease a 13 × 9-inch (3.5 L) baking dish (or pan).

2. In a large bowl, whisk together the flour, sugar, baking powder, baking soda, and salt.

3. In a medium bowl, whisk the eggs. Add the yogurt, melted butter, orange zest, orange juice, honey, and vanilla and whisk to combine.

4. Add the wet ingredients to the dry ingredients and stir with a rubber spatula just to combine; do not overmix. The batter will be quite thick.

5. Scrape the batter into the prepared baking dish (or pan) and smooth the top with the back of a rubber spatula. Bake until the cake is golden brown and springs back when lightly touched, and a wooden skewer inserted into the centre comes out clean, about 25 minutes. Cool the cake completely in the dish (or pan) before icing.

6. **Make the Yogurt Cream Cheese Icing:** In a medium bowl, combine the cream cheese, yogurt, icing sugar, orange zest, and vanilla. Using an electric mixer, beat on high speed until smooth and light, about 2 minutes. Store, covered, in the fridge until ready to use.

7. Spread the Yogurt Cream Cheese Icing over the cooled cake.

Vegan and Dairy-Free: Use dairy-free yogurt and vegan cream cheese. Use vegan butter.

Gluten-Free: Use a 1:1 gluten-free flour blend.

MAKE AHEAD | FREEZER-FRIENDLY

APPLE TURNOVERS

Vegan Option · *Vegetarian* · *Gluten-Free Option* · *Nut-Free*

Makes 8 turnovers

TIME	
Prep:	30 MINUTES
Bake:	15 MINUTES
Total:	45 MINUTES

6 cups (1.5 L) thinly sliced peeled Gala apples (about 5 apples)

¾ cup (175 mL) lightly packed brown sugar

2 tablespoons (30 mL) butter

1 tablespoon (15 mL) fresh lemon juice

1 tablespoon (15 mL) all-purpose flour

1½ teaspoons (7 mL) cinnamon

Pinch of salt

1 package (14 ounces/400 g) frozen puff pastry, thawed

Egg Wash

1 egg

1 tablespoon (15 mL) water

Glaze (optional)

½ cup (125 mL) icing sugar

1 tablespoon (15 mL) 2% milk

¼ teaspoon (1 mL) pure vanilla extract

STORAGE

Store cooled glazed turnovers in a resealable container at room temperature for up to 3 days or in the freezer for up to 1 month.

Turnovers are little pockets of joy—flaky, golden pastry filled with warm cinnamon-spiced apples. A touch of lemon adds brightness to the sweet, buttery filling, making these treats as delicious as they are portable—perfect for a picnic or an afternoon tea with friends. Serve them warm with a scoop of vanilla ice cream for an added touch.

1. Position the oven racks in the upper and lower thirds of the oven and preheat to 400°F (200°C). Line 2 baking sheets with parchment paper.

2. **Make the Filling:** In a medium saucepan, combine the apples, brown sugar, butter, lemon juice, flour, cinnamon, and salt. Cook over medium-low heat, stirring occasionally, until the apples have softened, 15 to 20 minutes. Remove from the heat and let cool.

3. **Make the Egg Wash:** In a small bowl, whisk together the egg and water.

4. **Roll Out the Pastry and Assemble the Turnovers:** On a lightly floured surface with a lightly floured rolling pin, roll out a sheet of puff pastry into a 10- to 12-inch (25 to 30 cm) square. Using a sharp knife or pizza cutter, cut the pastry into 4 squares. Place about 3 tablespoons (45 mL) of apple filling in the centre of each square. Lightly brush the edges with egg wash and fold half of the pastry square over the filing, forming a triangle. Trim the pastry edges, then press the edges with a fork to tightly seal. Using a metal spatula, transfer the turnovers to a prepared baking sheet. Repeat with the second sheet of pastry and remaining filling, arranging turnovers on the second baking sheet. Lightly brush the tops of the turnovers with the egg wash.

5. Bake until golden brown, 15 to 18 minutes, rotating the pans halfway through. Transfer the turnovers to a rack and cool slightly.

6. **Make the Glaze:** In a small bowl, whisk together the icing sugar, milk, and vanilla. Drizzle the glaze over the turnovers.

Vegan: Use vegan puff pastry and vegan butter. Use unsweetened plant-based milk.

Gluten-Free: Use gluten-free puff pastry.

Step-by-step photography continues . . .

MAKE AHEAD | FREEZER-FRIENDLY

CHERRY TURNOVERS

Vegan Option • Vegetarian • Gluten-Free Option • Nut-Free

Makes 8 turnovers

TIME
Prep: 15 MINUTES
Bake: 15 MINUTES
Total: 30 MINUTES

- 4 cups (1 L) fresh or frozen sweet cherries, pitted and halved
- ¼ cup (60 mL) sugar
- 1 tablespoon (15 mL) fresh lemon juice
- 1½ teaspoons (7 mL) cornstarch
- 1 tablespoon (15 mL) water
- 1 package (14 ounces/400 g) frozen puff pastry, thawed

Egg Wash

- 1 egg
- 1 tablespoon (15 mL) water

Glaze (optional)

- ½ cup (125 mL) icing sugar
- 1 tablespoon (15 mL) milk
- ¼ teaspoon (1 mL) pure vanilla extract

STORAGE
Store cooled glazed turnovers in a resealable container at room temperature for up to 3 days or in the freezer for up to 1 month.

These cherry turnovers are the kind of treat that feel fancy but are secretly so simple to make. Flaky, golden pastry wrapped around a sweet-tart cherry filling—what's not to love? Whether you serve them warm out of the oven or pack them for a picnic or coffee date, they're guaranteed to impress.

1. Position the oven racks in the upper and lower thirds of the oven and preheat to 400°F (200°C). Line 2 baking sheets with parchment paper.

2. **Make the Filling:** In a medium saucepan, combine the cherries, sugar, and lemon juice. Cook over medium heat, stirring occasionally, until bubbly and the cherries have softened, 5 to 7 minutes.

3. In a small bowl, whisk together the cornstarch and water. Stir the mixture into the cherries and simmer until the filling thickens, about 2 minutes. Remove from the heat and let cool.

4. **Make the Egg Wash:** In a small bowl, whisk together the egg and water.

5. **Roll Out the Pastry and Assemble the Turnovers:** On a lightly floured surface with a lightly floured rolling pin, roll out a sheet of puff pastry into a 10- to 12-inch (25 to 30 cm) square. Using a sharp knife or pizza cutter, cut the pastry into 4 squares. Place about 3 tablespoons (45 mL) of cherry filling in the centre of each square. Lightly brush the edges with egg wash and fold half of the pastry square over the filling, forming a triangle. Trim the pastry edges, then press the edges with a fork to tightly seal. Using a metal spatula, transfer the turnovers to a prepared baking sheet. Repeat with the second sheet of pastry and remaining filling, arranging turnovers on the second baking sheet. Lightly brush the tops of the turnovers with the egg wash.

6. Bake until golden brown, 15 to 18 minutes, rotating the pans halfway through. Transfer the turnovers to a rack and cool slightly.

7. **Make the Glaze (optional):** In a small bowl, whisk together the icing sugar, milk, and vanilla. Drizzle the glaze over the turnovers.

Vegan: Use vegan puff pastry and vegan butter. Use unsweetened plant-based milk.

Gluten-Free: Use gluten-free puff pastry.

Step-by-step photography continues . . .

STAPLES

MAKE AHEAD | FREEZER-FRIENDLY

PROTEIN CRUNCH SALAD TOPPER

Vegan Option • Vegetarian • Dairy-Free Option • Gluten-Free • Nut-Free Option

Makes 3 cups (750 mL)

TIME
Prep: 5 MINUTES
Cook: 10 MINUTES
Total: 15 MINUTES

¾ cup (175 mL) raw almonds
¾ cup (175 mL) raw pecans
½ cup (125 mL) raw pumpkin seeds
¼ cup (60 mL) raw sunflower seeds
¼ cup (60 mL) hemp hearts
2 tablespoons (30 mL) butter, melted
¼ cup (60 mL) pure maple syrup
¼ teaspoon (1 mL) salt
¼ teaspoon (1 mL) cayenne pepper (optional)

STORAGE
Store cooled salad topper in a resealable container at room temperature for up to 1 month or in the freezer for up to 3 months. If the mixture gets soft during storage, simply heat on a baking sheet in a 350°F (180°C) oven for 3 to 4 minutes.

This protein topper solves the boring salad dilemma and will be your best friend when it comes to eating (and enjoying) more salads. It's perfectly sweet, salty, crunchy, and nourishing. This also tastes amazing (without the cayenne pepper) as a topper for Greek yogurt with berries.

1. Preheat the oven to 350°F (180°C) and line a baking sheet with parchment paper.

2. In a food processor, combine the almonds, pecans, pumpkin seeds, and sunflower seeds. Pulse just until finely chopped. Transfer to a medium bowl.

3. Add the hemp hearts, melted butter, maple syrup, salt, and cayenne (if using) and toss until well combined. Transfer the mixture to the prepared baking sheet and spread in an even layer.

4. Bake until golden brown, 10 to 12 minutes, stirring halfway through. Cool completely on the baking sheet (it will harden as it cools).

Vegan: Use vegan butter.

Dairy-Free: Use vegan butter.

Nut-Free: Use the same volume of seeds of your choice to replace the almonds and pecans.

MAKE AHEAD | FREEZER-FRIENDLY

SOS SPAGHETTI SAUCE

Vegan · Vegetarian · Dairy-Free · Gluten-Free · Nut-Free

Makes 4 cups (1 L)

TIME — *Prep:* 5 MINUTES

- 1 can (28 ounces/796 mL) good-quality crushed tomatoes
- 1 can (5.5 ounces/156 mL) tomato paste
- 2 cloves garlic, minced
- 2 tablespoons (30 mL) extra-virgin olive oil
- 1 tablespoon (15 mL) dried oregano
- 1 teaspoon (5 mL) Italian seasoning
- 1 teaspoon (5 mL) red wine vinegar
- ½ teaspoon (2 mL) sugar
- ½ teaspoon (2 mL) salt

For those nights when you don't have a jar of marinara sauce on hand, this no-cook spaghetti sauce uses simple pantry ingredients and can be ready in a snap. It also doubles as a great pizza sauce. Buy good-quality crushed tomatoes for this sauce; diced tomatoes will work in a pinch (and can be blended if desired).

1. In a medium bowl, stir together the crushed tomatoes, tomato paste, garlic, oil, oregano, Italian seasoning, red wine vinegar, sugar, and salt.

STORAGE
Store cooled sauce in a resealable container in the fridge for up to 5 days or in the freezer for up to 3 months. If frozen, thaw in the fridge overnight, then heat on the stovetop or in in the microwave until warmed through.

WECK

MAKE AHEAD | FREEZER-FRIENDLY

BETTER-FOR-YOU BOLOGNAISE

Vegan Option · *Vegetarian Option* · *Dairy-Free Option* · *Gluten-Free* · *Nut-Free*

Makes 4 cups (1 L)

TIME

Prep: 10 MINUTES (NOT INCLUDING MAKING SOS SPAGHETTI SAUCE)

Cook: 20 MINUTES

Total: 30 MINUTES

- 1 pound (450 g) ground beef, chicken, or turkey
- 1 cup (250 mL) diced yellow onion
- 2 cloves garlic, minced
- ½ cup (125 mL) finely grated peeled carrot
- ½ cup (125 mL) finely grated zucchini
- 2 cups (500 mL) SOS Spaghetti Sauce (page 312) or store-bought marinara sauce
- ¼ cup (60 mL) heavy (35%) cream
- ¼ cup (60 mL) grated Parmesan cheese
- ¼ cup (60 mL) finely chopped fresh basil
- ½ teaspoon (2 mL) red chili flakes (optional)
- Salt and pepper

STORAGE
Store cooled sauce in a resealable container in the fridge for up to 4 days or in the freezer for up to 3 months. If frozen, thaw in the fridge overnight, then reheat on the stovetop or in the microwave until warmed through.

You need this bolognaise in your freezer or fridge batch-cooked to tackle a busy week. It tastes as good as the classic but is ready in a fraction of the time. Use this veggie-loaded sauce in recipes like my Bolognaise Flatbread (page 243) or on top of your favourite pasta. It freezes well. If you want to make the zucchini extra sneaky, peel it before shredding.

1. In a large frying pan over medium heat, cook the ground beef, stirring occasionally, until browned, about 4 minutes. Add the onion and garlic and cook, stirring occasionally, until the onion is soft and translucent, 3 to 4 minutes.

2. Add the grated carrot and zucchini and cook, stirring occasionally, until the vegetables have softened, about 5 minutes. Stir in the SOS Spaghetti Sauce, cream, and Parmesan and bring to a simmer. Stir in the basil, add the red chili flakes (if using), and season to taste with salt and pepper.

Vegan: Use veggie ground, Cashew Cream (page 332), and vegan parm.

Vegetarian: Use veggie ground.

Dairy-Free: Use Cashew Cream (page 332) and vegan parm.

MAKE AHEAD | FREEZER-FRIENDLY

ENCHILADA SAUCE

Vegan Option · Vegetarian Option · Dairy-Free · Gluten-Free · Nut-Free

Makes 2 cups (500 mL)

TIME
Prep: 5 MINUTES
Cook: 10 MINUTES
Total: 15 MINUTES

- 1 tablespoon (15 mL) cornstarch
- 1 tablespoon (15 mL) chili powder
- 1 teaspoon (5 mL) garlic powder
- 1 teaspoon (5 mL) ground cumin
- 3 tablespoons (45 mL) extra-virgin olive oil or avocado oil
- 2 tablespoons (30 mL) tomato paste
- 2 cups (500 mL) chicken or vegetable stock
- 1 teaspoon (5 mL) unseasoned rice vinegar
- Salt and pepper

STORAGE
Store cooled enchilada sauce in a resealable container in the fridge for up to 5 days or in the freezer for up to 3 months. If frozen, thaw in the fridge overnight before using.

I had no idea it was this easy to make my own Enchilada Sauce! It also gives me full control over the flavour and spice level for my family. This is my tried-and-true recipe, using simple ingredients. Once you've mastered your own sauce too, recipes like Skillet Enchiladas (page 186) and Black Bean Enchilada Soup (page 155) are only a few pantry staples away!

1. In a small bowl, stir together the cornstarch, chili powder, garlic powder, and cumin.

2. Heat the olive oil in a small saucepan over medium heat. Once hot, add the spice mixture and cook, stirring constantly, until fragrant, about 2 minutes (be careful it does not burn).

3. Stir in the tomato paste, then slowly whisk in the stock. Reduce the heat to a simmer and cook, stirring occasionally, until the sauce thickens slightly, about 5 minutes. Remove from the heat, stir in the rice vinegar, and season to taste with salt and pepper.

Vegan and Vegetarian: Use vegetable stock.

BUTTERMILK

Vegan • Vegetarian • Dairy-Free Option • Gluten-Free • Nut-Free Option

Makes 1 cup (250 mL)

TIME | *Prep:* 10 MINUTES

1 cup (250 mL) 2% milk

1 tablespoon (15 mL) white vinegar or fresh lemon juice

STORAGE
Store the buttermilk in a resealable container in the fridge for up to 4 days. Stir or shake before using, as it may separate over time.

Need buttermilk in a pinch? Try this easy hack. A couple of simple ingredients and buttermilk is made. Nothing beats using real buttermilk in a recipe, but for those days when you don't have it on hand, this recipe is a good runner-up.

1. In a small bowl, stir together the milk and vinegar. Let sit for 10 minutes before using.

Vegan and Dairy-Free: Use non-dairy milk.

Nut-Free: If using non-dairy milk, use a nut-free option.

FLAX EGG

Vegan • Vegetarian • Dairy-Free • Gluten-Free • Nut-Free

Replaces 1 egg

TIME | *Prep:* 10 MINUTES

1 tablespoon (15 mL) ground flaxseed or ground chia seeds

3 tablespoons (45 mL) water

You can use this flax egg to replace eggs in most baking recipes. While chia seeds and ground flaxseed both work well, I prefer the flax option, as it yields a slightly better texture. Both chia and flaxseed are a good source of plant-based protein.

1. Stir together the ground flaxseed or chia seeds and water in a small bowl. Let sit for 5 to 10 minutes before using.

MAKE AHEAD | FREEZER-FRIENDLY

CHICKEN STOCK

Dairy-Free • *Gluten-Free* • *Nut-Free*

Makes 8 cups (2 L)

TIME *Prep:* 2 HOURS

1 whole chicken carcass, meat removed

2 celery stalks, roughly chopped

2 carrots, peeled and roughly chopped

1 yellow onion, peeled and quartered

4 cloves garlic, smashed

4 sprigs fresh thyme

3 bay leaves

1 cup (250 mL) loosely packed fresh flat-leaf parsley leaves and stems

1 teaspoon (5 mL) black peppercorns

8 cups (2 L) water

Salt and pepper

If you dislike food waste like me, this recipe is a keeper. After enjoying my Roast Chicken Dinner (page 235), don't toss those bones; turn them into rich, flavourful stock that you can freeze to have on hand anytime. Your future self will thank you! Feel free to throw in extra veggie scraps and herbs for even more depth of flavour.

1. In a large pot with a lid, combine the chicken carcass, celery, carrots, onion, garlic, thyme, bay leaves, parsley, peppercorns, and water. Bring to a boil over high heat, then reduce the heat to medium-low, cover, and simmer for 2 to 3 hours. The longer you cook the stock, the deeper the flavour. Skim off any foam and impurities that rise to the top.

2. Cool the stock in the pot. Strain through a fine-mesh sieve into a resealable container. Season to taste with salt and pepper.

STORAGE

Store cooled stock in a resealable container in the fridge for up to 4 days or freeze for up to 4 months. If frozen, thaw in the fridge overnight before using.

GARLIC BREAD

Vegan Option · Vegetarian · Dairy-Free Option · Gluten-Free Option · Nut-Free

Serves 8

TIME
Prep: 5 MINUTES
Cook: 10 MINUTES
Total: 15 MINUTES

1 large soft French loaf

½ cup (125 mL) butter, room temperature

4 cloves garlic, minced

2 tablespoons (30 mL) finely chopped fresh flat-leaf parsley

½ teaspoon (2 mL) salt

½ cup (125 mL) grated Parmesan cheese (optional)

PREP AHEAD
The Garlic Bread can be made through step 3 up to 1 day ahead. Store in a resealable bag or wrap tightly in plastic wrap or foil and refrigerate.

STORAGE
Store cooled Garlic Bread in a resealable bag at room temperature for up to 2 days. Reheat in the oven on a baking sheet until warmed through.

This is the only recipe you'll ever need for homemade garlic bread. It's ready in just 15 minutes, perfectly crispy on the outside, garlicky, and is the ultimate side to any dish. You'll see it called for in saucy recipes like my Chicken Ricotta Meatballs (page 209) and Cajun Skillet Shrimp Boil (page 214) for good reason. It's not just for dipping though—use it as epic sandwich bread to make a Flank Steak Feta Salsa Sandwich (see page 181).

1. Preheat the oven to 425°F (220°C) and line a baking sheet with parchment paper.

2. Cut the French loaf in half horizontally and place cut side up on the prepared baking sheet.

3. In a medium bowl, mix together the butter, garlic, parsley, and salt until well combined. Spread the garlic butter evenly over the cut sides of the bread.

4. Bake until golden and crispy, 10 to 12 minutes. If using the Parmesan, sprinkle it on top of the bread in the last 1 to 2 minutes and bake until melted.

Vegan and Dairy-Free: Use vegan butter and vegan parm.

Gluten-Free: Use a gluten-free loaf.

MAKE AHEAD

PITA CROUTONS

Vegan • Vegetarian • Dairy-Free • Gluten-Free Option • Nut-Free

Makes 4 cups (1 L)

TIME	
Prep:	5 MINUTES
Cook:	10 MINUTES
Total:	15 MINUTES

2 pitas, cut or torn into 1-inch (2.5 cm) pieces

1 tablespoon (15 mL) extra-virgin olive oil

1 teaspoon (5 mL) garlic powder

1 teaspoon (5 mL) dried oregano

¼ teaspoon (1 mL) salt

STORAGE

Store cooled croutons in a resealable container at room temperature for up to 1 month.

Pita Croutons are such a simple and easy salad topper that add crunch and a dash of extra fibre. This is great way to use up stale or leftover pita. As an alternative, naan bread works well. Serve with Herby Green Salad (page 119) or Big Crunchy Greek Kale Salad (page 140).

1. Preheat the oven to 350°F (180°C) and line a baking sheet with parchment paper.

2. Place the bread on the prepared baking sheet and drizzle with the olive oil. Sprinkle with the garlic powder, oregano, and salt and mix together with your hands to coat. Spread the bread in a single layer and bake until golden brown, 8 to 10 minutes, stirring halfway through.

Gluten-Free: Use gluten-free pitas.

EXTRA VIRGIN
OLIVE OIL

MAKE AHEAD

CRISPY PANKO

Vegan • Vegetarian • Dairy-Free • Gluten-Free Option • Nut-Free

Makes 1 cup (250 mL)

TIME | *Prep:* 5 MINUTES

- 2 tablespoons (30 mL) extra-virgin olive oil or avocado oil
- 1 cup (250 mL) panko crumbs
- 1 teaspoon (5 mL) garlic powder

STORAGE
Store cooled Crispy Panko a resealable container at room temperature for up to 1 month.

Who needs croutons when you have crispy panko?! This is the ultimate lazy hack to add that perfect crunch to your salads for texture in every bite. Chances are you probably have all the ingredients in your pantry right now. Sprinkle these crispy crumbs on top of salads like my Ranch Cobb Salad (page 133) or Super Tuscan Salad (page 129), but don't restrict yourself to salads!

1. Heat the olive oil in a medium frying pan over medium-high heat. Add the panko and garlic powder and toast, stirring constantly, until golden brown, about 4 minutes. Transfer to a plate to cool.

Gluten-Free: Use gluten-free panko crumbs.

MAKE AHEAD

BUTTERY MASHED POTATOES

Vegan Option • Vegetarian • Dairy-Free Option • Gluten-Free • Nut-Free

Serves 4

TIME	
Prep:	15 MINUTES
Cook:	10 MINUTES
Total:	25 MINUTES

2 pounds (900 g) Yukon Gold potatoes, peeled and cut into 1- to 2-inch (2.5 to 5 cm) pieces

¼ cup (60 mL) butter

½ cup (125 mL) table (18%) cream or whole milk

Salt and pepper

STORAGE
Store cooled mashed potatoes in a resealable container in the fridge for up to 3 days. Reheat on the stovetop or in the microwave until warmed through.

My husband Charles is known in our circle of family and friends for many recipes, including these mashed potatoes. It's a classic side dish with just four simple ingredients that come together to create, true to its name, the most buttery, comforting mash. Perfectly versatile, they're a must-have side for meals like Pot Roast (page 231), Roast Chicken Dinner (page 235), or as the creamy top layer of Cottage Pie (page 169).

1. Place the potatoes in a large pot and add cold water to cover by 1 inch (2.5 cm). Salt the water. Bring to a boil, then reduce the heat to medium and cook until the potatoes are fork-tender, 10 to 15 minutes.

2. Drain the potatoes and return them to the pot. Using a potato masher, or potato ricer over a large bowl, mash or press the potatoes until smooth. Stir in the butter and cream to combine. Season to taste with salt and pepper.

Vegan and Dairy-Free: Use vegan butter and Cashew Cream (page 332).

MAKE AHEAD

QUICK PICKLED CABBAGE

Vegan · Vegetarian · Dairy-Free · Gluten-Free · Nut-Free

Makes 2 cups (500 mL)

TIME *Prep:* 10 MINUTES (NOT INCLUDING RESTING TIME)

⅓ cup (75 mL) unseasoned rice vinegar

1 tablespoon (15 mL) sugar

1 teaspoon (5 mL) salt

2 cups (500 mL) thinly sliced red or green cabbage

STORAGE
Store the pickled cabbage in the mason jar, sealed with the lid, in the fridge for up to 3 weeks.

If you're busy (and impatient) like me, then you'll like this Quick Pickled Cabbage. Why not enjoy your hard-ish work so much sooner and ditch the extra time and mess? It's fast and easy to make, and there's no need for sterilizing jars or gathering special equipment. I enjoy spending time in the kitchen, but for some reason the thought of canning makes me run for the hills. If you're like me, this recipe is for you!

1. In a medium nonreactive bowl (stainless steel, plastic, or glass), combine the rice vinegar, sugar, and salt. Whisk until the sugar and salt are dissolved.

2. Add the cabbage, stir to combine, and let sit at room temperature for 30 minutes, tossing occasionally.

3. Transfer the cabbage and the pickling juice to a mason jar. Seal with the lid.

QUICK DILL PICKLES

Vegan · Vegetarian · Dairy-Free · Gluten-Free · Nut-Free

Makes 2 cups (500 mL)

TIME | *Prep:* 30 MINUTES (NOT INCLUDING RESTING TIME)

Brine

½ cup (125 mL) water

½ cup (125 mL) white vinegar

1 tablespoon (15 mL) kosher salt

1½ teaspoons (7 mL) sugar

Pickles

1 teaspoon (5 mL) mustard seeds

1 small head of fresh dill (optional)

2 cups (500 mL) Persian cucumbers washed and quartered lengthwise

2 cloves garlic, peeled and halved lengthwise

These Quick Dill Pickles are crisp, garlicky, and full of bold, briny flavour, everything a good pickle should be. With just a few simple ingredients and a little patience, you'll have a jar (or two) of homemade pickles that taste far better than store-bought. Perfect for burgers, charcuterie boards, or straight from the fridge when a salty snack craving hits!

1. **Make the Brine:** In a small non-reactive saucepan (stainless steel or similar), combine the water, white vinegar, salt, and sugar. Bring to a simmer over medium heat, stirring to dissolve the sugar and salt. Remove from the heat and let cool.

2. **Make the Pickles:** To a 2-cup (500 mL) mason jar, add the mustard seeds and dill head (if using). Pack the jar tightly with the cucumbers and garlic.

3. Pour the cooled brine over the cucumbers to cover. Seal with the lid and refrigerate for at least 3 days before serving.

STORAGE
Store the pickles in the mason jar, sealed with the lid, in the fridge for up to 1 month.

MAKE AHEAD

QUICK BREAD AND BUTTER PICKLES

Vegan · Vegetarian · Dairy-Free · Gluten-Free · Nut-Free

Makes 2 cups (500 mL)

TIME | *Prep:* 30 MINUTES (NOT INCLUDING RESTING TIME)

- 2 cups (500 mL) Persian cucumbers washed and sliced ¼ inch (5 mm) thick
- 1 tablespoon (15 mL) kosher salt
- 1 cup (250 mL) thinly sliced sweet or yellow onion
- ¾ cup (175 mL) sugar
- ¾ cup (175 mL) white vinegar
- ⅓ cup (75 mL) apple cider vinegar
- 1 teaspoon (5 mL) pickling spice
- ½ teaspoon (2 mL) mustard seeds
- ¼ teaspoon (1 mL) ground turmeric

STORAGE
Store the pickles in the mason jar, sealed with the lid, in the fridge for up to 1 month.

My Quick Bread and Butter Pickles are sweet, tangy, and irresistibly crunchy—the kind of fridge staple you'll find yourself adding to everything. Made in minutes with just a handful of ingredients, they strike the perfect balance of vinegar, sugar, and spice. Whether you're piling them on burgers, tucking them into sandwiches, or snacking straight from the jar (no judgment!), they're a nostalgic classic made easy at home.

1. In a medium bowl, toss the sliced cucumbers with the salt. Transfer to the fridge and let sit for 2 hours. Rinse the cucumbers to remove the excess salt, drain, and return to the bowl. Add the onion and toss to combine. Transfer the cucumber mixture to a 2-cup (500 mL) mason jar.

2. In a small nonreactive saucepan (stainless steel or similar), combine the sugar, white vinegar, apple cider vinegar, pickling spice, mustard seeds, and turmeric. Bring to a simmer over medium heat, stirring to dissolve the sugar. Remove from the heat and let cool slightly.

3. Pour the warm brine over the cucumbers and onion to cover. Let cool to room temperature. Seal with the lid and refrigerate for at least 2 days before serving.

MAKE AHEAD

QUICK PICKLED JALAPEÑOS

Vegan • Vegetarian • Dairy-Free • Gluten-Free • Nut-Free

Makes 2 cups (500 mL)

TIME *Prep:* 30 MINUTES, PLUS RESTING TIME

- ⅓ cup (75 mL) unseasoned rice vinegar
- ¼ cup (60 mL) sugar
- 1 teaspoon (5 mL) kosher salt
- 2 cups (500 mL) washed and sliced jalapeños

STORAGE
Store the pickled jalapeños in the mason jar, sealed with the lid, in the fridge for up to 1 month.

Pickled jalapeños add a tangy kick to just about anything—from tacos and nachos to sandwiches and bowls. They're quick to make and easy to keep on hand. Once you try homemade, you'll never go back to store-bought!

1. In a medium nonreactive bowl (stainless steel, plastic or glass), combine the rice vinegar, sugar, and salt. Whisk until the sugar and salt are dissolved.

2. Add the jalapeños and stir to combine. Transfer the jalapeños and the pickling juice to a 2-cup (500 mL) mason jar. Seal with the lid and refrigerate for at least 1 day before serving.

QUICK PICKLED RED ONIONS

Vegan • Vegetarian • Dairy-Free • Gluten-Free • Nut-Free

Makes 2 cups (500 mL)

TIME *Prep:* 10 MINUTES, PLUS RESTING TIME

- ⅓ cup (75 mL) unseasoned rice vinegar
- 1 tablespoon (15 mL) sugar
- 1½ teaspoons (7 mL) salt
- 2 cups (500 mL) thinly sliced red onion

STORAGE
Store the pickled red onions in the mason jar, sealed with the lid, in the fridge for up to 1 month.

There's always a jar of pickled red onions in my fridge. They add the perfect pop of flavour to just about everything. Try them on Mango Coconut Shrimp Tacos (page 249) or in Dill Pickle Tuna Salad (page 130).

1. In a medium non-reactive bowl (stainless steel, plastic, or glass), combine the rice vinegar, sugar, and salt. Whisk until the sugar and salt are dissolved.

2. Add the red onion, stir to combine, and let it sit at room temperature for 30 minutes, tossing occasionally.

3. Transfer the red onions and the pickling juice to a mason jar. Seal with the lid and store in the fridge for at least 1 day before serving.

MAKE AHEAD

SPICY MAYO

Vegan Option · Vegetarian · Dairy-Free · Gluten-Free · Nut-Free

Makes ½ cup (125 mL)

TIME | *Prep:* 5 MINUTES

½ cup (125 mL) mayonnaise

2 tablespoons (30 mL) sriracha or chipotle hot sauce

1 teaspoon (5 mL) fresh lime juice

Whenever I'm craving a little extra zip on a dish, this is the condiment I turn to. For the nicest presentation, transfer the spicy mayo into a squeeze bottle to drizzle on, well, everything!

1. Whisk together all the ingredients in a small bowl until combined.

Vegan: Use vegan mayonnaise.

STORAGE
Store the Spicy Mayo in a resealable container in the fridge for up to 2 weeks.

CASHEW CREAM

Vegan · Vegetarian · Dairy-Free · Gluten-Free · Nut-Free

Makes 1½ cups (375 mL)

TIME | *Prep:* 20 MINUTES

1 cup (250 mL) raw cashews

STORAGE
Store the Cashew Cream in a resealable container in the fridge for up to 3 days.

I've been using cashew cream to replace heavy (or whipping) cream for years and am always so impressed with how incredible it tastes—better than dairy cream in some cases. Use this as a direct substitute in most recipes that call for heavy cream; baking tends to be an exception.

1. In a medium bowl, cover the cashews with enough boiling water to cover them completely. Let soak for 15 minutes (or for up to 12 hours in the fridge). Drain the cashews.

2. Combine the drained cashews and 1 cup (250 mL) cold water in a high-speed blender and blend until very smooth, 3 to 4 minutes. Add more water if needed to achieve the desired consistency.

MAKE AHEAD

CHANTILLY CREAM

Gluten-Free • Nut-Free

Makes 4 cups (1L)

TIME | *Prep:* 5 MINUTES

2 cups (500 mL) heavy (35%) cream, chilled

3 tablespoons (45 mL) sugar

1 teaspoon (5 mL) pure vanilla extract

STORAGE
The Chantilly Cream tastes best when served the same day it is made but can be stored in a resealable container in the fridge for up to 2 days. Adding a commercial whipped cream stabilizer (found in the baking aisle) will help prevent the whipped cream from separating as it sits and allow it to keep for up to 4 days once whipped.

Chantilly cream is a lightly sweetened version of whipped cream with a hint of vanilla. With French origins, it's my favourite simple way to elevate a dessert, waffles, or a bowl of fruit. For best results use heavy (35%) cream, but the recipe will also work with 33% cream. Be careful not to overbeat the cream—unless you want to make butter!

1. In a medium bowl with tall sides, using an electric mixer, or in a stand mixer fitted with the whisk attachment, combine the heavy cream, sugar, and vanilla. Beat until soft peaks form, 3 to 5 minutes.

Tip

Substitute almond extract for the vanilla to make almond Chantilly cream. Other extracts work as well.

EVERYTHING BAGEL SEASONING

Vegan · Vegetarian · Dairy-Free · Gluten-Free · Nut-Free

Makes about ⅓ cup (75 mL)

TIME | *Prep:* 5 MINUTES

- 2 tablespoons (30 mL) poppy seeds
- 1 tablespoon (15 mL) white sesame seeds
- 1 tablespoon (15 mL) black sesame seeds
- 1 tablespoon (15 mL) dried minced garlic
- 1 tablespoon (15 mL) dried minced onion
- 1 teaspoon (5 mL) flaky sea salt

Everything Bagel Seasoning really lives up to its name: you'll want to put it on everything! This flavourful blend of poppy seeds, sesame seeds, garlic, and onion turns the simplest of snacks into something special. It's the star of the Everything Bagel Salmon (page 257) and Everything Bagel Salmon Salad (page 120), but you can add a dash to anything from avocado toast to eggs or, of course, to a classic cream cheese bagel.

1. Combine all the ingredients in a resealable container.

STORAGE
Store the seasoning in a resealable container at room temperature for up to 6 months.

HERB BOMBS

Vegan · Vegetarian · Dairy-Free · Gluten-Free · Nut-Free

Tips AND THINGS TO CONSIDER

1. **Choose an oil:** Stick to neutrals—extra-virgin olive oil, avocado oil, and melted butter all work well. Choose one that suits your cooking style best!

2. **Label before freezing:** Once they're frozen, it will be hard to tell which herb is which.

3. **Mix and match:** Have fun with combinations! Combine basil and oregano for Italian dishes or mix thyme and rosemary for a classic herb blend.

4. **Storage:** Once frozen, pop the cubes out and store them in a labelled freezer bag to save space and make them easy to grab when needed.

I've been using this hack for years! Often by the end of the week, I have some sad-looking herbs that are almost destined for the compost bin. This simple trick gives them new life.

Chop up your leftover herbs, place them in an ice cube tray, cover with oil, and freeze; for bonus flavour, add minced garlic to each tray. For an instant flavour boost, pop a cube into your pan whenever you're cooking! Perfect for soups, pastas, stir-fries, you name it. No more wasted herbs. Try a few in place of the oil in Lemon Chicken Orzo Soup (page 146), Black Bean Enchilada Soup (page 155), or Shrimp and Feta Spinach Rice (page 173).

MERCI

ACKNOWLEDGMENTS

Thank you to all the incredible people who helped bring this book to life—especially my wonderful Fraîche team. It's a true gift to work with such a beautiful, fun, hardworking group of women. You inspire me every single day, and I feel so lucky to be in your company.

To my recipe testers—thank you for being my extra eyes, hands, and taste buds. Wendy Solway, I can always count on you. Your friendship and unwavering support mean the world. Lori Lawrie, Nadya Hrycak, Leah Menzies, Shannon Kray, and so many others (you know who you are!)—I'm endlessly grateful for your time, care, and feedback. I truly couldn't do this without you.

Mike Wilkins, your talent never ceases to amaze me. You have a gift for transforming the simplest dish into something extraordinary with just a twist or two—thank you for sharing that gift with me while bringing this cookbook to life.

To my talented, joy-filled photographer Rachelle Beatty—shoot days with you are such a highlight. Full bellies, big laughs, great music, and even better photos. I could wallpaper my walls with your beautiful images. Thank you for capturing the heart of this book so perfectly. We love you!

Andrea Magyar, from the bottom of my heart, thank you for giving me the opportunity to write a cookbook of my very own. Your guidance, patience, and belief in me over the years have meant more than I can say. I've learned so much from you!

To my sister-in-law, Brea Laurin—you've been with me since the first cookbook (and probably baked more lemon loaves than you'd care to admit). Your sweetness, support, and willingness to jump in wherever needed have not gone unnoticed. Thank you, from the bottom of my heart.

Shayna Kennedy, you have such a gift for storytelling and structure. Your creativity, dedication, and golden touch helped bring this book to life in the most magical way. I love working with you and am so grateful for your support through it all.

Victoria Bannerman, you are an absolute force. Your meticulous attention to detail, organization, and unwavering support behind the scenes made this book stronger in every way. Thank you for always having my back.

Aslinn Rogers, you arrived at the perfect moment. Hardworking, bright, and full of heart, you've been such a joy to work with. I'm so grateful for the energy and excellence you brought to this project.

To Charles—my taste tester, sounding board, and biggest supporter. Your honest feedback made every recipe better, and your support at home made this whole thing possible. Three cookbooks and we're still married—proof we can get through anything. I love you.

Charlie and Max—my sweet boys, thank you for being part of it all and for inspiring me daily. Everything I do is for you.

And to you—the reader—thank you for picking up this book and inviting it into your home. It is the greatest honour to share these pages with you. Your support means more than I can ever express. I hope this book earns a spot on your counter, with dog-eared pages, splatters of sauce, and memories made in between.

With love and gratitude,
xo Tori

BRONNLEY
LEMONS
PRODUCE OF ENGLAND
2 LB 4 OZ

INDEX

C

P

Q

R

S

T

V

W

Y

Z